RC
437.5
.H68
1977
R.D. LAING

WITHDRAWN

Date Due

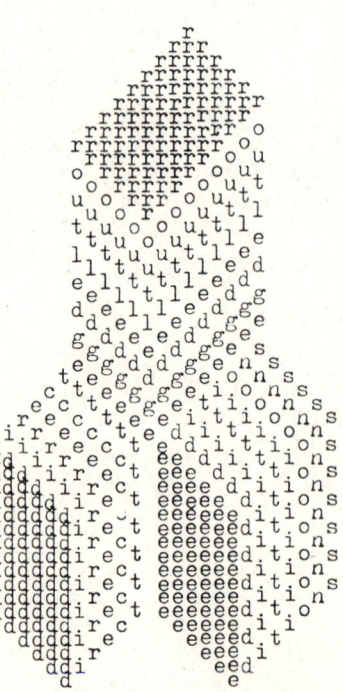

R. D. LAING
His Work and its Relevance
for Sociology

MARTIN HOWARTH-WILLIAMS

ROUTLEDGE DIRECT EDITIONS

ROUTLEDGE & KEGAN PAUL
London, Henley and Boston

First published in 1977
by Routledge & Kegan Paul Ltd
39 Store Street,
London WC1E 7DD,
Broadway House,
Newtown Road,
Henley-on-Thames,
Oxon RG9 1EN and
9 Park Street,
Boston, Mass. 02108, USA
Printed in Great Britain by
Thomson Litho Ltd
East Kilbride, Scotland
© Martin Howarth-Williams 1977
No part of this book may be reproduced in
any form without permission from the
publisher, except for the quotation of brief
passages in criticism

British Library Cataloguing in Publication Data
Howarth-Williams, Martin
R.D. Laing
1. Laing, Ronald David 2. Psychiatry
616.8'9'00924   RC461   77-30031

ISBN 0-7100-8624-5

For My Parents
And For Dave

The only way, the only way, we can define our aim is as this:
to reveal the greater glory of God. (R.D. Laing)

CONTENTS

	ACKNOWLEDGMENTS	viii
1	INTRODUCTION	1
	Laing: An outline biography	3
2	THE REVIEW, PART ONE: ANALYTIC	7
	Stage 1: 'The Divided Self'	7
	Stage 2: 'The Self and Others'	17
	Stage 3: Individual and Family Praxis	31
	Stage 4: Eknoia, Paranoia and Metanoia	49
	Stage 5: Political Radicalism	68
	Stage 6: The Politics of the Family	77
	Stage 7: Religious Sensibility	89
3	THE REVIEW, PART TWO: SYNTHETIC	105
4	LAING'S WORK AS A TOTALITY	136
	(i) The Totalization	136
	(ii) Philosophical Influences	141
	(iii) The Nature of Psychosis	164
5	THE SOCIOLOGICAL USEFULNESS OF THE CONCEPT OF INTELLIGIBILITY	174
	Introduction	174
	The Sociology of Schutz	175
	Laing and Schutz	180
	The Ghost of Schutz: or, Theses on Garfinkel	187
	Non-dialectical dialectics: The Case of Lévi-Strauss	197
	Laing and the Possibility of Sociology	201
	BIBLIOGRAPHIES	206
	Chronological order of Laing's texts	206
	Breakdown of texts by type, with source references	208
	Articles, etc., relating to Laing	211
	General bibliography	213
	INDEX	217

ACKNOWLEDGMENTS

The author and publishers are grateful for permission to quote from *Sanity, Madness and the Family: Families of Schizophrenics,* second edition by R.D. Laing and A. Esterson, © 1964 by The Tavistock Institute of Human Relations, Basic Books, Inc., Publishers, New York.

Chapter 1

INTRODUCTION

> You will not find on this planet a more fascinating man than
> Ronald Laing (Leary, 1970).

This book attempts to be an exercise in dialectical intelligibility. Naturally, then, the important terms cannot be defined in advance, but must be apprehended in the activity of reading. Nevertheless, it is in order to give the reader some idea of what is in store.

The bulk of the book (which was written as a thesis for Keele University Sociology Dept, and financed by the Social Science Research Council, to whom I am deeply indebted) consists of a 'review' of the 'work' of R.D. Laing. I have taken the term 'work' in its broadest possible sense; that is, I have included, where relevant, any source of statements that are unquestionably from Laing himself. These involve a number of media: in addition to one or two unpublished texts and interviews, I have used long-playing records, tapes of lectures, transcripts of television appearances, films, and even, on occasion, my own personal recollections of hearing Laing talk under informal conditions.

The structure of the review calls for some preliminary comment. The over-riding theoretical orientation employed in the review is that of Sartre, as expounded in 'La Critique de la raison dialectique' (1960). Indeed, the aim here is much the same as Sartre's stated aim for his proposed second volume of the 'Critique': 'I will simply try to show the dialectical intelligibility of a movement of historical temporalization' (Sartre, 1974b). In our case, the 'historical temporalization' is the span of Laing's career.

Following the Progressive-Regressive Method of Sartre, the review is presented in three moments. First, an analytic moment, in which all the sources are apprehended, in approximate chronological order, and, by a comparative reading of one source against another, breaks down this unstructured serialized collectivity - 'Laing's work' - into discrete 'stages'. A 'stage' is determined by two factors: chronological order and, more important, the mutual coherence of its contents.

Each stage - seven are isolated - is presented, in this analytic moment of review, as a period of theoretical stasis. A multiplicity of texts is unified, non-dialectically, and an 'essence' extracted:

this essence comprises the characteristic theoretical feature of that stage.

Recognizing, however, that progress in theoretical practice, as in any other form of practice, comes about through the transcendence of contradiction, the second moment of the review goes back, regressively, to discover contradictions inherent in each stage, and attempts to illuminate the historical development, so far only given metaphorically as successive stages, as a flow of transcendences. This second, synthetic, moment of review thus negates the negating stasis of the first moment, and reaffirms, at a higher level of inner clarity, the living flux of the totalization-in-process which is Laing's work. It is recognized, of course, that this development is 'uneven', and not linear, nor is it purely theoretical. A certain structuration of the stages is attempted, and certain biographical, historical and other overdeterminations are explored.

The analytic and synthetic moments thus comprise Chapters 2 and 3, respectively.

Chapter 4 attempts to grasp Laing's work as a totality. But this is not to be thought of as an inert summary. For we have taken advantage of the totalizing perspective of this chapter to look back, once more, and to examine some of the more prominent philosophical influences upon Laing's work, as well as the extraction of certain recurrent yet developing themes across the span of his work. These thematic considerations notwithstanding, this book concentrates on Laing as a theorist of the human scene; it is his theoretical methodology that is focused upon here, more than the substantive empirical side of his work. In particular, little attempt is here made to relate Laing's work *as a therapist* to either the theory or practice of orthodox Freudian psychoanalysis. This is partly because I felt I did not have sufficient familiarity with the latter to be worthy of the task, and partly because Laing *never, ever*, writes about how he *conducts* therapy. This, however, has not prevented some writers from attempting the task.

Throughout the review, we have attempted to show that there is so to speak a 'guiding light', the grasping of which illuminates the whole enterprise of Laing's work. This can be identified by the concept of Intelligibility. There is found to be a thread running through all the stages, concerned with this notion of Intelligibility. At certain points in his career, Laing's use of the term corresponds with Sartre's, and thus also with the present writer's. This book, or at least the review portion of it, consists of dialectical intelligibility as it were applied to itself and its precursors, as manifest over the span of Laing's career. Laing appears to have stopped using the term; a critique is included of Laing's most recent pronouncements, particularly in respect of politics and religious experience.

The last chapter establishes the relevance of our orientation on Laing as a theoretical social 'scientist'. Having established the centrality of the concept of intelligibility in Laing's work, we then examine this concept in relation to the broader problematic of interpretive sociology.

Laing called his theoretical orientation 'social phenomenology'. We begin our exploration of Laing's relevance to sociology by considering the work of Alfred Schutz, whose orientation could also have been described as a social phenomenology. In particular, Laingian insights are used in a critique of Schutz's assumptions and methodology.

Such a critique would seem timely in view of the recent resurgence of interest in Schutz, particularly from ethnomethodology. A critique of ethnomethodology follows, again using Laingian insights, which is itself followed by a brief consideration of structuralism.

The above mentioned critiques of existing sociologies all centre on the notion of dialectic. Lévi-Strauss's use of the term is severely criticized. In the case of Schutz and the ethnomethodologists, it is the tension between the implicit presence but actual absence of dialectical reason that is focused upon.

The book concludes with a view of the possibility of sociology. The prerequisites for a dialectical sociology are examined, as is the sociological usefulness of the concept of intelligibility. In doing so, the usefulness of sociology is brought into question.

Finally, we present a more or less exhaustive bibliography appertaining to Laing. In the first place, a thorough bibliography of Laing's work itself; this alone was a very difficult task, though a much needed one, as many of Laing's most important ideas do not, paradoxically, appear in his books but are tucked away in more or less obscure journals. Second, a reasonably comprehensive bibliography of articles and books pertaining to Laing; finally, of course, a conventional bibliography of works cited in the text.

There has never been a biography written of Laing, and he is known to be hostile to the idea. I certainly have no intention of attempting such a task; nevertheless, it will hopefully render what follows a bit more personally meaningful if at least an outline of biographical information is supplied at this juncture. It is to this task, then, that we turn, before embarking upon the review. (The main biographical sources are Laing, 1971, 1972a; Barnes and Berke, 1971; and Nuttall, 1970.)

LAING: AN OUTLINE BIOGRAPHY

1927   Born 7 October, the only child of lower middle class parents, at the edge of the Gorbals district of Glasgow. His parents were Lowland Presbyterian, his father apparently being the more religious partner.

1932   Very little is known of his childhood, except that it must have been an unpleasant environment for a child with his sensitivity and intelligence. According to Mezan (1972a) Laing decided quite self-consciously at an early age to be an intellectual, and worked hard at 'getting out' of his background. Reading, athletics and playing the piano appear to have been his main hobbies at school. He cites Darwin, Huxley, Mill and Voltaire - plus of course the Bible - as early influences, and says that 'by the time I was fourteen I knew that I was really only interested in psychology, philosophy and theology'. He went to a grammar school in Glasgow, where he had a 'Classical' education. He says elsewhere (Laing, 1973b) that 'I could read "Oedipus" in the original from the age of 14. I was also very impressed with Shakespeare's sonnets.'

1945   Went to Glasgow University to study medicine. Judging from autobiographical fragments, such as The Bird of Paradise, medical school was an equally unpleasant experience. He described university as 'largely a waste of time....I never felt completely comfortable as a doctor.' He reports that at the age of 22-23, he used to exercise himself 'by trying on the different psychoses to see how they worked and felt. Like intense paranoid schizophrenia, for example.' On another occasion he buried himself, naked, in snow on a freezing cold night, to test how far he could push his senses.

He tells us, in The Bird of Paradise, that he regularly read 'Horizon', an avant-garde intellectual journal of the 1940s, and records his violent rejection of their pessimism in the last issue (December 1949). It is interesting to examine the last issue. It contained, for example, a poem by C. Day Lewis, a long essay on De Sade, articles on Francis Bacon, and the atonal music of Dallapiccola. The editorial comment is particularly illuminating, as it goes over the ground covered in the magazine's ten years of publication. It is no surprise to find them noting (pp. 360-2. My emphasis)

> We became a display window for Sartre and Camus and the French writers;... and were in danger of becoming an advertisement for international fashions of the mind.... One can perceive the inner trend of the Forties [Age 13-23 for Laing] as maintaining this desperate struggle of the modern movement, between man, *betrayed by science, bereft of religion*, deserted by the pleasant imaginings of humanism.

If he rejected their conclusions, he was nevertheless influenced by their premises: that is, by whom and what they considered worthy of publication. Certainly, it is significant that he was so attached to a totally non-medical magazine.

1951   Graduated from medical school.

Drafted into the Army, during Korean War, after six months of a neurosurgical internship. Was apparently 'summarily informed' that he was now a psychiatrist. He reports that the only person in the Army Hospital he could have a reasonable conversation with was a man in one of the padded cells.

1953   Left the Army, and got a job at Glasgow Royal Mental Hospital. Conducted his first 'research' (see Laing et al., 1955).

1955   First publication.

1956   Started to write 'The Divided Self' and 'The Self and Others'.

1957   Moved to a post at the Tavistock, London. Having psychoanalysis from Charles Rycroft. Completed draft of 'The Divided Self'.

1958   Started work on the Tavistock Family Research Programme with Esterson. Being influenced by Bateson and communications research.

1960	'The Divided Self' published.
1961	'The Self and Others' published. Moved to Tavistock Institute. Experimenting with the (legal) use of hallucinogens such as LSD.
1962	Published 'Series and Nexus in the Family', employing concepts from Sartre's 'Critique'. Became director of the Langham Clinic, London. Finished Tavistock Family Research with Esterson. Began co-operation with Cooper on 'Reason and Violence'. Went to the USA to discuss his work with Bateson, Goffman and others.
1964	Published 'Reason and Violence', and 'Sanity, Madness and the Family'. Visited Timothy Leary. Becoming involved in the emergent British 'Underground' Movement. See Nuttall, 1970. Published articles of radically different orientation, using notions of hypersensitivity, transcendental experience etc.
1965	April. Philadelphia Association founded as Registered Charity. June. The PA took over Kingsley Hall, a large disused work house in East London as site for therapeutic community. Laing moved into Kingsley Hall himself, without his family (wife and five children). Reputedly taking (still legal) LSD very frequently. Left Langham Clinic after falling out with its founder Eric Howe, over the issue of drugs.
1966	Increasing ties with London Underground Movement. August. Laing and Esterson split. Esterson leaves PA and Kingsley Hall. August/September. Laing moved out of Kingsley Hall, and established a smaller community in his own home. Period of general family/personal crisis for Laing. Separation from family.
1967	Visits to the USA, including a course of lectures intended for publication. Published 'Politics of Experience', and started to become cult-hero amongst students, etc. Left the Tavistock Institute. Formed Institute of Phenomenological Studies with Cooper, Joe Berke and Leon Redler. Helped organize and run the Dialectics of Liberation Conference. Signed Legalize Marijuana advertisement.
1968	Gave lectures on Canadian networks, subsequently revised as 'Politics of the Family'.
1969	April. Finished work on 'Knots'.
1970	'Knots' published. Kingsley Hall closed down. PA operating other households. Arbours Association founded by ex-colleagues.
1971	July. Left England for Buddhist Monastery in Ceylon. Stayed six months.
1972	Visited India for seven months and Japan, briefly, to study Yoga and Zen. Lecture tour of the USA. September. Returned to England. Plans for therapeutic communities abroad. October. Public lecture in London 'Reflections on Psychotherapy'. December. Interview on ITV television.
1973	January. Lecture Reflections on Meditation. March. Broadcast musical/dramatized version of 'Knots'. Introduced and appeared in 'Asylum' and 'Breathing and Running' films.

Chapter 1

	Interest focusing on birth experiences and very early traumas. Co-operation with American therapists on re-living birth experiences. Still a regular visitor at PA communities.
1974	Spring. Married Jutta Werner. Writing a book on Birth and early experience.
1975	Televised version of 'Knots'.

So much for biographical details. The details have been only very sketchily dealt with here for the years after his first publication, as biographical details are dealt with in greater depth, where relevant, in the main body of the review. It is to the latter that we now turn.

Chapter 2

THE REVIEW, PART ONE: ANALYTIC

STAGE 1: 'THE DIVIDED SELF'

> And he was casting out a devil, and it was dumb. And it came to pass, when the devil was gone out, the dumb spake; and the people wondered....
> ...But he, knowing their thoughts said unto them, Every kingdom divided against itself is brought to desolation; and a house divided against a house falleth (Luke 11: 14-17).

We begin the review of Laing's work by noting what the first few publications of his were; and, through a comparative reading of each against each, discern what natural categories they fall into, chronologically speaking.

Laing's first publication was the paper Patient and Nurse Effects of Environmental Changes in the Care of Chronic Schizophrenics (Cameron, Laing and McGhie, 1955), at which time he was working at Glasgow University. It must also have been around this time that he started work on 'The Divided Self', as the latter was apparently completed by 1957. For this, and other reasons which will become apparent, we will group Patient and Nurse Effects together with 'The Divided Self' as constituting stage 1. They are certainly the first two fruits of Laing's synthesis of his academic and his psychiatric abilities.

The next text to be considered is The Collusive Function of Pairing in Analytic Groups, written by Laing and Esterson (1958). At this point, Laing had moved to Tavistock and met his new colleague, Esterson; it appears that this paper comes from the very beginnings of the massive research project which later produced 'Sanity, Madness and The Family' and 'Interpersonal Perception'; but in more immediate terms, we notice that it also forms the basis of chapter IV of 'The Self and Others'. As there is effectively nothing of interest to us in the paper that does not appear in the book, we shall rest content by merely stating that The Collusive Function forms a part of stage 2, alongside 'The Self and Others'.

Before reviewing the first paper, we should perhaps also note the existence of two other potential sources which date from the late 1950s or early 1960s. One is a lecture by the title of The

Development of Existential Analysis, given to the Royal Medico-Psychological Association in 1960. The other is an unpublished manuscript entitled Infancy and Ontological Insecurity. In view of their intriguing titles, it is a great shame that neither of these is available.

I shall begin by quoting at length the opening paragraph of Patient and Nurse Effects as it is a truly programmatic way of beginning one's first paper, and one whose assumptions have been proved so solidly by Laing's subsequent work.

> For a long time many have recognized that the familiar picture of the chronic deteriorated schizophrenic is not a necessary consequence of an inexorable process; even in the most disturbed wards of mental hospitals, occasional spontaneous remissions occur.... Believing...that the most important therapeutic element in the environment is the people in it, we have attempted an experiment in which a group of patients and nurses were given a chance to develop more or less enduring relationships with one another. This is an account of what happened over a year (p. 1384).

Now this does not strike us a desperately radical, or controversial point of view today: but it should be recalled that the opinions behind that statement must have been formulated at the very latest in 1954; a date that can be put in perspective by reminding ourselves that tranquillizers were not introduced into British hospitals until that same year, and then only on an experimental basis. Heavy sedation, electric shock and insulin therapies were the only technological forms of treatment available, excluding brain surgery.

Laing's 'experiment' consisted basically of providing the normal range of human facilities for a group of twelve schizophrenics, who were then treated simply as human beings. Laing, recalling the experiment some fifteen years later, mentioned with amusement the laborious sociometric statistics used to select the twelve most 'out-of-contact' chronic schizophrenics.

On the first day of the experiment, many of the patients, who had been mute and immobile for years, had to be wheeled into the experimental quarters. Laing recalls however, 'On the second day, an hour before the ward door opened, they had gathered around it talking, laughing, jumping up and down; it was enormously moving' (quoted in Gordon, 1971).

Clearly, the success of this experiment, in human terms, must have had a profound influence over Laing's subsequent career; it is strange that he has never, to my knowledge, mentioned the experiment in his own writings. At any rate we may note, in leaving this article, that its conclusion contains a pledge, so to speak: and it is one that would surely have seemed an unorthodox one at the time: 'Our experiment has shown, we think, that the barrier between patients and staff is not erected solely by the patients but is a mutual construction. The removal of this barrier is a mutual activity' (p. 1386).

Now, the realization of this pledge was to involve Laing in the realization and transcendence of a contradiction: the contradiction whose initial existential manifestation is, of course, the barrier spoken of. As we shall see in a subsequent chapter, this is a contradiction whose fundamental moments do not become apparent till much later; and one for which there is still no wholly adequate synthesis. But what concerns us now is the initial, confused, partial realization of it. This we find in 'The Divided Self', and it is to this book that we now turn.

The aim of the book is given clearly in the Preface; in Laing's own words:

> The present book is a study of schizoid and schizophrenic persons; its basic purpose is to make madness, and the process of going mad, comprehensible....A further purpose is to give in plain English an account, in *existential* terms, of some forms of madness.

Referring to the limited biographical material available on Laing, we find that the clinical material used throughout the book by way of illustration, was all taken from Laing's experiences as a doctor between the years 1951 and 1956, during which time he had worked in an Army Psychiatric Unit, and at Glasgow City Hospital. With his material complete by 1956, he completed the draft of the book in 1957, a year after he moved to Tavistock. The other main 'source' for the book, European philosophy, particularly existential phenomenology, appears to have been an interest of Laing's since his university days; at any rate, since the early 1950s.

As the aims quoted above suggest, the book can be viewed as an attempt to oppose and contrast two radically different viewpoints; the natural scientific, positivist approach of medical psychiatry, and the 'softer', more literary approach of continental philosophy, with its inclination towards idealism and metaphysics. Are these reconcilable? Laing obviously does not think so. Indeed, it will be the burden of this thesis to show how precisely this irreconcilability has led Laing to formulate a radically new approach; and he takes the first steps towards it in the first chapter of the 'Divided Self', to which we now turn.

Entitled The Existential-Phenomenological Foundation for a Science of Persons, the first chapter outlines very briefly the sort of approach Laing wishes to take, and contrasts it to the orthodox approach.

He starts by noting a major difficulty: 'how can I go straight to the patients if the psychiatric words at my disposal keep the patient at a distance from me?' For the technical vocabulary of psychiatry is one which splits man up, conceptually, without being able to 'put him together again', let alone put him 'back in world'. Any individual is seen, in isolation, as comprised of ego, id, and superego, or psyche plus soma, or a bundle of personality factors, and so on. Laing asks how this state of affairs comes about, and attempts to answer phenomenologically.

He notes that, in any relational system of human beings, the other(s) is the object of intentionality for the own person. That is, one can look at another person, or any aspect of the phenomenal world, in different ways. The *way* the looker looks at what he sees will determine in part '*What*' he sees. This is a basic tenet of phenomenology, and is denoted by the term intentionality.

Specifically, then, in the case of two people, say you and me, I can choose to see you as a person, that is, a being with consciousness, motivation etc., or I can see you as an organism, as a biological entity blindly obeying certain physico-chemico-biological laws.

One relates differently, Laing argues, to an organism and to a person. In the former case, one is concerned with complexes of things, 'its', with personally meaningless processes. But a science of persons cannot proceed on these lines, as to regard persons in that way is precisely to depersonalize them. He notes ironically:
> It seems extraordinary that whereas the physical and biological sciences of it-processes have generally won the day against tendencies to personalize the world of things,... an authentic science of persons has hardly got started by reason of the inveterate tendency to depersonalize or reify persons (p. 23. All page numbers refer to the 1967 Penguin edition).

He notes that 'scientific' tends to be equated with 'objective', an equation which does not hold for a science of persons. Unfortunately, he does not go into the epistemology of 'intersubjectivity', a term used in phenomenology which denotes the formal properties of the personal knowledge of persons. But he does proceed to state the aims of an existential/phenomenological approach to psychiatry:
'(the approach) becomes the attempt to reconstruct the patient's way of being himself in his world, although, in the therapeutic relationship, the focus may be on the patient's way of being-with-me' (p. 25).

When dealing with psychotics, this means reorienting oneself to radical different ways of being, ways which may strike one as bizarre in the extreme. Yet, one must do this without prejudging the issue of whose idea of the patient's being (yours or his) is the 'right' one.

The next chapter starts by noting that orthodox psychiatry automatically prejudges this issue. He quotes Van den Berg's phrase 'a vocabulary of denigration'. The schizophrenic is *mal* adapted, he has a *loss* of contact, a *lack* of insight.

He goes on to quote a classic passage from Kraepelin, 'father of psychiatry', which illustrates Laing's complaints admirably. Kraepelin is displaying a young catatonic, questioning him, and commenting on the meaninglessness of the replies he gets. But as Laing shows, if we are prepared to consider the boy's experience of Kraepelin, in that situation, his replies make a lot of sense.

But the clinical psychiatrist, wishing to be 'scientific', and 'objective', will not do this. In his eagerness to find 'signs' and 'symptoms' the psychiatrist has not time to simply try and understand the patient.

Understanding, however, is precisely what the phenomenological psychiatrist is aiming for. Laing by no means formulates the concept of understanding clearly but, at any rate, he means more than a purely intellectual process. We might, he says, substitute the word 'love'. He also speaks of empathy.

What Laing appears himself uncertain about here is *how* to achieve understanding; the 'what' of understanding is more defined. Namely, we must seek to know how the patient experiences the world and himself in it. But Laing has reservations: 'The kernel of the Schizophrenic's experience of himself must remain incomprehensible to us. As long as we are sane and he is insane, it will remain so (p. 38).

Let us move on now, as Laing does, to see how the clinical material is handled.

The whole study, Laing states, is concerned with issues arising in situations where the individual is lacking what [Laing calls] 'onto-logical security'.

Ontological security refers to the 'normal' sta[te of being] in which one experiences oneself as a real living per[son,] spatially co-extensive with the body; as a self, or ['I', that] persists temporally; as a being having inner consist[ency, substan-]tiality, moral worth and so on.

This state of being, however, is not always the ca[se. It seems] not to be 'inbuilt', but to be the result of 'normal' [nurturi]ng processes and physical development. There are those w[ho do] not experience themselves in these 'obvious' ways which we mostly take for granted. Such people may feel more unreal than real; they may be only precariously differentiated from the rest of the world, and thus lack a personal sense of individuality or autonomy. Generally his experience of *himself* is not *self*-validating. Such an ontological insecurity is reflected as a phenomenological insecurity; the world, as it appears to him, can be no more secure than he is. Ordinary everyday life thus constitutes a perpetual deadly threat to his shaky self.

Specifically, Laing isolates three forms of anxiety, generated by an external reality perceived as threatening, to which an ontologically insecure person is prone.

The first of these is termed Engulfment. This refers to a dread of losing one's already tenuous identity by interaction with other, more solid, identities (i.e. other people). The flimsiness of one's own identity is in permanent danger of being 'engulfed' by the others; a constant battle is necessary to 'keep afloat'. For example, a person in this state of being might invest colossal importance to an apparently trivial argument. Generally, interaction is dangerous for such a person, and he is likely to seek isolation as the only means to avoid total absorption by others.

The second form of anxiety is termed Implosion. It refers to a state where the individual experiences himself as hollow, vacuous, and thus lives in dread of the world 'breaking in' and obliterating his identity as a gas obliterates a vacuum. Although in some ways he longs to be filled, to be substantial, he dreads the possibility, as 'he' is the vacuum that would disappear if the world did crash in and fill him. Again, contact with the world is the threat, and isolation the means to avoid it.

The third form is termed Petrification, which, literally, refers to a dread of being turned to stone. Initially, therefore, this anxiety is one of being regarded as an object, an 'it', of not being considered really there, in a personal sense. However, it goes deeper than that, because such a thing is only possible if one regards other people as real people, in the way one fears they do *not* regard oneself. Only a human agency is capable of turning another to stone. One possible way, then, of avoiding being turned to stone by the others is to turn them to stone first. If I, for example, depersonalize you, regard you as a mere organism, not a person, then you cannot do the same back to me. The danger here, of course, is that what such an individual really wants is constant confirmation of his identity; but, because of his fear of disconfirmation, he has to disconfirm all those who might, given the chance, have confirmed him. As may be imagined, this form of anxiety can easily lead to

affect', i.e. a state where one does not display the
'ct' emotions towards certain people or situations. It is one
the 'early symptoms' of schizophrenia. Laing proceeds to give
several clinical examples illustrating these anxieties, and their
relation to ontological insecurity, and thus concludes part I of the
book.

Part II deals with how the schizoid individual copes with ontological insecurity, with the forms of being-in-the-world that are
devised to maintain a day-to-day existence.

Most people experience themselves as co-extensive with their
bodies; that is, that which is 'my body' is 'me', and that which is
not 'my body', i.e. the rest of the world, is 'not me'. Such a
person is said to be 'embodied'.

This need not be the case, however, for some people experience
their 'self' as quite distinct from their body. This usually leads
to a dual self system, whereby the body is experienced as a false
self ('it's not really *me*'), and their true self is experienced as
unembodied. This clearly has crucial import for one's being-in-the-
world. For the true self in this condition can in no way partici-
pate in the material world, as that is the domain of the false,
embodied self. The paradox here is that such an unembodied self is
both impotent and immune with respect to the world. It comes to be
occupied, then, with the functions of observation control and criticism with respect to the false-self/body system. It forms increasingly complex relations with itself, the false self, and the world.
For example, whereas the 'normal' person interacts with the world
thus:

$$(self/body) \rightleftharpoons world.$$

the schizoid interacts thus:

$$self \rightleftharpoons (body/world)$$

In such interaction, there can be no mutual confirmation, because
the self, although 'in relation' to the world, is only so in a very
limited sense. Specifically, to the extent of observation; it can
have no direct agency in the world. Consequently, both it and the
body/world system fail to achieve any mutual existential confirmation. If unchecked, this vicious circle spirals, and the entire
system becomes unreal and dead.

More clinical examples follow to illustrate the tortuosities of
such systems.

Part III deals with the transitions from schizoid to schizophrenic states, and the nature of the self-systems in a schizophrenic
state.

The true self, or 'inner self' as Laing terms it, is liable to
undergo certain changes, by virtue of its position in the structure
of the schizoid's total being-in-the-world. It will be recalled
that its primary functions, in the schizoid state, were observation
of the false self. By virtue of its 'distance', experientially,
from the false self, the inner self indulges more and more in a private world of its own making; direct participation in the external
world being impossible, its predominant mode of experience comes to
be phantasy. The irrelevance of the false self's perceptions of,
and actions in, the world lead to the world becoming increasingly
phenomenally unreal. In the face of such increasing lack of reli-
able information about the world, anxiety, initially avoided by

retreat from the world, returns, with ever more insidious strength. Generally, the deadness, unrealness, in fact, the nothingness, of the world/false self spreads, in this manner, to the inner self. The inner self, then, itself begins to disintegrate, split, and die.

Faced with such a situation, the schizoid/schizophrenic frequently, Laing claims, adopts the apparently paradoxical stance of killing the self in order that it may not be killed. In his own words:

> In impotence... the individual is afraid of losing his genital function, so he preserves its use (avoids castration) by appearing to be castrated....The psychotic has employed a defence on the same principles... but in respect of the self. It is the ultimate and most paradoxically absurd possible defence, beyond which magic defences can go no further. And it, in one or other of its forms, is the basic defence, so far as I have been able to see, in every form of psychosis. It can be stated in its most general form as: *the denial of being, as a means of preserving being*. The schizophrenic... is dead, in order to remain alive (p. 149-50).

By 'killing' himself, or putting himself in a state of numbness verging on death, the schizophrenic 'protects' himself from his fears and anxieties. If he is dead, he cannot feel the pain, he cannot hear the persecuting voices, he cannot see the ogres that populate his phantasy world.

In addition to the defence function, such existential suicide also serves to relieve a sense of guilt that many schizophrenics feel: the guilt of being in the world. Most schizophrenics, Laing suggests, have, associated with their ontological insecurity, an ontological guilt. That is to say, because they lack a sense of being-in-the-world, a being which is theirs, they experience the fact that they *are* in the world as a sort of ontological trespass. If, as Sartre says, man is a being such that its being is in question to itself, the schizophrenic is a man for whom the answer should have been 'no'. He is the original sinner.

The book ends with a whole chapter devoted to one case study, that of a girl of twenty-six, hospitalized for nine years. Without doubt, a large part of the impact of the book as a whole is due to this last chapter, which is no less than a masterpiece of empathic understanding. Particularly impressive is the interpretation of the girl's speech, conventionally regarded as gibberish, but, in Laing's hands, a mine of the most incredibly subtle yet illuminating puns, metaphors, double entendres etc.

This concludes our account of the content of 'The Divided Self'; we shall now attempt to characterize the approach taken here, that is to elucidate the formal properties of this, stage 1.

Laing claims to be presenting an account of certain forms of madness, and their dynamics, in existential and phenomenological terms. We must, therefore, be clear what these terms entail, though we cannot, of course, attempt to give a full or in any way extended account of these philosophies as such.

Phenomenology, as a school of philosophy, can be traced back to Hegel (though some phenomenologists, notably Husserl, would insist on tracing it right back to Descartes). Hegel could not accept, as Kant insisted, that a distinction should be maintained between phenomena and noumena; that is, between things-as-they-appear-to-

consciousness, and things-in-themselves. For, in the face of that
distinction, which implies the absolute unknowability of the noumenal realm, Reason, as the guiding force of the mind, was ultimately impotent to effect any influence on the (noumenal) world.
Hegel therefore denied the existence of the noumenal world, asserting that the phenomenal world was, so to speak, the whole of reality.
The appearance of the external world was for Hegel merely the alienation of man's consciousness; literally, a projection. Hegel was,
therefore, an idealist par excellence. Phenomenology does not,
however, imply of necessity an idealist epistemology (consider
Merleau-Ponty, for example); for one may abstract certain aspects of
this approach without retaining the whole systems. Indeed, many
people have done many things with Hegel; but what the phenomenologists have done, generally speaking, is to focus on two aspects of
Hegel's approach. First and foremost, phenomenology is always concerned with things as presented to consciousness, that is, with
'reality' *as experienced*. It is quite antithetical to, say, empiricist positivism. It has nothing to say about things as they are in
themselves, and would dismiss any attempts to talk on those lines as
meaningless. The essence of phenomenology is experience.

The second major concern of phenomenology is with the active
nature of the mind.

In contrast to the empiricist view, traceable to Locke, the mind
is not viewed as a passive receptacle of incoming sensory data, a
tabula rasa, but as an active agency which, so to speak, 'works' on
the experience given, of whatever modality, organizing it, and comprehending it, in terms of transcendental categories (see especially
Husserl, 1964, The Ideal of Phenomenology).

To give, then, a phenomenological analysis of x, is to give an
account of x as it is experienced by one or more human beings. When
dealing, therefore, with purely material, non-conscious objects, a
phenomenological analysis may be given merely to supplement an
objective, empirical analysis. On the other hand, when one is dealing with something which could not exist except by virtue of the
(logically) prior existence of conscious human beings, a phenomenological analysis is, I believe, an *absolute prerequisite* to adequate
knowledge of it. Madness, of course, is a perfect example of such
an object of study.

The exact origins of existentialism are a matter of considerable
dispute amongst philosophers, not least existentialists, and I would
not presume to judge the issue. At any rate, Kierkegaard and Sartre
(up to the 1950s) may be taken as fairly representative of existentialists. Probably the most important work in existentialism was
Sartre's 'Being and Nothingness' (1958), at least as far as influence is concerned.

The main doctrine of existentialism whence it derives its name,
is the assertion of the ontological primacy of existence over essence. By this, *very* roughly, is meant that the essential qualities
of a man are determined by his 'existence'; that is, by his various
modes of being: being-in-the-world, being-for-others, being-for-self
and so on. Implicit in this is that one makes one's own life, which
is to say that the qualities of a man, his essence, are the outcome
of his own personal *choice* of his general being in the world, i.e.
roughly, the way he chooses to live. Such a view obviously rests on

the premise that man has free will, and indeed a concern with the problems of freedom is characteristic of existentialists.

The general features, then, of an existentialist approach are, again, twofold.

First, a concern with the question of being, or rather, with different forms, or aspects of being. Hence we have: being-for-self, which refers to what a man is to himself, i.e. his own concept of his identity, or his perception of himself; being-for-others, which refers to what a man is in the eyes of other people, to the fact that his is a being in their experience; and so on. An existential analysis will usually involve, say, considerations of how these various modes of being go together to form a person's overall being, or of how one mode of being conflicts with another. In general, then, an existential analysis will usually be concerned with the ontology and/or ontogenesis of the individual.

Second, we may expect a concern with the issue of individual freedom, the right of the individual to choose and act out his own destiny. Even if 'freedom' is not explicitly an issue, we may expect, in an existential analysis, to perceive sympathy and tolerance towards the individual's general position; a respect for his views, if not agreement with them, rather than evaluation of them in terms of moral criteria external to his own position.

What, then, in the light of this all-too-brief account of these philosophical traditions, do we make of Laing's claim to be following, or at least, employing, them?

As regards existentialism, I think Laing's claims are most certainly justified. As we have seen, he is permanently involved in the question of the individual's being-in-the-world, and its relation to other aspects of his being. In particular, the problem of being-for-self was examined in great detail, by virtue of analysis of multiple-self systems, and their relation to the world. Despite his insistence that he is not using the word 'ontological' in the formally extended philosophical sense, ontological security is a typically existentialist concept; in particular, its affinities with existentialism of Tillich have not gone unnoticed by recent theological commentators (see, for example, Nicholls, 1969).

Similarly, the typically existentialist concern with the freedom of the individual is apparent in 'The Divided Self', as when Laing says: 'One must be able to effect this reorientation (towards the patient's scheme of things) without prejudging who is right and who is wrong' (p. 26). Such an attitude is quite foreign to orthodox psychiatry, with its ideology of positivism; existentialism has, as Maslow (1962) has noted, been strongly instrumental in opposing the orthodox view. Laing recalls, much later (Dialectics of Liberation Record DL 14) that in the early 1950s, from which time much material for 'The Divided Self' comes, he was regarded as either eccentric or extraordinarily dedicated - either way, most unusual - in his approach to his patients, in that he bothered to listen and talk with them, at great length, and did not automatically assume that their speech was senseless.

As regards the book's status as phenomenology, we must, I feel, be a bit more cautious in our assessment. It is true, certainly, that the approach is oriented strongly towards experience, and thus far may be termed phenomenological. However, unless one is to use the word merely trivially, 'phenomenological' must connote something more than mere references to experience. The crucial point here is that one can never observe anyone else's experience. This means that any such approach which claims to be factual, let alone scientific, must somehow incorporate a host of philosophical refinements, which deal with the considerable epistemological problems of others' experience as an object of knowledge. Laing does seem vaguely aware of the problem, as when he recognizes that natural scientific objectivity is not viable; but he does little to support the only alternative he mentions, subjectivity. Yet he talks about 'the foundations for a science of persons'.

I believe this oversight, which must be recognized as crucial, is related to a general feature of this stage that has not yet been focused on. I refer to the fact that, throughout, the book is located, theoretically, at what may be called the level of the individual. Every conceptual scheme that Laing develops here relates to the individual qua individual. True, he employs concepts of other (as in being-for-other) and recognizes the necessity of others in, for example, the maintenance of identity. But, despite that, he never develops a theoretical scheme as such to account for more than one individual at a time. The schemes he does develop concern either intra-individual structures, or more often, the relation of the individual to the world as an undifferentiated externality. As far as his existentialist learnings go, this is to be expected. The same cannot be said of phenomenology. For the latter, in so far as it is an applied philosophy, aims at verifiable knowledge, and is thus a science; specifically the science of experience. It has been forced, therefore, to examine its epistemology, and has found that it is unable to achieve these aims so long as it fails to conceptualize human beings as being specifically in relation to one another. It is from such considerations that the crucial concept in phenomenology of 'intersubjectivity' arises (Husserl, 1950); yet it is one that Laing nowhere hints at in 'The Divided Self'. This oversight, which goes hand-in-hand with his individualistic approach noted above, lies at the root of certain limitations to be found in the book.

We noted, for instance, a distinct lack of clarity in his concept of 'understanding', and now we can see why. For this concept, based as it is on phenomenology as Laing presents it, lacks any rigorous underlying epistemology which alone can give it the meaning it must have if it is to be, as Laing hopes, the central and active concept in a *science* of persons. Indeed, the whole notion of a science of persons requires far more philosophical groundwork than Laing provides here. (Which is not to deny, of course, that Laing has made a major break-through with what he *has* said here; simply a recognition that there is, at this stage, a long way to go.)

A further drawback to the individualist approach is that it *tends* to be a historical and undialectical. Undialectical in that it cannot, with its emphasis on one person versus the rest of the world, conceptualize the intrinsically mutual nature of human existence, or at least, can only view it from one end, so to speak. At any rate, it cannot conceptualize any social system as such, which leads on to the tendency to be a-historical. This charge should not be interpreted as implying that no concept of time, or dynamics is present.

Simply that it is impossible to obtain an adequate conception of the history of an individual without placing him in his context, and examining the history of that context as well.

Perhaps the most serious contradiction, however, that is generated by this approach, concerns, in a sense, Laing himself. For it is a fact that when Laing studies a patient, or conducts therapy with him, what he is involved with, is the patient in relation to himself (Laing). He is studying the patient's experience; yet at the time of study, the patient's experience is his experience of Laing. To be fair, Laing does note this (p. 25); but he makes no comment at all on its theoretical significance. This fact, however, must be taken into account, and Laing does indeed do so - at a later stage. At this stage, however, we shall merely note it as a serious contradiction.

In conclusion, then, we may say of this stage that it presents an account which is existentialist, limited phenomenologically, and conceptually rooted at the level of the individual and his relation to the world, rather than the level of the mutual interrelatedness of two or more individuals.

STAGE 2: 'THE SELF AND OTHERS'

> Is it unphilosophical to accept as a working hypothesis the idea that with the extension of human knowledge beyond the limits at present regarded as normal, there may arrive an expansion of consciousness which shall in some measure dissolve the hard line of demarcation between 'Self' and 'Others'? (Bligh Bond, 1924)

If 'The Divided Self' is to be first stage almost in its entirety, what then is to be included in stage 2? We have already noted that there were no publications between 'The Divided Self', and his next book, 'The Self and Others' (Laing, 1961). So we look to publications after the latter. It will be seen that the next in chronological order is the article in New Left Review entitled Series and Nexus in the Family (Laing, 1962). Now it is the explicit aim of this paper to introduce *new* concepts, derived from Sartre's 'Critique' - which was scarcely published when 'The Self and Others' was completed. As will become more apparent later, Series and Nexus marks very sharply the beginning of a phase radically distinct from anything previously characteristic of Laing. So it seems again that a single book must constitute a stage in its entirety. Here, however, we are in danger, I believe, of falling foul of the *theoretically* irrelevant contingencies of the Tavistock Institute, and Tavistock Publications Ltd. For I shall argue that a book co-written by Laing, although not published till 1966, belongs to this stage: in so far as it belongs anywhere, with respect to Laing's work itself (Laing, Phillipson and Lee, 1966a). For the moment, however, we shall concentrate on the primary constituent of this stage, 'The Self and Others'. (N.B. I am referring here explicitly to '*The* Self and Others', as opposed to 'Self and Others'. That is, to the first edition only; the second edition was 'extensively revised', as Laing puts it, in 1969. As this 'revision' will itself be the object of subsequent scrutiny, it is important at this juncture to keep the two editions distinct.) What, then, do we find in 'The Self and Others'?

The aim Laing has in mind is clearly stated in the Preface. To quote:

> This book attempts to depict the own person within a social system or 'nexus' of other persons; it attempts to understand the way in which the others affect his experience of himself and of them, and how, accordingly, his actions take shape.... No aetiological theory of madness that I subscribe to is stated in this book (p. ix).

Thus, there are in fact three 'aims'; two positive and one negative. To 'depict', and (hence) to 'understand', but without recourse to 'aetiological theory'.

We may expect, then, to be presented with 'depictions', i.e. verbal pictures or descriptions, of such a nature that in themselves, without recourse to causal hypotheses, they afford 'understanding' of interpersonal influences on experience and behaviour. We shall be examining the precise nature of these verbal pictures.

On a broad level first, what philosophical orientations and traditions are invoked as the canvas, so to speak, of these pictures? As far as pure philosophy goes, the situation seems much the same as in stage 1: phenomenology, and existentialism. The bibliography, for example, bristles with names such as Hegel, Buber, Sartre, Heidegger, Tillich and so on. And the chapters of the book bear out these influences; the first part, in fact, appears to be an attempt both to illustrate the need, and provide the presence of a phenomenology of the phantasy mode of experience. The second part, however, seems less phenomenological; rather, it seems to be a sort of social existentialism. But we are dealing very much in abstracts here: let us move on to consider how such philosophies are manifest by an examination of the concepts employed.

The starting point is explicitly the psycho-analytic term 'phantasy'. Laing insists on the need for a phenomenological investigation of this concept, as it embodies, he claims, a number of difficulties. These stem, ultimately, from the fact that phantasy is both an experience, and yet unconscious (or usually so). This leads, in the hands of phenomenologically naive psycho-analysts, to a teleological confusion whose details need not concern us. We shall be content to note that Laing restricts his use of the term strictly to the experiential realm - leaving aside 'as a problem for physiology' what the causes of phantasy are.

The next concept is introduced in the next chapter heading, Phantasy and the Social Nexus. A Nexus is defined here as 'a particular type of group characterized by the members of the group being connected by bonds of high valency' (footnote, p. 17). (Incidentally, Laing uses the wrong word here. 'Valency' refers to the numerical quantity of bonds, not their strength.) Before expanding upon this footnote definition, however, Laing considers the interpersonal nature of phantasy. It is not to be considered, phenomenologically, as necessarily private, unsharable and unreal. On the contrary, a given individual, (O), may share another's (P's) phantasy, thereby losing his individuality, albeit unconsciously. Nor is it restricted to dyads: a multivalent 'social phantasy system' (a term taken from Jaques, 1955) may be in operation.

Now, for any individual who is in such a system, his loss of individuality may not be experienced as such. Laing speaks of an 'alienation effect', and a 'false position', but stresses that the falsity of it is only apparent retrospectively; i.e. only after and in so far as the individual has managed to extricate himself from the system. For the system provides a strong sense of reality, and transcendence of it requires a derealization of this pseudo-reality and a rerealization of a new reality.

Hence, social phantasy systems provide, for individuals, false positions, in which their individual apperceptions are negated by an alienation effect.

A further concept is introduced by noting that one individual may be placed in two or more false positions which are mutually incompatible. He has to be, as it were, in two mutually exclusive nowheres, simultaneously. This bewildering region is termed an 'untenable position'. Attempts at derealizing-rerealizing such positions are considered especially likely to *go wrong*, and manifest themselves as psychotic delusions. Notice here, that the concept of psychosis is given a positive empirical connotation. Unlike stage 1, however, the psychosis occurs, still within the individual in a sense, but only in so far as the individual is not merely an individual, but an active member of a social nexus. It is the individual who is psychotic, but psychosis is a process, not a 'thing', and one that is unthinkable outside the context of the social nexus.

So far, then, Laing has elucidated an outline phenomenology of phantasy within its actual, social context. The next four chapters which comprise the rest of Part 1, are given over to an investigation of phantasy in relation to other modes of experience and forms of behaviour. Specifically, to hysteria, and masturbation, as discrete phenomena; to 'the counterpoint of experience', i.e. the blending or synthesis of multimodal experience; and finally, using the insights gained, an account of a psychotic case history is presented.

Hysteria is seen as an extreme form of an existential manoeuvre which Laing calls 'elusion'. Elusion is an important concept, if we consider that we need to know a person's relation to his behaviour, not just his behaviour itself: elusion is concerned with precisely this.

The dynamics of elusion are roughly speaking this. Person p is in a real situation. For some reason, he 'pretends' that the situation is not real, to such an extent that its unreality can be taken as basic. He then 'pretends' again, on the basis of this unreality, that the situation *is* real, after all. In other words, p is pretending to be what he is, instead of simply being it. From this phenomenological basis, Laing draws out, by means of examples from clinical practice and literature, the way in which practical complications arise, which in severe cases lead to hysterical 'symptoms'.

Similarly, he undertakes an analysis of masturbation, in terms of phantasy and imagination modes of experience; again, drawing on literary examples (notably Sartre's 'St Genet') to illustrate his points.

The next chapter sees Genet and Dostoevsky used to illustrate that 'experience as lived is always a blend of phantasy, imagination dream, of extraordinary complexity, and a constant destructuring-restructuring of their synthetic unity (p. 48). These insights are then applied in chapter VI to illuminate a woman's puerperal psychosis.

The second part of the book, Forms of Interpersonal Action, seems to have a rather different flavour to it. The approach is noticeably less phenomenological: rather, it appears to be a curious blend of existentialism and various sorts of basically *behavioural* theories, notably communications analysis. Let us see how this comes about.

After recognizing the inadequacy of 'monadic psychology' - i.e. psychology which considers the individual apart from his immediate social context - Laing introduces a rectifying concept, namely, Complementarity. This is defined as 'that feature of relatedness whereby the other is required to fulfil or complete the self' (p. 71).

Hence, to achieve a genuine social identity, one must have not only identity-for-self, but identity-for-others. Indeed, a coherent self-identity is impossible unless others define oneself in compatible ways. But this is not always realized in practice. Thus: 'A person will have considerable difficulty in establishing a consistent definition of himself in his own eyes if the definitions of himself given by others are inconsistent or even simultaneously and mutually exclusive' (p. 75). Two clinical examples are given.

What is at stake here is summed up in another pair of concepts, Confirmation, and Disconfirmation. Now confirmation (of one's identity) by others is obviously an act of communication, and the various channels through which it can operate are considered.

At this point Laing introduces an empirical finding of his work at the Tavistock Institute (subsequently published as 'Sanity, Madness and the Family'). This is that it appears to be a characteristic of families in which a 'child' (i.e. offspring, regardless of actual age) is diagnosed schizophrenic that there is very little positive confirmation of the parents by each other, and of the child by the parents. But neither is there usually direct disconfirmation. Rather, there is a sort of pseudo-confirmation, whereby confirmation is so to speak an empty ritual, or, if real is 'confirming' a fictitious child, with disregard for the authentic self of the actual child. Again, a variety of clinical examples are given.

As an interpersonal analogue of delusion, 'collusion' is next introduced. Collusion involves two or more people playing a 'game' with each other, such that they mutually deceive themselves. It is a co-operative venture, in which each 'player' participates willingly (that is, without being forced to) though without being aware that he is doing so. The particular function of collusion seems to be the mutual confirmation of the player's phantasy positions by each other. Thus, suppose p phantasizes that he is an intellectual and o that he (o) is a 'he-man', whereas in fact they are neither. Collusion would occur if p tacitly agreed to confirm o as a he-man in return for o confirming him, p, as an intellectual. This elaborate phantasy system is not, of course, made explicit by the players. If the group concerned is a group under therapy, however, the therapist (or at least, Laing) attempts to do just that, and 'expose' the social phantasy system for what it is. The example given by Laing to illustrate this is the previously mentioned rewrite of the

Collusive Function (Laing and Esterson, 1958).

In collusion, the players are all playing willingly; this cannot be said of all who occupy false positions. At this point, Laing introduces a basic distinction with respect to being-in-a-false-position: that between placing oneself in a false position, and being placed by others in a false position.

Concerning the former, it is important to be clear exactly what is meant by 'true' and 'false' in this context. For we are concerned here with phenomenology, the study of experience. Consequently, we are more concerned with how a person's behaviour (including speech) relates to his experience than with the absolute logical truth-value of his statements. Laing calls on Heidegger for clarification, and employs the latter's distinction between truth in the objective, natural science sense, and *aletheia,* which is truth in the sense of true-to-oneself. The importance of this distinction is apparent only when one considers their negations. For truth (i.e. the first usage) the 'law of the excluded middle' applies - a statement is either true or false. For *aletheia,* however, this is not so. Consider, in relation to it, the 'statements' of the outright liar, the hysteric, the actor, the drunkard, the hypocrite, etc. The subtlety of placing oneself in a false position, of not being 'aletheiatic to oneself', so to say, is that one does not realize that one is in such a position. Again, Dostoevsky is summoned to provide illustrations of the insidiousness of this phenomenon.

As regards being placed in a false position by others, the importance of this lies in the fact that it is an apparently common way of being 'driven crazy'. More specifically, the object of concern now is *untenable* positions, rather than merely *false* positions.

Laing singles out two studies in this field as being of special importance. The first is Searles' (1959) The Effort to Drive the Other Person Crazy. It seems to be Searles' view that pathogenesis is the likely outcome of conflicting attributions by others about one's personality or portions thereof. This Laing disputes, saying that it is only if conflict is not resolvable, and leads to confusion, rather than integration, that it leads to pathology. Thus Laing distinguishes between authentic and inauthentic conflict. The former is only possible if what is 'conflicting' is readily apparent, i.e. *not* on the level of unconscious phantasy. If the conflict is inauthentic, then the 'choices' are not 'real' choices, but phantasy choices and the person is in danger of becoming psychotic.

The ultimate in inauthentic conflict occurs when both choices are impossible. The position is then truly 'untenable'. The idea was developed first by Bateson et al. in their classic paper Towards a Theory of Schizophrenia (Bateson et al., 1956). Laing, noting that this theory is 'highly relevant to our considerations' quotes it at length. I shall paraphrase, rather than quote.

The necessary ingredients for a double-bind situation are:

1 Two or more persons. Of these, one is designated the 'victim'. In their account, it is the child of a family.

2 Repeated experience. The double bind is a recurrent theme in the experience of the victim, not a single trauma, such that its structure becomes a habitual expectation.

3 A primary negative injunction. This is of the form 'Do not do

x, or I will punish you'; or 'Do *x*, or else I will punish you'. They claim that their exact definition of punish 'is being refined'.

4 A secondary injunction conflicting with the first at a more abstract level. This is usually communicated via non-verbal channels, e.g. posture, voice intonation, etc.

5 A tertiary negative injunction prohibiting the victim from leaving the field. In the case of a young child, this injunction is not formally necessary, as the child is physically dependent on the parents. In older victims, however, it may be present in a number of ways; for instance, 'leaving home' is defined as being a rejection of parental love, and thus implicitly prohibited.

6 Finally, the above ingredients are no longer all necessary when the victim has come to habitually perceive his universe in double-bind patterns. Any part may precipitate the reaction.

So, the situation is such that the victim 'can't win'. Whatever he does, he is bound to be wrong. The long-term effects of repeated exposure to such communication patterns are likely to include the following:

1 Lack of ability in handling verbal and/or non-verbal communication.

2 Hence, confusion as to the real meaning of communications, which may in turn lead to

3 Withdrawal from communication.

4 Mistrust, and excessive speculation, concerning the intent of communicants.

5 Inability to detect, and thus respond to, the emotional content of communications.

6 Inability to distinguish different sorts of message, e.g. jokes, metaphors, serious comments, etc.

7 Particular inability to handle messages involving definition of self by others. Hence

8 Inadequate articulation and conception of identity for-self.

Laing notes that the double-bind hypothesis is really a number of hypotheses - but fails to quote, or even refer to explicitly, the one hypothesis which is formally stated by Bateson.

I refer to the passage where Bateson says: 'we argue... that a priori we must expect a pathology to occur in the human organism when certain formal patterns of breaching occur in the communication between mother and child (p. 251). This is the crux of the matter for Bateson: but not, it seems, for Laing. For Laing barely mentions this, and certainly does not comment; rather, he takes up the notion of existential positions rendered untenable by contradictory injunctions or attributions. Laing's use is altogether looser in that he formulates no hypotheses, nor agrees with any, and extends the use of the term double bind to contexts far outside the rigorously defined situations of Bateson, especially in the last chapter of the book.

That brings us to the end of our account of the concepts employed in 'The Self and Others'. It is time now to attempt a more global appreciation of the book.

The structure of the book, of being in two parts, seems totally confirmed by the contents. The first part seems eminently satisfactory when weighed against the stated aims. The title page proclaims the book to be one of several 'Studies in Existentialism and

Phenomenology', and indeed this is what Part 1 is. Specifically, the first two chapters outlined the need for and nature of, phenomenological insight into the concept of phantasy; chapter two ends with 'ten propositions that can, perhaps, clarify the phenomenology of phantasy'. (These will be examined in detail in a subsequent chapter, when we examine the development, in Laing's work, of the concept of phantasy itself.) We are given an account of phantasy both as a mode of individual experience, and, systematically, of social interexperience. Subsequent chapters illustrate the theoretical points via a wealth of examples drawn freely from clinical reports, philosophical investigations and literature.

However, we must note a limitation; Laing talks of 'depicting the own person with a nexus of other persons', and this he does. But the phenomenology of the nexual interexperience is severely polarized: as the title of the book suggests, the orientation is towards the self, or own person, in relation to others, in so far as self and others together comprise a system of interexperience.

The phenomenology here presented lies half way, so to speak, between the purely self-centred approach of 'The Divided Self', and the approach of, say, the later Sartre, which transcends all individual phenomenologies to include a phenomenology of the group or system as such. It calls to mind the opening chapters of Hegel's 'Science of Logic' (Hegel, 1929). For instance (granted that a person is 'something'):

> First, Something and Other each are determinate Beings, or Somethings. Secondly, each is also an Other....(Something) is *in relation to its otherness,* and is not simply its otherness. Otherness is simultaneously contained in and also separated from it: it is *Being-for-Other*.... It preserves itself in its non-existence, and is Being; not Being in general but as *relation to itself* as opposed to inequality to itself. Such a Being is *Being-in-Self*. Being-for-Other and Being-in-Self constitute the two moments of Something. (Hegel, 1929, Vol. 1, pp. 129, 131-2; my emphasis.)

As for Hegel, so here for Laing, the Self is not in unilateral opposition to the rest of the world. Each Self is an Other for each Other, there is no logical primacy of Self over Other. As Hegel puts it, 'each is also an Other. Which is mentioned first... is immaterial' (p. 129). But, although dialectical, this view is also fundamentally diadic. Self and Other co-exist in mutual relation; and one can posit endless numbers of binary relations. What is never attempted, however, is the conceptualization of the relations between all these relations, and thus the relations of them to the whole. For example, given a group comprising individuals A, B, and C (a family perhaps) Laing can here conceptualize the relations A-B, A-C, and B-C but not $(A$-$B)$-$(A$-$C)$ etc., or $(A$-$B)$-$(B \underline{A} C)$ etc. We must leave aside, for the time being, the question as to whether 'depicting the own person within the nexus' logically requires depicting the nexus itself as a system of relations of relations. Here, we simply note that if it does, Laing does, ipso facto, fail to thus depict the own person.

The same criticisms also apply, of course, to the second part of the book. Again, the Hegelian influence is apparent; although it is Buber that Laing quotes. The notion that identity is feasible only via, and in so far as there is, complementarity, whilst typically Buberian is more fundamentally (or at least, more originally) Hegelian. Illustrating this Hegelian dialectic with a specifically human example this time, we find: 'Self-consciousness exists in itself and for itself, in that, and by the fact that, it exists for another self-consciousness; that is to say, it *is* only by being acknowledged or "recognized"' (Hegel, 1949, 'Phenomenology of Mind', p. 229).

Are we saying, then, that Part II is of basically the same nature, epistemologically as Part I? I think not. For whereas Part I is concerned with 'modes of interpersonal experience', Part II deals with 'forms of interpersonal action'. As implied above, the second part is similar in its dyadic nature: the issues are the mutual (i.e. *two*-way) confirmation (or not) of identity, and the nature of the *self*'s existential position as a function of *others*' actions. *But*, 'others' as they are defined by determination of self, i.e. generalized others, other-as-related-to-self, rather than others as an internally structured system, simultaneously embracing self.

But the content here is action, rather than experience: the preoccupation is more and more with behaviour (albeit, as it relates to the individual's experience). The empirical substance that Laing draws on is derived increasingly from behaviourally oriented scientists. (Fittingly enough, Bateson's paper was published in a journal called 'Behavioural Science'!)

If this is so, however, Laing is presented with something of a problem. To be schematic: He is concerned with forms of action. He needs, therefore, data on human behaviour. This he finds, especially in 'American research in communication, person perception, and family process' (from his list of 'sources', p. ix). But, such research, whilst not 'behaviourist' in the Watson-Skinner sense, is certainly nearer to the latter than it is to European phenomenology! Specifically, it involves, or, more precisely, appears to utilize, the natural scientific paradigm of treating the object of study as truly 'objective' and governed by laws of cause and effect which are (in principle) discoverable. Yet Laing states 'no aetiological theory of madness that I subscribe to is stated in this book.'

Bateson's theory, to take the obvious example, is quite emphatically a causal theory: it postulates a hypothesized 'mechanism' to account for the aetiology of a 'disease' called 'schizophrenia'. And, of course, so long as behaviour is observed without theoretical consideration accorded to experience, this must be so. That is to say, behaviour isolated from experience is, to the extent of its isolation, behaviour without meaning or purpose; and any event (here, behaviour) which does not derive from purpose, or intent, must be viewed as an effect of a cause, if it is to be accounted for at all. (It is only fair to note, at this point, that Bateson has himself come to be aware of the critical nature of the double bind as an 'object' for consciousness for the 'victim', i.e. the question of experience. See, for example, Bateson (1969), where he admits 'our original paper on the double bind contains numerous errors due simply to our having not yet articulately examined the reification problem.' (Reprinted Bateson, 1972, p. 272).)

Chapter 2

The crux of the problem here lies in the behaviourist approach of conceiving communication, even verbal communication, as 'pure' behaviour, isolated from experience, and thus devoid, ultimately, of meaning. The problem for Laing, then, posed in the middle of this stage, is how can one retain the valuable information yielded by the study of communication without, at the same time, destroying it by viewing it as pure behaviour? How can the personal, experiential significance of communication be restored, theoretically?

The solution is to be found in crude form in the only part of 'The Self and Others' not yet considered: the appendix. Anticipating, the answer is to replace the behavioural concept 'communication' by a more phenomenological concept, 'perspective', which, so to speak, synthesizes the perception of incoming communication and the knowledge of outgoing communication, within the experience of the individual.

Entitled, A Shorthand for Dyadic Perspectives, the appendix presents what is basically a system of notation for expressing, concisely, complex chains of mutual perceptions and experiences. The basic elements are as follows:

$$p \quad \text{the own person}$$
$$o \quad \text{the other person}$$
$$p \rightarrow \ldots \ldots \quad \text{the way the own person sees} \ldots$$

Thus $p \rightarrow o$ represents the way the own person sees the other
And $p \rightarrow (o \rightarrow p)$, the way the own person sees the other seeing him (p).

In addition, the following copulae are defined:

$$> \quad \text{better than}$$
$$: \quad \text{compared to}$$
$$\equiv \quad \text{equivalent to}$$
$$\not\equiv \quad \text{not equivalent to}$$

A number of 'examples' follow. Let us be clear exactly what this impressive-looking calculus is *intended* to achieve.

Laing introduces the appendix by reminding us that one not only has phantasies about oneself, and one's other, but 'about his phantasies about one's phantasies about his phantasies about one's experience etc.' (p. 171). These are not merely theoretical complexities, Laing urges. Some people really do live their lives at several phantasy steps removed from 'immediate experience'. It is the job of the therapist to make inferences, as validly as possible, about his patients' phantasies. The shorthand, then, enables one to express, graphically, the complexities of which the above is an example - and by no means an extreme one. Incidentally, in this shorthand, it would appear as
$$o \rightarrow (p \rightarrow (o \rightarrow p \rightarrow o))$$
This can be compared easily with, say, a slightly different chain, of comparable complexity, and the differences noted. To do this on a verbal level would obviously be much harder and more laborious. The shorthand is indeed a labour-saving device; and no more. It gives us no new information; it merely allows us to perceive more readily the information that is already there.

In this respect, as well as in its superficial appearance, it is similar to the use of Boolean algebra in the solution of multi-premise syllogisms. (See also, Lewis Carrol, 1958, 'Symbolic Logic and The Game of Logic'.)

Let us note, however, that in the introduction to the appendix, Laing talks of the therapist using his capacity to make inferences about his patient's phantasies about him (the therapist). Now this is a dyadic situation, and one element of it, the therapist, is accurately described as 'the own person'. That is, the person who makes the inferences is one of the two parties comprising the dyad.

But by the time we get to the examples, the situation has changed, although no comment on the change is made. Specifically, the examples do not concern therapist (p) and patient (o); they concern, for example, a man (p) and his wife (o); yet, is is the therapist who *actually* uses the shorthand. In other words, the therapist who makes inferences about phantasies *is no longer* one of the parties comprising the dyad. We cannot comment here on the significance of this; we shall do so later. At the present we must simply move on to consider the other component of this stage, 'Interpersonal Perception'.

It is claimed that 'Interpersonal Perception' 'develops in detail this schema' (i.e. the shorthand system just considered). How should we go about assessing this claim?

In the first place, it would perhaps be useful to remind ourselves of some of the biographical background to the book.

The Tavistock Institute of Human Relations undertook, in 1958, a massive research programme into families of schizophrenics, and of non-schizophrenics; and also of married couples whose marriage was (by their own admission) 'disturbed', and of couples whose marriage was not. The exact history of this staggering programme is not known; but Laing appears to have been involved, to some extent, in all of it. The research into families of schizophrenics, of course, is well known, as 'Sanity, Madness and the Family', conducted and written with Esterson. The research into families of non-schizophrenics has never been published.

'Interpersonal Perception', which was written by Laing and two of his co-workers from Tavistock, Mr Phillipson (Chief clinical psychologist at the Tavistock Clinic) and Dr Russell Lee (from Palo Alto Clinic), comprises two parts. The second part includes a considerable quantity of empirical data; specifically, it presents the results (or parts thereof) of the Institute's research into disturbed and non-disturbed marriages. But it is not just a lump of bare facts. For the statistical findings are presented, not only or even primarily as facts in their own right, but as the content, so to speak, with which to illustrate the *form* of the method devised during the research. This method is called the Interpersonal Perception Method (IPM).

The first part of the book deals with the theoretical foundations for this method. So, the book is, in fact, tripartite: comprising theory; a method derived from that theory; and empirical findings, gathered and processed according to that method.

Now, it is not known to what extent Laing was involved in each of these three parts. Of course, technically, each of the co-authors is equally responsible for each part: yet the discrepancy between, say, the theory section, and the empirical section is so vast, stylistically speaking, that it is impossible to seriously believe that what is technically (i.e. vis-à-vis copyright etc.) the case, was actually the case (vis-à-vis who did what).

Considering the empirical side first, we know that the bulk of the data for disturbed marriages came from the Family Discussion Bureau of the Tavistock Institute. As for the data on 'normal' dyads, we are told that much of this 'was done by Aaron Esterson while engaged in family research under the auspices of the Tavistock Institute. Mr Sidney Briskin collaborated in this work' (p. vii). (Sidney Briskin, a social worker, was and is one of the directors of the Philadelphia Association.)

It seems, then, that the research done into 'normal' families was used not for the originally proposed second volume of 'Sanity, Madness and the Family', but for data on non-disturbed married dyads. We know that Laing was involved with this, though just how far is uncertain.

As for the theoretical side, i.e. Part 1, this is unmistakably Laingian. The first sentence sounds as if it comes from the 'Politics of Experience': 'The human race is a myriad of refractive surfaces staining the white radiance of eternity' (p. 3).

This leaves us merely in doubt about the method, the IPM itself. But before attempting to resolve this doubt, we must familiarize ourselves with the theory presented in Part 1.

As a matter of fact, we are largely familiar with it already; indeed, its familiarity - that is, its similarity, to 'The Self and Others' - is the very rationale for its inclusion in this stage.

After the Foreword, the Acknowledgments, and a reproduction of a 'Peanuts' cartoon strip, we find the first chapter; entitled, significantly, Self and Other. This begins with a recognition of the 'pivotal step in philosophy' effected by Feuerbach; namely, the discovery that all hitherto philosophy had been exclusively orientated around 'I', failing to recognize that 'you' is just as primary as 'I'; that all 'you's' and 'they's' are 'I's'. (Incidentally, I cannot agree with Laing in according this honour to Feuerbach; for it should surely go to Hegel, idealist though he was. Witness the whole of 'Phenomenology of Mind', and especially 'Science of Logic' Hegel, 1929 and 1949, pp. 129-35.)

The point is that I am not the only perceiving agent in the world; the others that I see are 'centres of orientation of the objective universe'.

Thus, my field of experience comprises not only my view of my self and the others, but also my awareness of the fact that the others are aware of, and have views about, me. This sort of awareness (which may be more or less veridical) is termed by Laing a 'metaperspective'.

By virtue of this, my identity becomes 'refracted through the media of the different inflections of "the other"' (p. 4), and thus it undergoes changes or 'alterations' in and through the others I become to the others. Thus we speak of 'meta-identities, acquired through meta-perspectives of oneself'.

Laing emphasized that in this context identity, meta-identity and so on are theoretical abstractions; in reality, these levels are almost inextricably linked. One's notions of what other people think of one have an unavoidable effect on one's view of oneself.

We need a theory, Laing insists, that is capable of conceptualizing this interconnectedness. But it must be one which allows not only for interaction but also for interexperience; unlike, for instant, games theory. Laing recognizes the philosophical advances made in this respect by Husserl and Scheler (but not, surprisingly, Merleau-Ponty), with their exposition of 'intersubjectivity', at the same time noting the *lack,* so far, of a practical employment of these advances in social science.

Chapter two expands on these themes, and takes the first steps to remedy this lack. Entitled Interaction and Interexperience in Dyads, it makes much the same points as 'The Self and Others' did, but in much more formal manner. The formality, the precision, the certainty, even, that characterizes 'Interpersonal Perception' as against 'The Self and Others' is only achieved by a strict limiting of the conceptualization to dyadic contexts.

But how is this formality expressed? Initially, by the following confident assertion of what was explicitly only *assumed* in 'The Self and Others' (p. 5): 'In a science of persons, we state as axiomatic that: 1, Behaviour is a function of experience; 2, Both experience and behaviour are always in relation to some one or something other than self' (p. 9).

The very basics of a situation in which one person can be understood is two persons and a common situation. The elements of the situation are the behaviour and experience of the understander and the person understood. Note that it is one person who is understood; not a relationship. As we shall see, this is a very serious limitation. At the moment, however, we shall rest content to see how this limitation allows a formalizing advance over 'The Self and Others'.

It will be recalled that one of the problematical issues in 'The Self and Others' was the term 'communication'. Specifically, it was not at all clear to what extent this is an objective, behavioural concept, or a subjective, experiential concept. If it was one to the exclusion of the other, then clearly it is an inadequate concept for expressing a human dyadic situation. On the other hand, if it incorporates both moments, it in no way illuminates their conjugation; indeed, it obscures it.

By means of the concept 'perspective' however, this dilemma is overcome; when placed, that is, in the context of the aforementioned axioms. For the perceptual implications of the term point irrevocably to experience. Behaviour, axiomatically, is a function of experience, and thus of the perceptual experience posited by the term perspective. And finally, that behaviour constitutes itself as the 'some one or something other than self' of the second axiom, which exists in relation to the experience (and thus behaviour) i.e. the perspective, of the other person in that situation.

All this, as is readily apparent, was to be found, implicitly at least, in the appendix of 'The Self and Others'. But it was not to be found, verbally, in the text.

In a similar fashion, we may trace the fate of the notion of 'alienation effect'. This, it will be recalled, was expressed loosely, frequently in literary terms, in the text of 'The Self and Others', and referred to the degree of removal from immediate direct interaction and interexperience by absorption in phantasy systems.

It was expressed concisely, but non-verbally, in the appendix. (In fact, it was expressed quantitatively: the 'degree' of alienation is symbolically represented and measured by the number of brackets involved in writing the situation in shorthand.)

Here, however, in 'Interpersonal Perception', the issue is dealt with in a manner simultaneously formally rigorous and verbal, under the heading The Spiral of Reciprocal Perspectives. This allows, for the first time, a formal definition of the term 'Understanding' to be given: 'Understanding can be defined as the conjunction between the metaperspective of the one person and the direct perspective of the other.'

, A understands B, relative to issue X, when A's view of B's view of X coincides with B's view of X.

We may sum up the personal geography of Understanding, then, by saying that it occurs *in a dyad of a monad*. That is, understanding is limited to the understanding of an individual; the possibility of understanding a relationship is precluded.

So much, then, for theory. To what use is this theory put? Luckily, there is no need for a comprehensive review of the methodology deployed in the book; I shall summarize very briefly.

The investigators constructed a questionnaire (Laing, Phillipson, Lee 1966b) comprising sixty 'issues'. Each issue (e.g. 'is sorry for') is expressed four times, in the following fashion:

1 She is sorry for me
2 I am sorry for her
3 She is sorry for herself
4 I am sorry for myself.

The subject has to state how true each of 1-4 are. He then repeats the procedure, stating how he thinks 'she' would answer. Thus:

How would she answer the following?
1 I am sorry for him
2 He is sorry for me
etc.

And finally, the subject answers how he thinks she would think that he has answered the first four items. Thus there are twelve elements of data for each issue, which yield the direct perspectives, meta-perspectives and meta-meta-perspectives of both members of the dyad on four relationships defined by the issue. (The four relationships being She-He, He-She, She-She, and He-He.) The issues themselves supposedly deal with six categories: interdependence and autonomy, warm concern, disparagement, contentions, contradiction and confusion, and extreme denial of autonomy.

Analysis of the total 1,440 bits which comprise a full answer by two people to the questionnaire gives a profile of their relationships with each other and themselves. It tells the investigators (a) whether they agree or not (over issue X); (b) whether they understand that they agree or disagree; and (c) whether they realize, or fail to realize, that they understand (or misunderstand) that they agree (or disagree). Scores can thus be obtained for the percentages of issues (i) which they agree about, (ii) on which they understand their agreement, and (iii) over which they realize their understanding. (I have omitted all the negative alternatives in (i)-(iii), i.e. misunderstanding etc.)

That, basically, is the methodology of the IPM. In the book it is illustrated, empirically, by contrasting the mean scores (i-iii) of significant numbers of married couples who felt their marriages disturbed enough to seek help, with married couples who did not consider themselves so disturbed. Statistical tests were run, and it was found that IPM scores were significant in distinguishing between disturbed and non-disturbed couples.

Obviously, there is no question of doubting the figures given. Nevertheless, I feel I have to register my personal doubts; not about the theory, which is impeccable as far as it goes, but about the questionnaire itself.

I had decided that the only way to assess the IPM was to do it myself (and seek the co-operation of my co-habitee!) Our overwhelming impressions, having done it (expressed in writing independently, i.e. without prior discussion), were the same: that 99 per cent of the questions were meaningless to the point of being unanswerable other than totally arbitrarily. On lengthy consideration and discussion we concluded that the vast majority of the questions only related in a meaningful way to couples whose interpersonal life was extremely disturbed. Only in extreme situations, we felt, would it be meaningful to answer yes or no to such propositions as 'She blames me' or 'She can face up to my conflicts'.

Thus, it is no surprise that the IPM can and does distinguish between disturbed and non-disturbed couples. But it claims to do much more than that: it claims to reveal the texture of the interaction and interexperience of non-disturbed (indeed, any sorts of) couples. From my experience of it, I am afraid I cannot accept this. I hasten to add, however, that this is merely an attack on the actual questions used, not on the method itself, still less on the theory behind it.

So much, then, for 'Interpersonal Perception'. I think we have established that it embodies substantially the same concepts as 'The Self and Others', though in a fashion which is more rigorous, and thus, more circumscribed. It constitutes, I would argue, the logical culmination of the premise structure of 'The Self and Others'. That is to say, its dyadic nature is here revealed in its essentiality. The sociality of 'The Self and Others' (social phantasy systems etc.) was illusory, being merely the result of lack of rigour in its formulation. The premise structure of 'The Self and Others' is dyadic; but the inevitability of this is only made apparent in 'Interpersonal Perception'.

We must now attempt to summarize the characteristics of stage 2 as a whole.

As regards aims, they are, as with stage 1, basically heuristic. The *object* of Understanding, however, has changed: it is now interaction and interexperience, as opposed to the purely subjective 'intra-experience', so to speak, of stage 1. Initially, this new notion of understanding was formulated and achieved in nexual terms, but only vaguely, and, as the next chapter will show, not without contradiction. A more rigorous formulation was forthcoming, however, in dyadic terms.

Philosophically, the approach was existential-phenomenological in the first instance: the influence of Hegel and Buber was apparent, as was that of Sartre; less so, Heidegger. Later the approach becomes, implicitly at least, dialectical- or non-ego-centric as Laing puts it. The main influence here is Feuerbach; but also Buber, Husserl, Mead, and even Talcott Parsons. (One could say, therefore, though without stretching the point too far, that at the end of this stage, Laing is, philosophically speaking, at the interface of the confrontation between Hegel and Feuerbach, with a bit of existentialism thrown in. Yet there are still people who do not understand Laing's subsequent movement in the exact direction of Sartrean Marxism!)

There is no need to go over all the main concepts of this stage: mostly, they derive from 'Self and Other'. Of paramount importance, however, was the concept of 'phantasy', née psycho-analytic, but now of the critical phenomenological status of unconscious experience. The concept of Communication was observed to undergo reformulation in terms of perspectives thereby at least partially overcoming the problems of the behaviouristic implications of the former.

The double-bind paradigm was found to have been abstracted from its original formulation by Bateson, where it was profoundly aetiological, to serve as a basically *descriptive* term for denoting certain 'existential positions'.

The exact nature of the notion of 'psychosis' was found extremely hard to pin down in this stage: the standard psychiatric use of the term is emphatically rejected, yet Laing uses the word: without explicit formulation. Tentatively, however, we may say that it refers to the result of an attempt, by an individual, at self-liberation (from a social phantasy system) that has in some way 'gone wrong'. The exact status of the word 'wrong' in this context is highly problematical: and not commented on by Laing. We shall be returning to this problematic in a subsequent chapter.

This concludes our account of stage 2.

STAGE 3: INDIVIDUAL AND FAMILY PRAXIS

> If we look at it closely, we see that the basis of terror is the fact that the group has not, and cannot have, the ontological status that it claims in its praxis: conversely, it is the fact that each and every person is produced and defined on the basis of this non-existent totality (Sartre, 1960).

We move on now to consider the third stage: by what criteria have we determined its beginning?

As noted earlier, the next published work was an article which appeared in 'New Left Review', entitled Series and Nexus in the Family (Laing, 1962). In a sense, this is an epochal paper: it is the first occasion that Laing uses what can properly be called 'Marxist' concepts; for the entire purpose of the paper is to introduce four concepts derived more or less directly from Sartre's 'Critique de la raison dialectique' (Sartre, 1960) which endeavours to lay bare the a priori foundations of a concrete dialectical anthropology (using the word in the broader, Continental sense). As such, it must rank among the first attempts to employ Marxist theory in psychiatry (as opposed to psycho-analysis).

At any rate, this shift, (if not rupture, or break) to a Marxist rather than *merely* existentialist problematic, is the criterion for its being placed at the beginning of a new stage. In fact, the use of Sartrean Marxist concepts is to be considered as the defining feature of stage 3.

The next work by Laing also falls into this stage, being an attempt to actually employ certain of Sartre's concepts in the analysis of clinical and research data: I refer to 'Sanity, Madness and the Family', Vol. One: 'The Families of Schizophrenics' (Laing and Esterson, 1964). (Co-written with Esterson, his research colleague. The impact of Sartrean Marxism appears to have been more thoroughly lasting upont Esterson. See Esterson, 1970.)

The year 1964 also saw the publication of 'Reason and Violence' (Laing and Cooper, 1964); this book falls outside the continuum of psychiatric work represented by Laing; it purports to be an account of 'A Decade of Sartre's Philosophy' (the book's sub-title). The bulk of the book, in fact, is taken up by a precised translation of Sartre's 'Critique'. As its relevance is highly tangential with respect to the continuity of our review, it is not a work we shall focus on here. (The sole reference to mental illness is to be found, ironically, in the Preface, written specially by Sartre!) How it *is* useful, however, is as a reference book, against which Laing's *practical use* of Sartre's terms can be assessed. (For the record, other valuable references for understanding this 'monument of unreadability' (Mary Warnock), the 'Critique', which I have used are, in order of preference: Desan, 1966; Turner, 1973; Cooper, 1967a; Esterson, 1970 and Lafarge, 1970. Several important sections of it are available in translation in Cumming, 1965.

Finally, the paper entitled Mystification, Confusion and Conflict (Laing, 1965a), although not published till 1965, does, it will be argued, fall more logically into this stage than any other.

We begin the review of this stage, then, by examining the Series and Nexus article.

Laing states his aims quite clearly: '(to) give an account of two theoretical polarities developed by Sartre in the 'Critique', namely praxis and process, and series and nexus, using the family as a point of concrete reference (p. 7).

Laing notes that he employs 'certain minor modifications of Sartre's position' notably in so far as nexus is not a term used by Sartre. It does correspond closely, he claims, however, to Sartre's grouppe assermenté, or bonded group. What, then, is Laing's employment of these terms?

Taking praxis and process first, Laing says:
Events, occurrences, happenings, may be deeds done by doers, or they may be the outcome of, or parts of, a continuous series of operations that have no agent as their author.

In the first place, Sartre speaks of such events as the outcome of praxis: in the second case, as the outcome of process.

When what is going on in a group can be traced to the authorship of its members it will be termed praxis, and it will be thus far comprehensible. Behaviour, however, may have become too far alienated from anyone's responsibility to be directly comprehensible in terms of the deeds of any identifiable agents. But it will still be intelligible if one can retrace the steps from 'what is going on' (process) to 'who is doing what' (praxis) (pp. 7-8).

Thus, the entire distinction between praxis and process, for Laing at any rate, is found in the fact praxis has human authorship, it assumes intentionality, whereas process does not, being the blind outcome of physical, rather than conscious forces. For example, the delirious mutterings of a person with a severe fever could be said to be the outcome of process; if the same man, a few weeks later, pronounced (of his own free will), say, wedding vows, that would be the outcome of praxis.

Now the crucial point here is that praxis, being the outcome of human intention, is intelligible - it can be understood, in human terms. It can be identified with. Process, on the other hand, can be explained, by empirically verifying hypothesized cause and effect contiguities, but it can never be understood in human terms; that is, by reference to human motives, intentions, desires etc. There can be no question of responsibility - credit or blame - when dealing with processes.

However, as Laing points out, behaviour may be too alienated from individuals' responsibility to be directly comprehensible as praxis; but that same behaviour can be rendered intelligible by tracing the apparent 'process' back to 'praxis'. He goes on:

> Group actions appear to be generated without anyone's express desire and without anyone being able to see the possibility of an option, much less to exercise it.... In what sense, or to what extent, is this or that 'social fact' intelligible as praxis, or explicable as process?
>
> If an idea, for instance, has become a social fact (my neighbours object to 'coloured' people), if it appears to be a thing, its intelligibility is in the retracing of the steps from thing → social fact → idea → the men who thought it up: its apparently uncontrolled power, its anonymity, its unavowed authorship, are intelligible to the extent that one can discover the way it is a deed estranged by doers from themselves (p. 8).

I find this quite amazing. What Laing is actually saying, at least up to the colon, is that we can understand racial prejudice by working back from the more or less overt behavioural manifestation of prejudice, through the pure idea of it, to some specific occasion when someone brewed up the idea of hating black men. I find this extremely unconvincing; it seems like a sort of 'social anti-contract theory'. Certainly nothing like it appears in Sartre. The second half of the sentence is scarcely more illuminating. However, let us continue with the exposition.

Laing notes that a group *as such* can never actually *do* anything, except through the praxis of an individual. That is, process cannot be attributed to a group as a whole; or rather apparent group process can *always* (in theory) be traced to a multiplicity of individual praxes. However, such individuals are not 'de-situated, extrapolated, alone'; every human being is 'metamorphosed and transmuted in the interstices of his being in and through his modes of involvement with other human beings'.

Now, two extreme modes of involvement can be conceptualized; it is to these that we now turn.

The first extreme is a form of group termed a series:

> The series is a type of human multiplicity in which no person is essential, where everyone is quantitatively inter-changeable.

Yet the members of the series are united in a negative unity, by their reciprocal qualitative indifference to each other, and, simultaneously, by their quantitative concern (p. 9).

Laing quotes briefly Sartre's original example, that of a bus queue. The members of this primitive group have only the bus as a common object of unification. They relate to each other only in so far as they all relate to a common external object. (Sartre, of course, is referring to Parisian bus stops. The word 'queue' implies, in English, a structured, rank-ordered line; this would *not* be a series in Sartre's sense. A Sartrean queue is typically Continental: unstructured, chaotic, first-come-first-served.)

An interesting situation arises, Laing says, when this external object is a human group, defined by some criterion. For example, anti-Semites are united by a common object to which they are all anti, namely, Jews. The Klu Klux Klan are similarly united against American communists (among other things). This last example should alert us to an important feature of the series: *the common object does not actually have to exist*. It is sufficient that the members of the series believe it to be so. This point, which seems to me to be crucial, is, strangely, never explicitly pointed out by Laing. It is implicit, however, in his next example, that of scandal, an example which brings out other important features of the series.

With scandal, or public opinion, a certain act must be avoided because of what 'they' will think or say. It is always 'they', never 'us'. For example, 'we don't mind a coloured lodger, but what would the neighbours say'. Now the interesting point here is that the groups, 'they', is always 'there', never 'here'. It is ubiquitous, but it is a ubiquity of 'theres' (theirs). As Laing puts it:

The members of such a series are unified, for instance, by serial ideas which are never held by anyone in his own person. Each person is thinking of what he thinks the other thinks. The other, in turn, thinks what yet another thinks.... This serial collection is united by the fact that each person is a neighbour of his neighbour.... Since such a series is always the others, and always elsewhere, each member of the series feels unable to make any difference to the series (p. 9).

As we shall see, Laing is here using the Sartrean concept of sérialité in a highly refined, or at least restricted, way. But before we turn to Sartre himself, we must look at the last term to be introduced, that of nexus.

Laing starts by considering briefly what is involved in group formation.

If I think of certain others as together with me, and certain others as not together with me, I have already undertaken two acts of synthesis, resulting in we and them.

However, in order that we have a group identiy, it is not enough that I regard, let us say, you and him as constituting a we with myself. You and he have to perform similar acts of synthesis, each on his own behalf (p. 11).

Thus, each member of such a group interiorizes every other members' syntheses of the group. A perfectly formed group, then, for each member is both the synthesis of the multiplicity of the members, and the synthesis of the multiplicity of the syntheses made and maintained by each member. Hence, the group, in so far as it exists, exists as a perpetual synthesis of syntheses, a multiplicity of praxes; never as a thing, an object as such, a process. It can never be conclusively grasped as a whole. In Sartre's language, it is a continual totalization, never a totality. (These terms will shortly be examined.)

Now Laing defines a nexus as 'a group, whose unification is achieved through the reciprocal interiorisation by each of each other, in which neither a common object, nor organisational or institutional structures, etc., have a primary function as a kind of group "cement"' (p. 11).

That is, a nexus is a group whose bonding is entirely mutual, and entirely not serial. In distinction to a series, the nexus is a structure which is a ubiquity of heres. The nexus only exists in so far as it is present in each person, including the own person.

Families, Laing argues, are frequently of the structure of a nexus. Now if a family is a nexus, it follows that any threat to the group is a threat to each member, and vice versa. In particular, if one individual member decides to leave the group, the group as a whole is threatened; partly because, before any member can even wish to leave, he must have dissolved the interiorizations in himself of the group synthesis.

Hence, the united family, if it is nexual, depends on each member continuing to act on the basis of already established group syntheses. How is this achieved?

> The condition of permanence of such a nexus, whose sole existence is each person's interiorization of it, is the successful re-invention of whatever gives such interiorization its raison d'être. If there is no external danger, then danger and terror have to be invented and maintained. Each person has to act on the others to maintain the nexus in them.... The 'protection' that the family offers its members seems to be based on several preconditions: (i) a phantasy of the external world as extraordinarily dangerous; (ii) the generation of terror inside the nexus at this external danger. The 'work' of the nexus is the generation of this terror. This work I shall call violence (p. 12).

Thus, the close knit united family commonly supposed to be based on love, is based on violence and terror. Yet, we should not talk of family pathology, Laing insists. He notes that the rigidity of such nexual families is 'explained' (not understood) by social scientists by conceptualizing the family as an organism, with its own physiology and pathology. Such rigidity, which so to speak, brings about an atrophy of its organs (members) is seen as being due to an excessive homeostatis being in operation. However, family pathology, Laing claims, is 'an even more corrupt concept than individual psycho-pathology'. For what is being done by so viewing the family is to assert that the family is a thing, a totality; it is to obscure the fact that what happens in the family is, in reality, praxis. It extends the unintelligibility of the individual to the group. For only a process can be pathological, and only praxis can be intelligible. Of course, phenomenologically, the family can and does *appear* to be an organism; but that should not make us lose sight of the fact that ontologically it is not and cannot be such, just as, ontologically, a person is not an organism, but an origin of action, an agency with consciousness.

So much, then, for the concepts as outlined by Laing in this paper; we must now turn to examine the source of these concepts, for Laing claims to use them as Sartre does, with only a few 'minor modifications'.

It cannot be our aim here to give a summary of the 'Critique', or of all the concepts introduced in it; rather, we shall restrict ourselves only to those which Laing employs, plus any that are found necessary to give a sufficient account of those.

Laing uses six concepts from the 'Critique': Praxis, process, series, bonded group (nexus), intelligibility, and totalization (plus related words: totality, detotalization etc.). How does Sartre define or use these terms? We start with praxis and process.

Praxis refers to human action, and *very* roughly can be taken as synonymous with it. So we ask, how does Sartre see human action?

As may be expected, praxis is a dialectical concept; specifically, praxis is seen as the dialectical synthesis of two moments: the field of possibilities, and the individual's project. Now project refers to the subjective inclination or intention of the individual to transcend his existing material circumstances; roughly, to create an event by his own agency in the world. But men do not exist in a vacuum; the 'existing material circumstances' determine what the possible choice of action is, in a physical way. They constitute, in fact, the 'field of possibilities' *within* which the individual is free to choose his project.

Thus, through praxis, the individual transcends his environment, or as Sartre says, he 'depasses' it. That is, he destroys it (in so far as he changes it) yet he conserves it, by absorbing it (in so far as it is one of the determinants of the outcome of his action) and he goes beyond it (in so far as he creates a new state of affairs).

Praxis, then, is in effect the passage from the objective (field of possibilities), through interiorization (project) to the objective (event in the world). By virtue of the fact that human intentionality is involved, praxis is characterized by the fact that it 'possesses' an end, an 'objective'; i.e. that towards which the individual 'pro-jects' himself. As such, it is the free constitution of an end or ends.

Process, on the other hand, is action which does not have human agency as its origin. It is action which does not stem from project. It is nevertheless dialectical, Sartre maintains, by virtue of the fact that it has the dual, contradictory aspects of being at once a form of action, and yet a form of passivity, lacking, as it does, any agency. (I remain far from convinced of this point: it sounds suspiciously like a dialect of nature. However, the point is not crucial in this context.)

It is possible to distinguish two sorts of process; that which is the result of purely physical matter in states of energy disequilibrium (e.g. a star going nova, or a rise in body temperature when the body is infected with certain viruses); and that which is the result of a multiplicity of human action, where the result cannot apparently be traced to any specific human agency or intention. In this latter instance, the process is only apparently process; it can, in theory at least, be traced to human praxis. However, such praxis cannot be said to be the free constitution of ends (as nobody freely, intentionally constitutes them); on the contrary, the action is itself constituted by the unintentional action of a multiplicity of individuals. As such, it is said to be action unfreely constituted, and the praxes involved are said to be 'alienated praxes'.

So far, then, it seems that Laing is using Sartre's term as Sartre does himself, though we may perhaps wonder why Laing makes no mention of their dialectical nature, nor the crucial concept of project.

We move on now to consider the term totalization, and its related terms.

First, we should note that Sartre uses the word 'totalization' to refer both to the *act* of totalizing, and to the product yielded by this act.

In this second sense, we may state initially that: a *totalization is a dialectically produced structure*. In terms of the nomenclature Marx borrowed from Hegel, it is a 'synthesis'. Thus, a totalization is *always* to some degree 'complex', in so far as it is a 'structure', not a monad.

In the first sense, a totalization is always a form of *human* activity, praxis in fact, because it is dialectically *produced*. As Althusser would say, it is an 'instance of practice'.

Praxis, as we saw, is regarded as the outcome of a dialectic between human consciousness (project) and the field of the given (which may be the material world, or it may be 'raw' concepts upon and through which *theoretical* practice is exercised, to yield knowledge).

Thus all and only praxis yields totalizations.

For example, the painting of a picture yields a totalization. The artist's 'raw materials', in this instance, are on the one hand, his paints, canvas, brushes, etc. (his 'means of production') and on the other, his ideas, preconceptions, unconscious phantasies etc.; these are 'totalized' in the praxis of producing the painting, which is the resulting 'totalization'.

Note, however, that it is not only the production of the painting that both is and yields a totalization: the act of perceiving and grasping it as a painting is likewise a totalization; specifically, of the painting as a 'raw material' and the observer's total consciousness which he so to speak brings to the painting. Even to grasp it merely as 'a painting' fulfils this criterion in that it is a totalization of the observed *form* of the object (though here, not its 'contents') and the observer's past experience of recognizing and calling objects manifesting that form 'painting'. And this is true epistemologically for any sort of conscious grasping of reality.

A crucial form of totalization occurs when what is totalized is a human multiplicity; this has been discussed above, with respect to series and nexus. The nexus, we saw, was an extreme form of social relation, where the raw material for the totalization, that is the group, is *purely* the members of that group.

Totalization tends to appear as totalities. To examine the

nature of this illusion (which is of crucial import to this book - for it is basically this illusion which is later referred to as 'Durkheim's Illusion') will thus clarify further the nature of 'totalization' itself. Sartre defines a totality in the following way:

> Totality is defined as a being, radically distinct from the sum of its parts which is complete, in each of its parts, and which relates to itself either through its relation to one or several of the parts, or else by its relation to connections between the parts themselves.... By its very definition, it claims the ontological status of the in-itself, or the inert. The synthetic unity which will produce its appearance of totality cannot be an act, but only what remains of an act.... When practical objects are concerned (i.e. tools in the broadest sense) our present action is what gives them the appearance of totalities by reviving the praxis which attempted to totalize their inertia. These inert totalities have a major importance... and create among men that type of relation... called the practico-inert (Sartre, 'Critique de la raison dialectique', pp. 138-9, trans. J. Atkinson in Cumming, 1965).

Totality is thus rather a relative term, paradoxically, in so far as a constant totalization is necessary to maintain the appearance of a totality. For any totalization is immediately detotalized, by being put in opposition to a new project, and subsequently retotalized. As Sartre says: There are no final totalities in history. Further, in the case of social relations, the apparent 'totality' of a group of which I am a member - 'us' - involves not only my own totalizations (of myself and the others as a group) but also the others' totalizations of my totalizations, and mine of theirs; i.e. it is always a *totalization-in-progress*. The time-transcending illusion of totality thus resides in the subjectivity of the individual as against the social field's mode of being, which is intersubjectivity.

Sartre also talks about totalization in another pair of ways: ontologically and epistemologically. The former refers to the creation of 'objects' (human or otherwise); the latter to knowledge. In the second sense here, totalization refers to the praxis of totalizing given information with the awareness of knowing it, to yield the 'product', which is self-conscious knowledge. The significance of this distinction will only become apparent when we turn our attention formally to the concept of Intelligibility.

However, we have seen that it is of the essence of a totalization to be dialectical. Thus, in the epistemological sense, a totalization so to speak 'embodies' dialectical reason; whereas ontologically, a totalization is dialectical reason in action, that is its very mode of being proclaims its dialectical nature, precisely because the human social world constitutes and transcends itself in the acts of totalization performed by its members, these being dialectically related as explained above.

On the issue of complexity, Sartre is a little less forthcoming. His rejection of essentialist simplicity, including all forms of reductionism, is apparent in 'The Search for a Method', particularly in his treatment of 'dogmatic Marxism' and in his appraisal of Flaubert; but his alternatives seem to lack the precision and vigour that have (wrongly) earned Althusser the criticism of being 'structuralist'. While Sartre asserts the multiplicity of contradictions determining a given situation, he offers nothing equivalent to Althusser's concepts of overdetermination and structure-in-dominance. Sartre, in a somewhat hostile interview with 'New Left Review' (Sartre, 1974b), half-heartedly defended himself against such charges, ultimately resorting to a 'wait for next week's thrilling instalment' technique (i.e. vol. II of the 'Critique'). The gist of his thinking seems to be that every situation is so unique that no structural generalizations about situating contradictions within a whole can be substantial enough to be worth making. This is of course related to Sartre's insistence on tracing all forms of praxis back to individuals. Complexity in fact only becomes problematic at a relatively high level of totalization, notably within the unity formed by opposing classes. Sartre could never agree with Althusser here that history is a process without a subject. It is rather for him the very opposite - nothing but totalized-totalizing praxis. However, the point does not seem to me to be a crucial one for either party. For surely Althusser would admit that it is frequently necessary to delve into *how* certain groups participating in struggles are constituted, sometimes down to an individual level (did not Marx do this in 18th Brumaire?). Equally one would hope that Sartre would agree that in practice one cannot hope to literally trace the praxis of, say, the Chinese peasant class in 1949 to the individual praxis of each peasant, however theoretically sweet it would be to do so. For Laing's purposes (and ours in this thesis), which are biographical/ psychological more than sociological, Sartre's attitude seems more relevant.

It would perhaps be advisable at this juncture to remind ourselves of the distinction between dialectics, as conceived here, and other intellectual disciplines which handle what is called 'complexity'.

Piagetian structuralism, for example, certainly handles complexity. But structural evolution is by no means the same as dialectical development. For the latter is quite literally unthinkable without consciousness; dialectics, as Sartre uses the term, can only be manifest through totalization, and these as we have seen, invariably and necessarily involve some degree of human intentionality.

For example, the development of the genitals of a child in puberty would be considered an aspect of structural evolution by Piaget, but not a totalization by Sartre: the development is a biological one, that is largely independent of the child's consciousness. It is in fact, *process not praxis*. To the minimal extent that the child's consciousness, through his behaviour, does effect the development, to precisely that extent there is praxis and a dialectic.

Similarly, to the extent that Piaget deals with biological and conscious aspects of development in the same 'natural', non-dialectical way, to that same extent he fails to draw the vital distinction between process and praxis. It is not that either approach is wrong: both are fully and solely adequate in their own sphere of reference.

In so far as Piaget restrains himself to applying his methods to those realms where they are appropriate, one can say that Sartre and Piaget are talking about a different kind of complexity. For Sartre, complexity is the specific dialectical structure of a given social situation, which is constituted by the actors' mutual totalization of that situation. For Piaget, complexity is constituted not by praxis but by forces; his is a sort of cybernetic complexity (or else a dialectical one misconstrued as a cybernetic one).

We must now return to the 'Critique', and an exposition of the next term, the practico-inert.

Although Laing does not employ the concept of practico-inert, I shall deal with it here as it does lead on, for Sartre, to the next concept Laing does use, that of series.

It is to be stressed that in themselves objects have merely an inert status; it is only in so far as they relate to, *and lead to relations between,* human beings, that the status of practico-inert arises. What are these relations?

Sartre considers the object known as a bus stop. At a bus stop we have a multiplicity of individuals who collect together with an inert object as their mutual centre of orientation. That is, each relates to the object, the bus stop, but none relate to each other directly. Hence, they form a group, but of a very weak kind. For each individual, every other individual is replaceable by any other. All qualitative differences are irrelevant. Put abstractly, each individual has become an other for and among the others. This is the essence of this sort of group, which Sartre terms a 'series'. In a series, each individual has his internal qualities, his uniqueness, negated, in so far as he is quantitatively interchangeable with the others. He becomes merely an object, a unit, his status for the others is that of a being-in-externality. This sort of relation, in which men are united by a common external object, only to regard each other as objects, is termed practico-inert.

How does this relate to Laing's use of the term? I think we can see that, in essence, their uses are the same, though Laing considers almost exclusively the special case where the common external object is a (real or imagined) human group (e.g. the reds, the black, witches, and so on). Laing does not, of course, *derive* the concept, in the formal way that Sartre does, but then he really has no need to do so; generally, I find his account of it satisfactory for his purposes.

As already noted, Sartre does not himself use the term nexus, but as Laing claims, Sartre's bonded group does resemble nexus as conceived by Laing.

I shall not detail Sartre's account of the features of a bonded group as such, but rather look at the *relation* between such a group and a series, and contrast that with what we find in Laing.

Sartre devotes a large part of the 'Critique' to showing how and in what conditions a series changes into a group proper. This is indeed a crucial point for Marxism in general in that if one views the exploiting class as a common external object, the exploited class are *at least* a serial group. The point is, then, how does a serial group of exploited workers, each one isolated from each other, come to form *direct* links between themselves, and create a bonded group, with class consciousness? This 'apocalypse' as Sartre terms it, is probably the most important part of the 'Critique', at least for Sartre. Yet Laing does not mention it; on the contrary, series and nexus are for him polar opposites, and that seems to be that. More important, perhaps, is the related point that the role of terror in partially nexual families is thus, obviously, not considered.

The importance of this lies in the fact that, as Sartre has shown, the basis of terror in a group is to be found in the fact that, in moving from seriality, through the group-in-fusion to 'nexus', the negation of seriality permits *individual* praxis, whereas in its genesis the nexus is denied group praxis. Hence, conformity in individual praxis is essential, which requires terror. *It is significant that Laing nowhere tries to relate praxis to nexus*. Considering his concern with the maintenance or decay of family unity these facts are surprising.

We come now to the hardest, yet most important concept that Laing takes from Sartre: Intelligibility.

We have already noted that dialectical reason has so to speak a dual aspect; human history itself is a dialectical totalization, it is dialectical reason in action; and dialectical reason is also, epistemologically, the permeability of that totalization to knowledge, that knowledge itself being a totalization within the individual.

Similarly, Intelligibility has a dual aspect, and is itself dialectical.

In the first place, we may speak of the intelligibility of history that is, recalling our definition of history, the intelligibility of human action in the world.

In the second place, we may speak of the intelligibility of dialectical knowledge itself. Thus, not only is human reality intelligible, but the praxis of rendering it intelligible is itself intelligible. Hence we speak of the translucency of dialectical reason - its second intelligibility.

Now we may ask, what is involved in creating this dialectical intelligibility?

Sartre utilizes what he calls the 'progressive-regressive method'. This consists of the two moments, implied in its name. The first moment, the regressive, involves a return, in thought, to the circumstances prior to the action which is to be understood, to establish what were the real possibilities - the field. It is the discovery of the original context of the project. This can be expressed verbally.

The second moment, the progressive, involves a sympathetic moving through the field of possibilities, again in thought, to re-live the project, the end of which the praxis concerned constituted. Cooper (1967a) has summed this up very well.

> There are, first, the acts by which a person presents himself to us; in these acts we trace an intention that relates to a prior and more basic choice of self: this presentation of self... is the *constituted dialectic*. From a phenomenological description of this constituted moment we proceed by a *regressive movement* to a *constitutive dialectic:* by this latter term we mean all the socio-environmental (intra-familial, extra-familial, economic-class, social-historical) conditioning factors in their

inter-penetrating fullness. But we cannot end here. By a *progressive movement* we must attain the personal synthesis, the total totalization - the person's unique totalization of the conditioning totalization on the basis of its totalization of him. We have then attained the 'truth' of the person's life, or of some specific sector of his life (p. 25).

The recreation of the project is termed by Sartre 'comprehension'; he defines it as 'that movement of the human consciousness by which it reproduces the project of the other' (Sartre, 1960, p. 171). It is to be distinguished from knowledge in that as a form of lived experience, it cannot be rendered in terms of verbal symbols. It cannot be a form of 'intellection', which is Sartre's term of conceptually formulated knowledge. Both comprehension and intellection are essential for full dialectical intelligibility. Thus, the social scientist who wishes to render intelligible the actions of those he studies must, for Sartre, re-live the projects of those he studies. (This is what we meant, but could not say, when it was claimed (Chapter 2, stage 1) that 'a phenomenological analysis is... an absolute prerequisite to adequate knowledge'.)

In the light of these considerations, one cannot help but feel that Laing's account of it is hardly adequate in the Series and Nexus article. For he says that as soon as what is going in a group can be traced to praxis it is 'thus far comprehensible'. But comprehension involves more than that; specifically, the re-living of the project 'behind' the praxis. Project is not even mentioned. Similarly, to say, as he does, that the intelligibility of a social fact is in the retracing of the idea behind it to the people who thought it up is, to say the least, a very crude account of a highly intricate concept.

The crucial problem, one would think, in all this is how does one re-live an alienated praxis? That is, granted that someone is involved in a 'group process' (i.e. a situation involving mass alienated praxes), even when this process is traced back to the praxes concerned, how does one comprehend them? It seems one cannot, as they lack project; yet, Sartre maintains, comprehension is essential for intelligibility, and all human actions are in theory intelligible.

Let us recapitulate; intelligibility involves the totalization of the individual's comprehension of what he is studying, with his own awareness of him doing it. For example, to render a family's actions intelligible, the social scientist must not only come to be aware of their totalizations of each other, and of the family itself, but also be aware of his own totalization of their totalization; of the way he constitutes himself as a part of the field that he is studying.

This, I think, can give us a clue to the problem just stated. The individuals concerned may not experience themselves as active agents in 'what is going on' (i.e. as possessors of projects); the investigator's task, then, is to discover what their totalizations of the situation are. That is, the very *absence* of projects, on their part, with respect to their (alienated) praxis, is what must concern him. In producing overall intelligibility, then, a totalization is required which takes into account not only comprehension but the lack of it; the lack of experienced awareness on the part of the actors concerned. This appears to contradict Sartre's criteria; on close examination, however, it can be seen that it does not. If an alienated person does something (alienated praxis which has no conscious project), then for the investigator to 're-live', or better, realize, its lack of lived meaning for that person is exactly what constitutes its 'comprehensibility' for the investigator. The paradox of alienated praxis is that through realizing its incomprehensibility one comprehends it, and one is thus able to render, the context of which it is a part, intelligible.

However, as far as Laing is concerned, we are anticipating too far. As noted, no remarks of this kind are to be found in the Series and Nexus article. We leave the article, then, with the concept of intelligibility extremely ill-defined, and move on to the next work, 'Sanity, Madness and the Family' (Laing and Esterson, 1964).

Before discussing what is said in 'Sanity, Madness and the Family' it would be advisable to recall a few historical facts about the book.

First, it was not published till April 1964, although it was completed in August of the previous year. The research behind it, which provides the direct source for the bulk of the book, was conducted largely at two mental hospitals where Dr Esterson was a member of staff, and was started in 1958, as part of the Tavistock Institute's research programme. The actual research was completed in 1962, after which Laing went to the USA to discuss it with a host of well-known scientists, including Bateson, Goffman and Speck. It is worth recalling at this point, that Sartre's 'Critique de la raison dialectique', was not published till 1960, by which time the research programme was half over at least; this may in part account for the fact that the Sartrean concepts, which, the Introduction claims, form the theoretical framework, do appear in the text to be rather 'stuck on', almost as an afterthought.

The book falls naturally, for our purposes, into two sections: the Introduction, which is purely theoretical, but comprises a mere twelve pages; and the bulk of the book, which comprises eleven 'case histories', of families which contain one adult female diagnosed as schizophrenic. The families were selected on the basis of numerous criteria, which are listed in the Introduction.

The theoretical discussion, brief as it is, concerns two main areas: the nature of 'schizophrenia', and the theoretical framework used by the authors to render the clinical material 'more socially intelligible', this being their primary aim.

Concerning schizophrenia, they outline very briefly the conventional view, that the behaviour and experience of certain people is taken to be symptomatic evidence for an underlying pathology, this being identified as the disease schizophrenia. They then note the total lack of any evidence *for the 'disease' itself*, as opposed to its supposed symptoms, and on the basis of this lack, claim that, *at most*, schizophrenia as a disease should be regarded as a hypothesis, not a fact or assumption.

Their approach is different altogether, as they do not even take over this hypothesis: 'the issue is simply bracketed off' (p. 19). What they do is to try and show that the supposedly symptomatic behaviour and experience 'makes sense' when placed in the context in which it arose.

Theoretically, their starting point is the 'person'.

Each person not only is an object in the world of others, but is a position in time and space from which he experiences, constitutes, and acts in *his* world. He is his own centre with his own point of view, and it is precisely each person's *perspective* on the situation that he shares with others that we wish to discover (p. 19).

They go on to show how one individual may be different people, experientially, according to whom he or she is interacting with. Jill, for example, may be daughter, sister, wife or mother according to context.

The total context of all these contexts is the family as a whole, or the family nexus (which may include individuals not strictly part of the kinship network, but who are nevertheless regarded as 'one of the family' - godparents might be an example).

The authors go on to note that one of the most serious theoretical difficulties involved in 'the apparent discontinuity between the processes of the system and the actions of the agents who comprise the system'. It is here that they find Sartre's concepts of praxis, process, and intelligibility useful. There follows a rewrite of that part of the Series and Nexus article which deals with these terms, plus the rejection of the concept of family pathology. Their exposition is almost identical, except in that the illustration, criticized earlier, of racial prejudice is, happily, omitted.

They claim, then, to have developed a method which enables them to study 'at one and the same time (i) each person in the family; (ii) the relations between persons in the family; (iii) the family itself as a system' (p. 23). They go on to note, however, two reservations. The first concerns the level of analysis:

Inferences about experiences that the experiencers themselves deny, and about motives and intentions that the agent himself disavows, present difficulties of validation that do not arise at that phenomenological level to which we have restricted ourselves .... The reader will find documented the quite manifest contradictions that beset these families, without very much exploration of the underlying factors which may be supposed to generate and maintain them (p. 26).

This clearly relates to the problem we isolated at the end of the discussion of the previous article. Expressed formally, the phenomenological reduction that is undertaken moves from process to praxis but stops there. They do not descend to the level of individual project. Formally, then, one cannot but conclude that they do not achieve (and did not in fact aim for) full dialectical intelligibility as conceived by Sartre.

This is recognized implicitly when they state 'within the terms of phenomenology itself, this study is limited.... Subsequently we hope to go much further in interpreting data' (pp. 25-6). We may sum this limitation up by saying that their analysis of the constituted dialectic falls considerably short of that envisaged by Sartre.

The second reservation concerns the constitutive dialectic, that of totalization.

Our totalization of the family itself as a system is incomplete. Our account of each family is to a considerable degree polarized around the intelligibility of the experience and behaviour of the person who has already begun a career as a schizophrenic. As such, the focus remains somewhat on...the person-in-a-nexus, rather than on the nexus itself. This we believe to be historically unavoidable (p. 26).

This again, of course, falls short of the formal requirements laid down by Sartre. An attempt to meet the requirements was subsequently made, however, by Esterson, who took the analysis/synthesis for one of the eleven families very much further in his book 'The Leaves of Spring' (Esterson, 1970).

Having recognized their limitation at this juncture, the authors go on to restate their aim: 'We have tried in each single instance to answer the question: to what extent is the experience and behaviour of that person... intelligible in the light of the praxis and process of his or her family nexus? (p. 27).

It is beyond the scope of this thesis to attempt to measure that extent; for one thing, there is only Esterson's (ibid.) example of a more complete study, of only one family, plus Cooper's (1967a) study (though the latter is said to require 'psycho-analytic interpretation...To achieve a full comprehension') against which to compare the intelligibility here achieved. We may say without hesitation, however, that the authors succeed in rendering their subjects remarkably intelligible, even with this partial analysis. Indeed, one is left wondering how orthodox psychiatrists can be so stupid as to define the individuals concerned as unintelligible in the first place.

It is perhaps worth mentioning that the first edition of 'Sanity, Madness and the Family' was subtitled 'Part I, the Families of Schizophrenics'; by the second edition (1969), the 'Part I' was dropped. Part II, as far as can be ascertained, was to have been a similar investigation into 'normal' families. Judging from the few comments made by Laing on the matter (for example, the ITV programme, Something to Say; reprinted in 'The Guardian', 27 December 1972) this work was actually carried out, though never published. One may perhaps speculate that Laing's intense involvement in Kingsley Hall, and his subsequent split with Esterson when he (Esterson) left the Philadelphia Association, are responsible for the project being 'shelved'.

The next work to examine is the book, written by Laing and Cooper, entitled 'Reason and Violence' (Laing and Cooper, 1964). Subtitled 'A Decade of Sartre's Philosophy, 1950-1960', it consists of an exposition, rather than an evaluation or application, of three recent works by Sartre: 'St. Genet', 'Search for a Method', and the 'Critique'. Laing's contribution was to the Introduction, and 'Search for a Method', which were co-written with Cooper, and the account of the 'Critique', which is his own. The latter consists of little more than a decimal précis, a translation-cum-reduction, to about one tenth its original length. The end product is so compressed, not to say difficult, as to be virtually incomprehensible, at least as an introduction to the 'Critique'. To those already acquainted with the 'Critique', or the concepts propounded in it, it does, however, serve as a very useful guide.

I can see very little point in attempting to assess Laing's

rendering of the 'Critique'; apart from the sheer vastness and complexity of the 'Critique' itself, it has never been translated. The task is unnecessary, anyway; for it has already been done, by Sartre himself. In the foreword, written by Sartre especially for inclusion in 'Reason and Violence', he has this to say:

> I have read attentively the work that you have been willing to entrust to me, and I had the pleasure to find in it a very clear and faithful exposition of my thought. Even more than the perfect understanding of the Critique, what appealed to me in this book, as in your previous works, is your constant concern to achieve an 'existentialist' approach to mental illness....I attach the greatest value to your researches, in particular to the study you attempt of the family milieu takes as nexus and as series (Sartre, November, 1963, p. 7, trans. Dennis Moore).

In the light of that, any further comment would seem superfluous.

We move on, then, to examine the last work of this stage, an article entitled Mystification, Confusion and Conflict (Laing, 1965a). Although not published till 1965, it does fall naturally into this stage, as it employs concepts like praxis and process; it labels and defines concepts so far only implicit in this stage, but undoubtedly present; the clinical material used for illustrations is taken directly from 'Sanity, Madness and the Family', and finally, there are no hints of those features which we shall come to see are characteristic of the next stage.

The article starts as follows:

> Marx used the concept of mystification to mean a plausible misrepresentation of what is going on (process) or what is being done (praxis) in the service of the interests of one socioeconomic class (the exploiters) over or against another class (the exploited)....We can employ Marx's theoretical schema... in the field of the reciprocal interaction of person directly with person (p. 343).

The aim of the paper is to present the concept of mystification, plus some related concepts, as developed by Laing and his colleagues at the Tavistock Institute, with clinical illustrations to demonstrate 'the heuristic value of the theoretical discussion and its crucial import for therapy (p. 344).

Mystification is used both actively and passively; that is, to connote both an act and a state. Actively, to mystify is to mask whatever is going on, and thus to lead to 'confusion', i.e. a failure to perceive what is going on. Passively, the state of being mystified may or may not entail a *feeling* of confusion. That is, confusion may or may not be experienced as such.

Related to these terms is 'conflict'. Mystification frequently seeks to avoid authentic conflict, i.e. the working out of real contradictions perceived as such, but does not necessarily avoid all conflict. On the contrary, it may institute conflict over nonexistent issues, thereby clouding the real issues.

The first example Laing gives of mystification concerns a mother and her child. The child is playing noisily, and is getting on the mother's nerves. She wants him to go to bed. Now she may say, 'I am tired, go to bed', or 'Go to bed because I say so.' These are straight injunctions, which the child may obey or disobey. On the other hand, the mother may employ mystification and say: 'I'm sure you feel tired, darling, and want to go to bed, don't you?'

The mystification here resides in several aspects: first, what is apparently a factual description of the child's condition is really a command; second, the child's feelings are being defined for him regardless of how he actually feels; and third, what he is 'supposed' to feel is what the mother actually feels.

Laing goes on to note that it is implicit in the theory of mystification that demystification must occur before enlightened action can occur. What theoretical schema, then, does Laing propose for demystification in therapy?

He starts by noting that in many families, particularly those who contain a person diagnosed as schizophrenic, all actions on the parts of the members, are evaluated with respect to certain axes of orientation. In many cases a single axis may be of such importance as to virtually act as a lynch pin that keeps the family together.

Conflict arises over issues; and issues may be about members' actions in relation to axes; or they may be about what the 'right' axis really is. If mystification serves, then, to obscure issues, it is the job of the therapist (demystifier) to discover the real issues, and contrast these with the false issues. As Laing says:

> Our axis of orientation both as researchers and as therapists is to pick out what the axes of orientation and issues are for each member of the family in turn.... There are as many issues as people can invent, but we have come to regard the issue of person perception as central in all the families we have studied.
>
> Although this issue may be central as we perceive it, we have to recognize that it is not necessarily seen or accepted as such by the family members themselves.... (The method) is to present the perspectives of everyone in turn (including our own) on 'the shared situation' and then to compare the evidence for the validity of different points of view (p. 347).

An example follows concerning a teenage girl and her mother. Her mother perceived any signs of maturation on the part of her daughter as symptoms of either badness or madness (e.g. going out with boys, and the questioning of accepted religious beliefs). Her axes, then, were simply good/bad, and sane/mad, these being identified with her daughter's behaviour, chronologically, then/now. 'Good', for the mother, was the girl's behaviour as an obedient child. She lacked any historical perspective, both of her daughter, her relation to her daughter, and of the family as a whole. Consequently, she was not able to use the axis of, say, immature/mature, which would have corresponded, objectively, to the girl's developing biological maturity.

Laing goes on to argue that the misrepresentation of praxis as process is a form of mystification, and that this misrepresentation is itself a form of praxis. He notes ironically that this form of mystification occurs not only in families but equally in the so-called social theory that deals with the results of such mystification. Hence, a person is repeatedly treated as a thing by its parents, who deny it autonomy, agency, etc. The person reacts in certain ways, only to be viewed and treated by the 'experts' as a thing again; namely an 'infected', or 'diseased' organism.

We have already noted that the immediate function of mystification appears to be to mask real conflicts. As the example of the mother/daughter showed, however, what is really at stake behind the masking of conflicts is a concern to maintain the status quo of the family. It will be recalled that the family, viewed as a nexus, was seen to be based on violence and terror; any threat to the nexus resulted in pressure being brought to bear in the direction of the status quo. Mystification, then, in so far as it masks conflicts which are seen as threatening the nexus, serves as a form of violence used against such threats, and serves the nexus as a system.

Mystification also serves to maintain rigid stereotyped roles, on an individual level. A mystified relationship rules out the genuine reciprocal conformation of identity, and substitutes a pseudo-mutuality in which false fronts are induced, and an overall system of pseudo-identities arises based on phantasy. Such systems are found to be almost universal in the families of schizophrenics; Laing states that 'we are currently investigating the extent to which, and the manner in which, pseudomutuality and mystification occur in the families of non-schizophrenics (p. 352). This presumably refers to an unfortunately never-published sequel to 'Sanity, Madness and the Family'.

The paper is concluded with extracts of case histories taken from 'Sanity, Madness and the Family', rewritten using the term 'mystification' to refer to the confusion of praxis as process.

This completes our review of the material for this stage. How are we to sum it up in its generality?

First and most important, this stage was characterized - indeed, defined - by its use of *dialectical* concepts. These derived from Sartre in the first place and later direct from Marx; though in both cases, Laing's use of these concepts was adapted to his own needs, and restricted by limitations of theoretical practice (these being held to be historically overdetermined limitations).

The main function of these concepts was seen to be rendering intelligible the experience and behaviour of individuals, considered in their more or less immediate group context. This stage partially confirms, then, our notion that there is a fundamental concern running throughout Laing's work that can be described as a 'heuristic consistency'; namely, the project of the understanding of persons. In fact, this is the first stage in which we find Laing himself using the term 'heuristic', with reference to the 'value of theoretical discussion and its crucial import for therapy (Laing, 1965a, p. 344).

A second aspect of the use of dialectical concepts concerns the possibility, occasioned by their use, for the conceptualization of the investigators' relationship to the field they are investigating. In fact, this dialectic lies still-born in thought unless it is lived: the contradictions of living it are still not overcome. These issues will be discussed at greater length subsequently.

The nature of dialectical reality and thought was seen to be totalization: the level to which epistemological totalization can *in practice* be taken were seen to be less than that level at which totalizations already are: we cannot think reality in its reality. This contradiction will be focused upon in Chapter 3.

Before moving on to the next stage, let us just remind ourselves of a fact that so far may seem obvious: for it will shortly cease to be a fact. The almost exclusive emphasis of Laing's theorizing is still on finding alternative, more satisfactory ways, vis-à-vis the

49   Chapter 2

orthodox medical way, to approach and handle clinical and research
material. That is, Laing is dealing still with what are normally
called 'mentally ill people' - even if he would be unwilling to call
them that: the *object* of Laing's reference, and orthodox psychiatry's
reference, are the same - even if the shape of their frames are
radically different.

STAGE 4:   EKNOIA, PARANOIA, AND METANOIA

> At midnight all the agents
> And the superhuman crew
> Come out and round up everyone
> That knows more than they do
> Then they bring them to factory
> Where the heart-attack machine
> Is strapped across their shoulders
> And then the kerosene
> Is brought down from the castles
> By insurance men who go
> Check to see that nobody is escaping
> To Desolation Row
> (Bob Dylan, from the LP 'Highway 61 Revisited, 1965.)

What more shall I say, lunacy is a confusion of the understanding - but it is also the emancipation of the mental faculties
from the control of a natural but often erroneous, that is,
already confused judgment; so that the talents become free which
have before been cramped, and those discover themselves which
were before smothered (John Perceval, A Narrative of the Treatment Experienced by a Gentleman, During a State of Mental De-
rangement, in Bateson, 1961).

We move on now to consider the next stage that can be isolated; and
it is one which paradoxically is the most 'obvious' as a stage, and
yet perhaps most artificial in its isolation. Obvious, because it
is the stage for which Laing has become most notorious, and which
probably accounts for the bulk of his popularity outside the strictly
psychiatric context. Yet artificial, because, as will be shown
later, much of what he says in this stage was implicit in earlier
stages; because, at least as far as texts are concerned this stage
starts very much where stage 3 left off; and because much of what
follows in later stages can be traced, more or less directly, to
ideas conceived in this one. More of this later, however; our concern here is to isolate and analyse.
   The span of this stage is considerable; the first published work
which can be seen to be radically different from the previous stage
appeared, ironically, on 16 April 1964 (Laing, 1964a) - the day
'Sanity, Madness and the Family' was published. Indeed the article
is, as Laing notes, 'partly based' on the latter; yet it contains
ideas of great importance not found there.
   In terms of the number of publications 1964 was Laing's most pro-
lific year, although there is very considerable repetition in his
published articles. At any rate, all articles and papers published

in 1964 and 1965 are to be regarded as belonging to this stage (with the exception of 1965a) as is the book 'The Politics of Experience'. This book, which constitutes the end of stage 4, can be regarded as a synopsis of the previous three years of Laing's work. Every chapter in it is based to a greater or lesser extent on previously published material - mostly dating from 1964.

We start our analysis of this stage, then, by examining the article mentioned above (Laing, 1964a).

Entitled Schizophrenia and The Family, the article starts by quoting a conversation between two schizophrenics, (Haley, 1963) but unlike before, there is no attempt to understand the *'schizophrenics' themselves,* but rather the social event of diagnosis itself. This marks a very considerable change of approach, with many implications, as we shall see. Laing goes on to record the paucity of evidence for schizophrenia being a disease which people have got. This is familiar, being taken more or less straight from the Introduction to 'Sanity, Madness and the Family'. He again recognizes his debt to Szasz, with his crucial statement that schizophrenia as pathological process is either a fact, a hypothesis, an assumption or a judgment. Only the second of these is legitimate, and it is lacking in conformation.

We thus are presented with an example of the erroneous method of psychiatry from Kraepelin (1905) - the same sourse as provided the first example in 'The Divided Self'. The rest of the article deals with familiar ground; Goffman's 'Asylums', the Double Bind, and Laing's own previous work.

So the criterion for including this article in this stage is simply the shift of emphasis mentioned earlier. Specifically, it points the way to a more sociological level of reference; it is not the experience of individuals, either singly or collectively, that is under scrutiny here, but rather the 'social act' of the diagnosis of schizophrenia as such.

With this in mind, we can now consider the next paper, which forms the basis of several later publications (Laing, 1964g, 1967a, chapter 5), entitled Is Schizophrenia a Disease? (Laing, 1964b). Also published in April, this was a paper read by Laing at the First International Congress of Social Psychiatry, in which he takes over where the previous article left off. It starts almost identically, with the quote from Haley, and the question of what the diagnosis means, but (and here we have the essence of this stage already) now we are told that 'before I shall be able to put forward the alternative point of view (concerning schizophrenia), however, I shall have to examine some of our prevailing attitudes about normality and sanity' (p. 185). He starts in a familiar way; but soon we have a totally (or almost so - see next chapter) new notion. Consider:

When a person finds himself in a total impasse, if he does not commit suicide, Nature sometimes calls upon a healing process that has been available to mankind at all times and in all places. *No age, however, has so lost touch with this process as has our own.* I refer to ceremonies of initiation practised all over the world until very recently, when a person was conducted through an experience of (i) death; (ii) of journeying in the Other World; of (iii) rebirth from that Place and that Time back into this world with its here and now. *Schizophrenia is a confused attempt to conduct such a sequence* (p. 187).

I take this to be the most important quote in the whole of Laing's work. It contains the essence of stage 4 in pure undiluted form; it could be taken as an initial formulation of the theoretical basis of all Laing's practical work thereafter; I believe it could be one of the most decisive and revolutionary (in the Kuhnian sense) statements in the history of psychiatry. Though not the first statement of its kind (for example, Bateson, 1961), the degree to which such an approach is active today, is largely due to the influence of Laing.

The whole of stage 4 can, I believe, be seen fundamentally as an expansion of this initial statement; and the expansion begins in this article.

In the first place, there are two aspects, as it were, involved; these being represented by the two sentences put in italics (by me) in the above quote. They concern first, the notion that the prevailing form of experience in our age, i.e. 'Sanity', ('eknoia', as Cooper, 1971, puts it) is to a great extent out of touch with the totality of possible human experience. Expressed in a single word, we are 'alienated'.

Second, 'schizophrenia is now regarded as 'a natural healing process' that has somehow lost its way. The crucial point here is that it is something that one goes through, positively, (hence Laing's term for it: 'metanoia') rather than, say, a deterioration that must be arrested and hopefully reversed.

Considering the first point first, one may remark that a concern with the multiplicity of modes of experience is nothing new for Laing, remembering 'the counterpoint of experience' of 'The Self and Others'; that, at most, we have a quantitative difference here, Laing having perhaps discovered a few more parts in the experiential polyphony. I would beg to differ. True, he has done that; but also. and more important, he now recognizes, at a sociological and incipiently political level, that these 'new' levels of experience are ones that are not 'normally' available to 'sane' people. The emphasis is not so much on the *nature* of the particular modes of experience, as on the fact that, sociologically, some, or even most levels, are not available and in some cases outrightly suppressed and invalidated. As he says 'we come to realize that we have to begin from a position wherein we are largely alienated from experience' (p. 190). This again reflects the shift of emphasis noted in the Schizophrenia and the Family article.

It would be misleading, however, to pretend that Laing devotes *no* attention to the particular nature of these lost modes of experience. For he says
> we have to realize the phenomenal existence of an 'inner' world, that goes beyond the realm of imagination, reveries, dreams and personal unconscious fantasy.... I still can think of no better word for this experiential domain that lies 'beyond' the usual level... than the spiritual world - of the domain of spirits, Powers, Thrones, Principalities, Seraphim, Cherubim, the Light (p. 191).

Once again, in this extraordinary paper, we see the beginnings of a subsequently amplified area of Laing's interest - in this case, the religious.

Turning now, as Laing does in this paper, to the second point, we find a set of 'telegramatic remarks on therapy'. These are initial statements of his new approach to schizophrenia, now viewed as an inner voyage. In fact, very little is actually said here about the nature of this voyage; much more is said in a rewritten version entitled What is Schizophrenia?, which we shall examine shortly. But he does note that the normal clinical/medical approach is grossly unsuited as a context for such journeys. 'Increasing numbers' of people, himself presumably included, feel the need, he maintains, for a place in which such journeys can be undertaken, without the interference of misguided medicine.

Referring to the limited biographical material available (Nuttall, 1970; Barnes and Berke, 1971) we can see that such a need was apparently very much in Laing's mind at the time - as it was in his colleagues' Esterson and Cooper. For by April 1965, the three of them became the founder-members of the Philadelphia Association, a registered charity in this country, and the equivalent in the USA. ('Philadelphia' means literally 'city of brotherly love'.)

The stated aims of this organization, as given in its Articles of Association, appear orthodox enough; almost surprisingly so, considering the time they were drawn up. For example:

To relieve mental illness of all descriptions, in particular schizophrenia.

To undertake, or further, research into the causes (sic) of mental illness, the means of its detection and prevention, and its treament.

To provide, or further, the provision of residential accommodation for persons suffering or who have suffered from mental illness (from The Philadelphia Association Report, 1969).

In practice, the Association provided the means to the realization of what Laing now, in this stage, regards as a pressing need; the creation of an 'asylum' in the true sense of the word. And indeed, two months later, the Association took over Kingsley Hall in London, and set up a community along the lines envisaged by Laing and his colleagues. The history of this place is documented in 'Mary Barnes: Two Accounts of a Journey through Madness', by Mary Barnes and Joe Berke. (See also Schatzman, 1970, and The Philadelphia Association, 1969.) We cannot go into the details of the Kingsley Hall experiment here, but a few points about it do help to shed light on the nature of this stage.

In the first place, Kingsley Hall could be seen as a reaction against the more or less admitted failure of David Cooper's Villa 21. The aim of this was to break down the role structure of the conventional mental hospital, especially the patient/doctor dichotomy which was regarded as an unnecessary strait jacket preventing genuine encounter. The failure of Cooper's experiment, situated as it was, as a ward *within* a conventional hospital, presumably played a part in shaping their ideas on Kingsley Hall. (For an account of Villa 21, see Cooper, 1967a.)

At Kingsley Hall, the dichotomy was transcended. Laing himself lived there for over a year, in the same conditions as the other residents. The degree of success in this matter can be partially gauged by the fact that visitors, including professional psychiatrists, and other 'experts', were frequently unable to tell who would, in a 'normal' hospital, have been 'patient' and who 'doctor'.

Laing himself was apparently frequently mistaken for a 'schizophrenic'!

This concern with breaking down role structures reflects very well the broader context of Laing's thinking that we have noted as a feature of this stage; though perhaps one should say that his writings are a reflection of the practical issues he found himself dealing with. At any rate, we can see in Kingsley Hall the fulfilment of a desire expressed in an article to be examined shortly (Laing, 1964f): 'Psychotherapy must remain an obstinate attempt of two people to arrive at a re-covery of the wholeness of being human through the relationship between them.' It was fitting, in the light of this, that Laing should have said to his model resident, who confirmed so many of his beliefs, Mary Barnes, 'you need therapy 24 hours a day' (Barnes, 1970).

If such is the relevance of the internal nature of Kingsley Hall, so too, its relation to other movements outside it are relevant to our considerations. For a great many activities not associated with psychiatry in the orthodox sense took place at Kingsley Hall. It was associated intimately with the New Left, and the emergent 'underground' movement (Nuttall, 1970), and also with the artistic avantgarde. It formed a focus, so to speak, for the vast array of apparently disparate fields of interest which are reflected in the writings of Laing at this period. Today, we do not find it difficult to think of say, Yoga, Marxism and LSD as topics of at least arguable connections with each other. Such was not, however, the case in 1965, at least for most people; and it is perhaps in part due to people like Laing that this sould be so. For this period was one of great synthesis for Laing, and Kingsley Hall appears to have been, as I say, the geographical focus which enabled such a synthesis to progress. It is interesting that two writers who knew Laing well should, apparently independently, have compared him to the Master Glass Bead Game Player, of Hermann Hesse (Leary, 1970, p. 96 and Berke, in Barnes and Berke, 1973, p. 280).

Having noted, then, these two aspects of Laing's practical affairs at Kingsley Hall, of breaking down interpersonal barriers, and of a catholicism of interactional interest, we return to a consideration of the texts of this stage.

It would perhaps be appropriate, having discussed practical issues, to return to the texts via those that express Laing's views on his profession generally. One source that springs to mind is the Preface to the Penguin edition of 'The Divided Self', written in September 1964. Laing says:

> Psychiatry could be, and some psychiatrists are, on the side of transcendence, of genuine freedom, and of true human growth. But psychiatry can so easily be a technique of brainwashing, of inducing behaviour that is adjusted by (preferably) non-injurious torture.... Lobotomies and tranquillizers... place the bars of Bedlam and the locked doors *inside* the patient. Thus I would wish to emphasize that our 'normal', 'adjusted' state is too often the abdication of ecstacy, the betrayal of our true potentialities (Laing, 1964e, p. 12).

And again, in the Foreword to 'Estrangement and Relationship', by Macnab (Macnab, 1965), Laing indites psychiatry when he says 'when the world has itself gone mad, we should not too readily suppose

that it is just the schizophrenic who is "the ruined man"'. The
implication being, presumably, that the orthodox psychiatrist is, so
to speak, doubly ruined; in himself, and in so far as he 'ruins' by
'curing' those who attempt to reconstruct themselves out of their
own existential rubble. As he says elsewhere (Laing, 1965g),
'... they will try and cure us. They may succeed. But there is
still hope that they will fail'.)

It will be recalled that Is Schizophrenia a Disease?, the main
text so far considered, was originally a paper read at the First
International Congress of Social Psychiatry. Sedgewick (1971) in
his review of this period denigrates this gathering by referring to
it as 'an inconsequent jamboree': a 'jamboree' it may have been, but
'inconsequent' is hardly the adjective I would have chosen, in view
of the enormous subsequent interest in the ideas that Laing was propounding. For it was also at this jamboree that Laing first delivered the paper entitled Transcendental Experience in Relation to
Religion and Psychosis, subsequently reprinted (Laing, 1965e) in
Leary's journal 'Psychedelic Review', and rewritten as chapter six
of 'The Politics of Experience'. I shall here be considering the
1965 version.

As the title implies, the paper is basically an attempt to explore
whatever similarities there may be between religion and psychosis,
vis-à-vis the possibility in each for the occurrence of so-called
'transcendental experience'. It was undoubtedly the most polemical
(to put it mildly) of Laing's outputs at the time; it must have
shaken the international social psychiatrists to whom it was delivered considerably. It contains the first account, for me at any
rate, of what it is really like to be mad that invokes more than
mere sympathy or compassion: it is a frightening document.

The central issue, which defines the term 'transcendental' is the
question of ego loss. Laing states, somewhat bluntly perhaps, that
non-egoic, transcendental experiences of the divine are 'the Living
Fount of all religion'. I suspect that sociologists of religion,
assuming they understood the assertion at all, would beg to differ:
but then, so, I am sure, would Laing beg to differ over what constitutes religion. Or, more accurately, he would wish to make a
distinction between true religion and false religion - using 'true'
in the sense conveyed by Heidegger's use of the word 'aletheia' (see
above, the review of 'The Self and Others'). Indeed, such a distinction is in effect what Laing is making in his discussion of faith,
belief, and experience of the Divine. For instance:

> Nowhere in the Bible is there any argument about the *existence* of
> gods, demons, angels. People did not first 'believe in' God:
> they experienced His Presence.... There is everything to suggest
> that man experienced God. Faith was never a matter of believing
> He existed, but of trusting in the Presence that was experienced
> and known to exist as a self-validating datum....(Today) Few are
> made to believe by their experience. Paul of Tarsus was picked
> up by the scruff of the neck, thrown to the ground and blinded
> for three days. This direct experience was self-validating (pp.
> 13-14).

In our time, the verbal attributions concerning God, which are
secondary to these self-validating experiences, have come to be primary: because of the poverty of our experience. Most of us do not

know the infinite richness of the 'spiritual', (for want of a better word) realm, because we are too firmly clutching on to our egos; and as Laing says, the ego is an 'instrument for living in this world'.

Now, the religious books and teachings of the world contain limitless accounts of the techniques available to overcome the ego, and of the phantasy geography of the non-egoic realms. (Strangely, Laing does not point out that these are, to a large extent, culturally specific. This, I should have thought, was a crucial point.) Madness, he argues, is, or rather, involves, some sort of ego loss. As such, it is possible, *though by no means inevitable,* that transcendental experience may be a component of the experience of madness. Thus, he comes to make a distinction which appears to particularly annoy conventional psychiatry: between madness and illness. The schizophrenic is indeed mad; but he is not ill (p. 11). The social attribution of illness is only possible because transcendental experience *in general* is regarded as at best extremely suspect. The predeliction that psychiatrists seem to have for announcing that certain historical characters, notably prophets, and mystics (including Jesus) were almost certainly 'schizophrenics' or 'manic depressives' testifies to the accuracy of Laing's point.

Laing talks at somewhat greater length about the notion of an Inner Voyage; insisting of its naturalness:

> The process of entering into *the other* world from this world, and returning to *this* world from the other world, is as 'natural' as death and childbirth of being born. But in our present world, that is both so terrified and so unconscious of the other world, it is not surprising that, when 'reality', the fabric of this world, bursts, and a person enters the other world, he is completely lost and terrified, and meets incomprehension in others. In certain cases, a man blind from birth may have an operation performed which gives him sight. The result: frequently misery, confusion, disorientation (Laing could have added, forcefully, suicide). The light that illumines the madman is an unearthly light... it may burn him out (pp. 11-12).

The second notion of this stage, i.e. normality as alienation is, as can already be seen, strongly expressed in this paper. But nowhere has he ever expressed the idea in such apocalytpic terms as he does at the end of this paper:

> We live in a secular world... (and) we are expected to have faith. But this faith comes to be a belief in a reality which is not evident. There is a prophecy in Amos that there will be a time when there will be a famine in the land, 'not a famine for bread, nor a thirst for water, but for *hearing* the words of the Lord.' That time has now come to pass. It is the present age (p. 15; Amos 8: 11).

A famine starting in the head, as Brian Aldiss (1969) put it.

It is also in this paper that Laing makes some statements which in their rewritten form, were to be much-quoted, usually out of context, and much misinterpreted - whether favourably or otherwise. I refer to the passage where he states 'I am not merely spinning senseless paradoxes when I say that we, the sane ones, are out of our minds' (p. 11). (A comparable passage in the 'Politics of Experience' is: 'From the alienated starting point of our pseudo-sanity, everything is equivocal. Our sanity is not "true" sanity (p. 118).)

Such statements have been interpreted as meaning that Laing considers 'normal' society is sick and mad, and 'mentally ill' people truly sane. Laing is not, fortunately, so simplistic. Let us return to the article in question and look further.

He notes that it is still widely believed that some forms of insanity are caused by the psyche being 'overwhelmed' by the 'unconscious'; that, by implication, there is a correlation between sanity and being unconscious, or at least, not too conscious of the 'unconscious'. He goes on to argue, however, that what Freud and Jung regarded as 'the Unconscious' is simply what, 'we, in our historically conditioned estrangement, are unconscious of.... The mind is what the ego is unconscious of. We are unconscious of our minds' (p. 11). That is, our 'minds' are simply all our experiences. But 'we', being alienated from so many of experience, are unconscious of much of our 'minds', hence the illusion of 'having', an 'unconscious'. He illustrated this with reference to dreams. 'The Dreamer who dreams our dreams knows far more of us than we know of it.... The mind of which we are unaware, is aware of us. It is we who are out of our minds' (p. 11). This is not simply an inversion of the 'good guys/bad guys' duality, although unfortunately, it has often been interpreted along these lines. Possibly it was as a result of such simplistic interpretations that Laing later took the trouble to spell out quite explicitly the fallacy of a naive Us/Them inversion - see Politics of the Family', pp. 123-4.

This general notion of normality as alienation from experience was investigated by Laing in more specific detail in a lecture given to the Institute of Contemporary Arts in 1964, and reprinted as Violence and Love, and The Massacre of the Innocents (Laing, 1965c and d). 'More specific detail', because they deal explicitly with the aetiology of this state of affairs.

These articles, which considerably revised and expanded, form chapter three of 'The Politics of Experience', form the basis of a critique of the socialization processes dominant in our society. The 'innocents' that are 'massacred' are simply babies. To quote from Violence and Love:

> The baby is subjected to forces of outrageous violence, called love, as its mother and father have been, and their parents, and their parents before them. These forces are mainly concerned with destroying most of the baby's potentialities. This enterprise is on the whole successful. By the time the new human being is fifteen or so, we are left with a being like ourselves, a half-crazed creature, more or less adjusted to a mad world. This is normality in our present age (p. 417).

Strong words: how does Laing justify them? Strangely, he says that he 'cannot give examples either from my consulting-room or my own research' (p. 418); instead he cites the work of Jules Henry (Henry, 1963). (Henry was, incidentally, one of the speakers present at the Dialectics of Liberation Conference - see Cooper, 1968.)

Henry's work in fact concerns the classroom, not the family; though by the time Laing's paper was rewritten for 'Politics of Experience', it included a severe criticism of the work on family development by Lidz. The burden of Henry's writing is that schools provide a context in which children can internalize mystifying patterns of personal violence, which form paradigms for existing in the outside world. He pays attention to the way that one child's failure (to solve a problem) is the sole condition for another's success; that the one's misery is necessary and sufficient for the other's rejoicing. '(The child) was not learning arithmetic only; he was learning the essential nightmare also. To be successful in our culture one must learn to dream of failure (p. 420).'

In more general terms, 'education' is seen as the means of binding children, and negating their natural curiosity, creativity, etc. About the strategy involved, Laing has this to say:

'I have called this strategy mystification, taking the concept from the definition given by Karl Marx of the way the exploiting classes seek to bemuse the exploited by representing forms of exploitation as forms of benevolence.'

The issue is that socialization is Violence represented as Love. Laing notes that we are in imminent danger of annihilating ourselves; but that if we are to stop destroying each other, we must first stop destroying ourselves. And this brings us, full circle, back to alienation from experience, because the 'average man of 25... is almost totally estranged from inner experiences': a half-crazed creature, destroyed, mutilated, doomed 'to this travesty that we call love'.

Now, while Laing's descriptions of the horrors of our society may well be entirely justified, he gives very little indication of what is to be done about it. In particular, he pays no attention to an agonizing paradox that has surely preyed on the mind of anyone who has enough sensibility left to realize that 'something' needs to be done about the state of human existence. The paradox, as I see it, is this: Something is wrong with people because something is wrong with society. Therefore, society needs changing. Granted that society is comprised of people, this requires that people be changed. But, if it is the society that causes people to be alienated etc., one cannot change people without changing society first. Yet, equally; one cannot change society except through changing people, and the relations between them. The problem is bad enough on a purely theoretical level; though it can at least be grasped coherently if one adopts a dialectical stance. But when it comes down to actually *doing* something, to the level of individual praxis, then many people at any rate, feel depressed beyond words at the insignificance of any possible personal action in the fact of the staggering enormity of the irrational totality. I shall leave this point here, for the question of individual praxis is one that is returned to, indeed focused upon, in the next stage, that of Laing's political radicalism. At this juncture, we will simply note that this problem is deeply implicit in the things that Laing is writing.

It was promised earlier that we would consider the rewritten test What is Schizophrenia; this we must now do. Published in the November 1964 issue of 'New Left Review', it contains perhaps Laing's most radical ever statements on schizophrenia.

The first section deals with the by now familiar topic of the baleful history of 'schizophrenia' as a hypothesis, plus a superb specimen of Laing's vitriolic sarcasm:

It would be an interesting experiment to study whether the

syndrome of 'labelling' others runs in families. A pathological process called 'psychiatrosis' may well be found, by the same methods, to be a delineable entity, with somatic correlates, and psychic mechanisms... etc.' (p. 64).

The second section of the paper, A Political Event, is noteworthy for its opening, in which Laing commits himself on the schizophrenia issue. Whereas before he would say that schizophrenia was an unproved hypothesis, that was unnecessary, he now is prepared to state: 'I do not myself believe that there is any such "condition" as "schizophrenia"' (p. 64). He goes on to argue, however, that the diagnosis of schizophrenia is not merely a social act, but a political act.

(How does such a procedure serve for the maintenance of the civic order? These questions are only beginning to be asked, much less answered. ....Socially, this work (of the Tavistock Institute of Human Relations, e.g.) must now move to further understanding ...(of) the meaning of all this within the larger context of the civic order of society - that is, of the *political* order, of the way persons exercise control and power over one another (p. 65).

The final section is entitled Exploring Inner Space, in which he again presents the arguments about our estrangement from the 'inner' world. He also talks about the need, on an institutional level, for a context for inner voyages.

Instead of the mental hospital, a sort of reservicing factory for human breakdowns, we need a place where people who have travelled further and, consequently, may be more lost than psychiatrists and other sane people, can find their way *further* into inner space and time, and back again.... Instead of the *degradation* ceremonial of psychiatric examination we need ... an *initiation* ceremonial, through which the person will be guided.... Psychiatrically, this would appear as ex-patients helping future patients to go mad (p. 67).

Laing then, for the first time, gives us a list of what is involved in this inner voyage:

What is entailed then is:
   i   a journey from outer to inner
   ii from life to a kind of death
   iii from going forward to a going back
   iv from temporal movement to temporal standstill
   v   from time to eternity
   vi from the ego to the self
   vii from being outside (post-birth) back into the womb of all things (pre-birth).

and then subsequently a return journey
   1 from inner to outer
   2 from death to life
   3 from the movement back to a movement once more forward
   4 from immortality to mortality
   5 from eternity back to time
   6 from self to a new ego
   7 from a cosmic foetalization to an existential birth (p. 67).

He leaves it to others, he says, to translate the above into the terms of psycho-pathology. Without wishing to use any terms which invoke 'pathology', it is obvious that the death referred to is an existential death, namely the death of the ego, experienced in ego loss. Rebirth occurs when the individual 'returns' to this world, establishing a new ego in the process. Existential death is of course a familiar concept already in his work, but rebirth through death is an idea which really only enters in this stage. And it is one of obvious importance, in that it presents itself as a practical solution to the 'problem' of schizophrenia. Therapy, now, becomes a matter of guidance, into, through, and ultimately out of these transcendental realms. Laing notes that this role of guide is traditionally the role of the priest, or guru; but in our society, at least, the priest does not himself (usually) have direct experience of this realm, and is consequently unsuitable. The orthodox psychiatrist, of course, is even less suitable, being positively antagonistic to the process.

In 1965 Laing published an article entitled a Ten-Day Voyage (Laing, 1965f) which gave for the first time from Laing a detailed account of an actual 'inner voyage' so far only described in fairly general terms. (A revised version of this article formed chapter seven of 'The Politics of Experience'.) There is no need to recount the details of this voyage here; but it is interesting to note that the subject of it, a sculptor by the name of Jesse Watkins, was largely responsible for arranging the exhibition of Mary Barnes' paintings, as she was very much a prototype case of the supervised death-rebirth cycle for Laing, she being one of Laing's first residents at Kingsley Hall. The success of the exhibition appears to have been one of the most powerful factors in Mary Barnes' 'rebirth' (Barnes and Berke, 1971).

There is another 'aspect' of this stage as a whole, which was not referred to in the initial article examined, but which we must now look at.

In concerns methodology. The term 'social phenomenology' was introduced in 'Sanity, Madness and the Family', but did not there receive much elaboration. Elaboration was forthcoming, however, in a speech delivered in 1964 to the Sixth International Congress of Psychotherapy entitled Practice and Theory: The Present Situation (reprinted Laing, 1965b). It was also considered in an article published in 'New Society' in October 1964 (Laing, 1964f). These papers deal, as implied, with both theoretical and practical issues. On the theoretical side, the most notable feature is a total *absence* of reference to the work of Sartre. Laing notes that Freudian theory has no constructs in which the encounter of two individuals can be expressed. Games theory, although interactional, is not, in Laing's view, inter*personal*, in so far as 'games' (as defined by games theory) can occur equally between electronic systems as between humans. We need, claims Laing, a *specifically* human theory, which can conceptualize behaviour, experience, and the relation between them, in the individual *and* between individuals.

The very opposite of this is found in so-called behaviour therapy, which is dismissed as 'schizoid' and 'a lie and a betrayal of man' (Laing, 1964f, p. 13). In fact, the tone of these papers is, as these remarks indicate, predominantely negative. A more positive approach is taken in the last and most formidable work of this stage (possibly of Laing's work as a whole) - 'The Politics of Experience'. It is to this book that we now turn - not without trepidation.

As already noted, the majority of this book appeared as papers at previous dates. Only Chapter one appears substantially new, and even here parts of it are recognizable from the papers just discussed. Thus it will not be necessary to go right through 'Politics of Experience', extracting 'points', or establishing the theoretical schemata that Laing deploys. Rather, after a brief account of Chapter one two tasks await us; and they are related. First, we must examine the book as a whole, as an entity in itself, for thus is it read, and thus are the ideas (which originally were scattered in journals as diverse as the 'International Journal of Social Psychiatry', 'New Left Review', and 'Psychedelic Review') absorbed. Each idea, each influence, each approach, is a context for each other. So to answer this question we must ask not only what are all these different perspectives, but also how do they 'hang together' to form a coherent whole (if, indeed, they do), and what effect does this integration of disparate elements have on the reader.

Second, we must examine, in some detail, *how* Laing achieves the effects he does with his writing: for it will be argued that the effects are profound. How, in fact, does Laing use words in this, his most powerful book?

But turning first to chapter one, what do we find here?

The chapter is entitled Persons and Experience, and is divided into six sections. The first of these, Experience as Evidence, deals explicitly for the first time, with social phenomenology. To quote:

> The task of social phenomenology is to relate my experience of the other's behaviour to the other's experience of my behaviour. Its study is the relation between experience and experience: its true field is inter-experience.... I do not experience your experience. But I experience you as experiencing (pp. 15-16).

Basically, we are presented with familiar ideas - spirals of perspectives, the distinctions between natural and human science, and so on - but they are presented in a new style. Gone is the super-academic jargon of stage 3; instead, we find Laing actually building a model of the situation, using very basic conceptual building bricks, such as 'experience', 'behaviour', 'I', 'you' and so on. There is thus an element of structuralism inherent here, at least as far as defining the field of social phenomenology goes. Having done that, Laing goes on to talk about the terms 'inner' and 'outer'. Experience is not inner as opposed to outer; rather we experience in different modalities. Nor are any of these any more inner or outer than any others. Least of all, is experience 'intrapsychic processes' as this dualistically assumes that there *is* a psyche that the experience is in. Experience *is* psyche, and vice versa. Similarly, my experience (say, of this room) is not in my head, or brain - it is out there in the room, or better, it *is* the room. Amidst the howls of protest from empiricists, we can see here a number of influences: Hegel's notion of consciousness of the world as an alienation or externalization of consciousness, Husserl's transcendental phenomenology of the Lebenswelt, and the Buddhist idea of the indissoluble unity of the observer, the act of observing, and the field observed.

The rest of the chapter really serves either as a synopsis of earlier work, or an introduction to subsequent chapters. Thus sections II and IV repeat the 'axioms' of social phenomenology and the nature of phantasy, respectively (see stage 2) whereas III and V anticipate Chapters three and four.

Section VI really defies a brief exegesis. Entitled The Experience of Negation, it consists of a series of attempts to use words to point to that which cannot be expressed in words thus: 'We are afraid to approach the fathomless and bottomless groundlessness of everything. "There's nothing to be afraid of." The ultimate reassurance, and the ultimate terror' (p. 33).

Or again, when considering the apparently innocuous sentence 'The sky is blue', Laing discovers that

None of the things that are united by 'is' can themselves qualify 'is'. 'Is' is not this, that or the next or anything. Yet 'is' is the condition of the possibility of all things. 'Is' is that no-thing whereby all things are (p. 35).

Here again, Buddhist influences are apparent - Nirvana (no-thing) as the pre-condition of all phenomenal appearances; and also, again, Hegelian ones, notably that a thing, (a 'determinate something' as Hegel would say) can only be itself in relation to that which is other than itself.

It would seem, at first sight, that Laing is submerging himself in pure idealism, especially when one reads: 'Man, most fundamentally, is not engaged in the discovery of what is there, nor in production, nor even in communication, nor in invention. He is enabling being to emerge from non-being' (p. 36).

Statements like the above have tended to polarize reactions to 'The Politics of Experience'. Those of a mystic/poet/psychedelic persuasion have welcomed them, breathing a sigh of relief at the (apparent) demise of Sartrean phenomenology. On the other hand, those of a scientific/political/psychiatric persuasion have decried such statements as being metaphysical, idealist, meaningless or just plain rubbish. I hope to convince the reader that both sets of attitudes represent at best an incomplete view, and in any case, one that fundamentally fails to realize *how Laing is using words*, and *for what purposes*. So we turn now to the two tasks already outlined above; initially, an examination of the book as a whole.

If 'few books today are forgivable', then even fewer book reviews are forgivable. However, we must, as Laing notes, begin to think, feel and act from the starting point of our own alienation, being the murderers and prostitutes we are. I wish neither to 'murder' nor to 'stand for' Laing, merely to clarify; for it is apparent, if only from Laing's own subsequent reiterations and rephrasings, that 'The Politics of Experience' has been grossly misunderstood. If I earn forgiveness in the process, so much the better.

So what is the overall conception of the book? As the Introduction suggests, the central theme is alienation; specifically, alienation from various modalities of experience, and the political pseudo-rationality of these alienations. Thus, to consider the most obvious aspect of its structure, the existence of discreet chapters, we find the following:

Chapter one is concerned with the 'fundamental' nature of experience and alienation. The analysis here is essentially *logical* rather than concrete; a strong but perhaps misleading flavour of idealism is thus imparted to the whole enterprise.

Chapter two: The Psychotherapeutic Experience, deals with
alienation in psychotherapy. It seeks to explore the implications
of the *universal* alienation characteristic of our age for psychotherapy today, viewed in its historical context.

Chapter three: The Mystification of Experience deals with alienation in families, particularly in 'Love' and in schools, with an
emphasis on the family and the school as paradigm institutions for
the experiencing of society at large.

Chapter four: Us and Them, concerns alienation within and between
groups, ranging from the family to international relations. One
might say the focus is on alienation in political experience.

Chapter five: The Schizophrenic Experience, traces a brief history of approaches to schizophrenia, calling for a radical inversion
of conventional attitudes. Again, one might say the focus is on
alienation in psychiatric experience. As with Chapter two, there is
an exploration of the *implications* of alienation in this sphere, set
against both the historical background, and the contemporary function of psychiatry.

Chapter six: Transcendental Experience, examines the very wide
spread alienation from the transcendental realm, or modality, of
experience. So widespread is this that the chapter consists largely
of a polemic arguing for the very existence of this modality. Here,
it is the relevance of such an alienation for psychotic experience
that is focused upon.

Chapter seven: A Ten-Day Voyage, is, so to speak, a 'case study'
of the very interplay of all these alienations, particularly transcendental and psychiatric.

In each chapter, then, we see a specific and a general reference:
A special form of alienation is considered, in its context of the
general alienation typical of our society. In some instances, a
historical context is also provided. Considered globally, then, the
purpose of the book, on this level, is to document the political
suppression of several specific realms of experience, this suppression itself being experienced - or rather, left unexperienced - as a
range of specific alienations, all within the broad context of
general alienation inevitable within a capitalist system. It is,
indeed, the politics of experience....

But these alienations are by no means described 'from outside',
as it were. We have already noted the presence of polemic, of non-scientific language and so on. Is this, as some people seem to
think, mere incompetence or feeble-mindedness on Laing's part? I
think not. Let us return to a consideration of the quote concerning
man as 'most fundamentally' involved in 'enabling being to emerge
from non being'.

Man, it seems, is at the helm of Hegel's first dialectic (Hegel,
1929, pp. 94-5). If this is the first move in 'a thoroughly self-conscious and self-critical human account of man', that will bring
about the science of social phenomenology, then I, at least, an mot
impressed. For to talk about 'being' and 'non-being' as 'most fundamental' in relation to man, is to adopt a *logical,* i.e. ideal,
concept of fundamentality, rather than a material one. One cannot
escape the conclusion that Laing is moving headlong into a totally
metaphysical idealism - if he insists that what he is saying is
imparting knowledge; that these are preliminaries to the *science* of

social phenomenology. In fact, I do not believe he is doing this. Laing is speaking in strictly irrational ways - and I believe that to the extent that what one says is not rational, one is either wrong or a poet. I believe that a good case can be made out for large parts of this book to be considered as poetry. Consider:

> At the point of non-being we are at the outer reaches of what language can state, but we can indicate by language why language cannot say what it cannot say.... In using a word, a letter, a sound, OM, one cannot put a sound to soundlessness, or name the unnameable (p. 35).

Laing is concerned here with what Huxley (1959) has described as 'the antipodes of the mind', and there is really very little point in taking issue with what he sayd. One can only agree to accept it, or reject it; presumably according to whether one has oneself experienced the ecstatic terror of whatever one labels the unlabellable. The point is that Laing is trying to establish the fact that such experiences occur; the majority of the book deals with the social contexts in which such experiences are generated, suppressed, invalidated: the politics of experience....

Be all that as it may, there is, I think, an interestingly rational point to be extracted here. It will be remembered that, in the previous stage, Laing was deemed to have failed to employ Sartre's term Intelligibility in the full dialectical sense; that this required not only intellection, but also comprehension, the lived experience of human consciousness 'by which it reproduces the project of the Other'; that, by their own (implicit) admission, Laing and Esterson did not descend to that phenomenological level. The situation here, however, would appear to be different. For although there is none of the technical academic language of Sartre's 'Critique', I think we can see that Laing is, to an extent, now achieving this - or at least, aiming specifically for it. For instance, he says 'Our task is both to experience and to conceive the concrete, that is to say, reality in its fullness and wholeness (p. 19). The words are different, but the idea seems to be the same.

But you and I cannot experience Laing's experiences, however much he experiences reality in its wholeness. Consequently, if the book is to be active in creating Intelligibility in the full Sartrean sense which includes experience, it, the book, must generate, or in some way open the door, for such experience *'in' the reader* - you and me. It must also, of course, convey knowledge, the intellection side of Intelligibility.

This means that it must be a very strange book. For the experiences that are to be rendered intelligible are precisely those experiences from which, Laing argues, we are most radically estranged and alienated. Hence, the book must enable one to experience experiences, the non-experiencibility of which the book is about! Or else, it preaches to the converted, which in fact is probably a large part of the truth.

But how exactly does Laing go about inducing this experience? Wherein lies the potency of what I have termed his 'poetry'?

Reading a book is a pretty ordinary, conventional, activity. To induce not merely quantitatively more, but radically and qualitatively *different sorts* of experiences via a book requires the 'upsetting' of the reader's normal relation to words. For example, most so-called scientific facts are responded to essentially on a conscious intellectual level. The sort of 'upsetting' I am thinking of would occur if those *same* scientific facts could somehow also induce an intense emotional reaction of, say, disgust, or a 'transcendental' reaction of wordless awe. This is just the sort of thing Laing does. Let us consider some of his techniques, with examples.

Generally, the basic technique seems to involve the sudden, unexpected juxtaposition of radically different orders of word forms. One quite common form of this involves the laying out of a situation in accordance with strict logic, which is then suddenly negated. For instance:

> They will say we are regressed and withdrawn and out of contact with them.... And because they are humane, and concerned, and even love us, and are very frightened, they will try to cure us. They may succeed. But there is still hope that they will fail (p. 137).

Here, the entire psychiatric experience is 'flipped over', in one sentence. The tension of the contradiction involved in hoping that the cure fails can only dissipate itself in the sudden dissolving of the (unspoken) category 'illness'. The dynamic here seems much the same as that exploited by Zen Koans: the disciple/reader is presented with an immediate verbal contradiction; the only way out is to reject the apparent reality of the concepts involved - in this case illness and cure. In so far as a large part of the experience of psychiatric alienation is the unquestioning belief in psychiatric concepts, to that extent the example quoted can cut across such alienation.

A more common technique is the juxtaposition, not of strictly contradictory terms, but of forms of discourse expressing wildly different sorts of conceptual experience. This induces a sort of synaesthesia of experience modalities, as opposed to the 'normal' one-dimensional experience of words. Thus we find sudden interjections of religious forms of expression in the middle of a predominantly scientific discourse, poetic imagery in the midst of a philosophical passage, or mystical notion hand in hand with political ones. Thus,

> The family is, in the first place, the usual instrument for what is called socialization, that is, getting each new recruit to the human race to behave and experience in substantially the same way as those who have already got here. We are all fallen Sons of Prophecy, who have learned to die in the Spirit and be reborn in the flesh (p. 57).

Or again:

> As war continues, both sides come more and more to resemble each other. The uroborus eats its own tail. The wheel turns full circle. Shall we realize that We and Them are shadows of each other? When will the veil be lifted? (p. 83).

Elsewhere, a critique of positivist moral philosophy is torn asunder by 'Meanwhile Vietnam goes on.'

Another powerful technique Laing uses in 'Politics of Experience' (and a great deal, in subsequent works) is to repeat the syntactical structure of a sentence or passage, merely altering the semantic content. This has the effect of laying bare the underlying similarity of two intellectual positions that at first sight seem unconnected, or even opposed. Thus, an otherwise 'unthinkable' connection between Naziism and Christianity is established in the following example:

Rudolf Hess proclaims: We are the Party, the Party is Germany, Hitler is the Party, Hitler is Germany, and so on.

We are Christians in so far as we are brothers in Christ. We are in Christ and Christ is in each one of us (p. 78).

I have so far only considered techniques that operate on the level of sentences; But Laing also obtains comparable effects from single words. One aspect of this, of course, is a judicious selection of 'potent' words. In its crudest form, this merely takes the form of a barrage of words considered taboo in 'serious' books, as in the 'Bird of Paradise', for example: 'How to inject nothing into fuck all? How to come into a gone world? No piss, shit, smegma, come, mucoid, viscoid, soft or hard, or even tears of eyes, ears, arse, cunt, prick.... ', etc.

More subtle, however, is the use of archetypal words or images. Thus we find Mandala, The Lotus, Earth Mother (as the fat She-Buddha), Inner Light, Alpha and Omega, the Wise Old Man (Guru), The Wheel, The Snake, Immortality, Cosmos, and, of course, Death-Rebirth. It is impossible to analyse the effect of using such words; clearly, they leave many people cold - some indeed are put off by their presence - whereas for others (myself included) they act very much as triggers, potentiating a sensitivity that I can only allude to as 'higher' than that invoked by, say, scientific, or political terms. I can only assume that Laing and many others share this sort of reaction to archetypal imagery. This is not necessarily a mere 'preaching to the converted', a possibility noted earlier. For there may be many people with such a sensitivity who simply never have access to what might be called 'archetypal stimulation', at least, not of the strength found in 'Politics of Experience'. This could perhaps explain the book's overriding popularity, even relative to Laing's other writings, with people called schizophrenic, who, if Laing's ideas are correct, might well have a lower 'threshold', as it were, for such stimulation.

Perhaps a more significant aspect of Laing's use of single words, is his ability to, so to speak, take one right 'into' the word. This technique involves looking afresh at a common word, usually in etymological terms, to discover new, or often, very *old*, meanings, which are literal, thereby sweeping away, or at least, relativizing, the conventional meaning. (Cooper, of course, is the master at this word game; whole chapters in 'Death of the Family' and 'A Grammar of Living' have been devoted to following up etymologies or puns - it seems as good a way to relate to words as any.) Though Laing's most impressive examples of this are to be found in The Obvious, he uses the technique here to subvert the clinical meaning of three terms: 'disturbed' (p. 93), 'orientation' (p. 136) and 'schizophrenic' (p. 106). Thus, the term orientation, with its usual connotations of adjustment to the 'outer' reality, is reduced to its 'obvious' but invisible meaning, to know where the Orient, or East is. Thus orientation in *'inner'* space and time, means to know the 'East', i.e. mythically, the source or origin of one's experience. (Cf Hesse, 1960, Journey to the East.)

Another, perhaps surprising, technique used to considerable effect in 'Politics of Experience' is the sudden insertion of relevant, and usually appalling, statistics. In the section on Normal Alienation Laing is discussing normality as a state of chronic alienation, saying how much society values the 'Normal Man', when he slips in the following bombshell: 'Normal men have killed perhaps 100,000,000 of their fellow normal men in the last fifty years' (p. 24). Even if the figure is exaggerated - and it may not be - the sheer bluntness of such a fact is overwhelming, and more important, it makes an utter mockery of the concept of normality. In an instant, the concept of normality is 'flipped over' to one of atrocious mass insanity. Or, alternatively, one can accept it at face value, that mass genocide *is* normality in our age - in which case, the same instant sees the utter destruction of one's last tottering delusions that perhaps man is capable of rationality, peace etc. Either way, it is very hard to be unmoved by such a sledgehammer statistic.

Although far less devastating, the fact that a child born in the UK today stands a ten-times greater chance of going to mental hospital than university operates in a similar manner.

And finally, of course, it must be said that Laing is a very competent writer, in a more conventional sense than we have just been analysing. He has an extraordinary power to summon simple but powerful analogies and metaphors to illustrate his examples, though here again, the most notable ones are those that subvert one's usual way to looking at things. Thus, he quotes a transcript of an amazing conversation between two so-called schizophrenics, which, as he noted earlier (1964a) reads like a Pinter play, and asks what does the diagnosis mean? He answers himself:

> To regard the gambits of Smith and Jones as due primarily to some psychological deficit is rather like supposing that a man doing a handstand on a bicycle on a tightrope 100 feet up with no safety net is suffering from an inability to stand on his own two feet (p. 85).

Endless similar examples can be found in 'Politics of Experience'.

In conclusion, then, we have seen that the style of writing, initiated in the 1964-5 papers, and carried to the *n*th degree in 'The Bird of Paradise', and used in the 'Politics of Experience', is no literary accident. It seems to have been quite deliberately 'constructed' in order to 'destruct' normal patterns of word usage. We cannot go in depth here into the dialectic between language and consciousness; but I suggest that what Laing was trying to do was to break down (a) unquestioned conventional meanings of specific and in fact *repressive* concepts; (b) similarly unquestioned barriers between different modalities of experience, and (c) the mediating intrusion of (essentially static) language on the immediate flux of experience. Further, I suggest the reason for doing this was to facilitate (a) a less 'filtered' perception of the positive facts and ideas presented in the book, and (b) the actual experiencing, on the part of the reader, of some of the things that he is talking about. Here at last, I think, is the meaning of the phrase that Laing chose to end the book with. 'If I could turn you on, if I could drive you out of your wretched mind, if I could tell you I would let you know.'

Two comments can perhaps be attached to this analysis. First, it does seem that Laing is pursuing something recognizable, in spirit if not in terminology, as Sartre's notion of Intelligibility. That is, in principle *both* a rigorous verbal account of individual experience, (the moment termed Intellection by Sartre) and a sympathetic re-living in thought of the experience of the other (i.e. Comprehension for Sartre). I say in principle, for in practice, 'The Politics of Experience' *has* to concern itself primarily with establishing even the *possibility* of experience in these critical modalities, rather than concentrating on specific concrete 'cases'. It is also a large part of the book's purpose to examine *why* this possibility it not already a certainty.

The second comment is that the book can itself be seen as an exercise in social phenomenology. To be sure, we cannot in any way get directly at Laing's experience of writing it; but we *can* experience his behaviour of writing, and make inferences concerning his experience (see chapter one: section 1). Moreover, referring back to the two reasons (a and b) just mentioned, the entire enterprise of Laing-writing-reader-reading matches very well Cooper's definition of phenomenology as 'the description of experiences from the 'inside' with as little intrusion as possible by conceptual thinking' (Cooper, DL 3).

We now have the unenviable task of summing up the characteristics of this 'stage'.

In general terms first, we find here a concern that is located on a more sociological level than earlier stages. The phrase 'politics of experience' really does sum up this stage very well: for what is involved is an examination of the *ways* certain sorts of experience arise and are invalidated, or are prevented from arising at all, by society; why it is that certain sorts of experience are held to be intolerable in the eyes of society. Specific reference was made to transcendental experience, which was held to *sometimes* arise in religion and psychosis.

It is impossible to isolate a set of concepts, theoretically related to form a schema, which express Laing's views here. We must again, therefore, speak in generalities. In so far as a philosophical 'position' is employed, it is a curious blend of dialectical phenomenology, and existentialism. However, we should remember that theoretical positions are not so much *posited* here as *used*; specifically, certain verbal forms are exploited in order to generate, in the readers, certain sorts of experience. This is, of course, always the case to some extent with writing. But scientific discourses tend to attempt to eliminate this factor and concentrated on the imparting of objective knowledge. Here, however, the emotive aspects are concentrated upon; as the blurb on the back of the book points out 'he does not hesitate to call on science, rhetoric poetry and polemic to support his points'. We have attempted to relate this concern to certain aspects of Sartre's position in relation to human sciences.

Turning to look more specifically at what is involved in this stage, we found two related issues returned to time and again. These were the notion of schizophrenia as an inner voyage, and the notion of normality as predominantly a state of alienation. The 'inner voyage' conception, of existential death and rebirth, was termed by Laing 'metanoia'. The term, which comes from Old Testament Greek literally means 'change of mind'. The metanoic sequence of uninterrupted 'schizophrenia' was related to accounts of similar sequences found in other cultures by Laing, particularly in lectures and informal seminars held at Kingsley Hall. Unfortunately, Laing has not published much in the way of such accounts. His notion of alienation, however, has been much more fully spelt out. It is primarily alienation from experience, and thus from the total real possibilities of being human. We might say, therefore, that it is an alienation of man from his species being (i.e. that which in essence he could be). Although Laing never relates his conception of alienation to that of Marx (or of anyone else), I think it is closest to Marx's sense; in particular to the third aspect which Marx isolates, that aspect which

> make the species-being of man, both nature and the intellectual faculties of his species, into a being that is alien to him, into a means for his individual existence. It alienates man from his own body, from nature exterior to him, and from his intellectual being, his human essence (Marx, Economic and Philosophical Manuscripts. From 'Early Texts', ed. McClellan, 1971, p. 140).

Of course, Marx is tracing this alienation more or less directly to certain economic features of our society, whereas Laing traces them to more social or cultural features. Still, no doubt Laing would agree with Marx that both sets of features exist in dialectical relation to each other.

Can we say, in conclusion, that this stage, like previous ones, is ultimately concerned with the understanding of individual's experiences? I think we can, but not in the same way. Unlike in previous stages, Laing does not take 'samples' of supposedly incomprehensible experience and behaviour, and then render them intelligible. The 'clinical' content of this stage is almost negligible. However, I think very broadly, his aim is the same in so far as he is arguing for the existence and validity of certain types of experience which are generally invalidated or otherwise denied. The difference here is not so much one of aim, as one of the level at which the argument is conducted. This stage can be seen as a sort of 'stepping back', to allow a broader perspective in which his more detailed, individualistic observations can be located. We conclude, then, by saying that we find the primary aim of Laing's work as a totality, as it is conceived in this thesis, verified yet again by this stage, albeit at a significantly different level of conceptualization.

STAGE 5: POLITICAL RADICALISM

> No matter how obvious the irrational character of the whole may manifest itself and, with it, the necessity of change, insight into necessity has never sufficed for seizing the possible alternatives' (Marcuse, 1964).
> Just remeber the Bhagavad Gita! (Laing, 1967).

The next stage we have to discuss is, in some ways, scarecely a stage at all, at least, in the temporal sense. I present it here as a stage because Laing made a number of statements, within a fairly clearly defined space of time, relating directly to 'Politics' (in the more usual sense of the word) which, on the one hand, should not be ignored in a review of his work, and, on the other hand, do not fit directly into the stream of his theoretical work. As we shall hopefully see in the next chapter, however, they *do* 'fit' when one considers Laing's career more broadly. For the time being, however, we shall concentrate on the statements themselves.

The time span involved includes the years 1967-8; specifically, we start in July 1967, with the Dialectics of Liberation Conference.

This 'conference' was convened by Drs Joe Berke, Cooper, Laing and Redler of the Institute of Phenomenological Studies 'in order to figure out what the hell is going on' (Berke, 1971, p. 410), but was actually run by Joe Berke and Leon Redler, rather than Laing and Cooper, as is commonly supposed. Laing himself delivered a paper entitled The Obvious (reprinted in Cooper, 1968) but also took part in several seminars, recordings of which are available as LPs from the Institute. Laing's paper, and his contributions to the seminars, constitute the first source for this stage. Other sources will include literature on the Anti-University of London, which arose out of the Conference, and was sponsored by an interest-free loan from the Institute of Phenomenological Studies; plus various interviews with Laing which appeared in the underground press at this time.

The defining feature of this stage is the concern with 'political' action; our first task, then, is to examine, in general terms, the theoretical framework in which such action is conceptualized as taking place. We will then move on to examine specific forms of action.

The theoretical status of the action concerned is more or less defined in a passage in The Obvious, which I shall now quote.

> In our society, at certain times, this interlaced set of systems may lend itself to revolutionary change, not at the extreme micro or macro ends; that is, not through the individual pirouette of solitary repentance on the one hand, or by a seizure of the machinery of the state on the other; but by sudden, structural, radical qualitative changes in the intermediate system levels: changes in a factory, a hospital, a school, a university, a set of schools, or a whole area of industry, medicine, education, etc. (Laing, 1967e, p. 16).

What we are concerned with, then, is the level of discrete Institutions rather than classes or other economically defined units; a concern which, although antithetical to orthodox Marxism, was characteristic of the thinking of the so-called New Left at that time. Before considering what is involved with this concern, however, we must first place it is the theoretical context that Laing himself does.

> The fabric of sociality is an interlaced set of contexts, of sub-systems interlaced with other sub-systems, of contexts interlaced with metacontexts and metametacontexts and so on until it reaches a theoretical limit, the context of all possible contexts, ... what one might call the total social world system. Beyond this... there is no further *social* context to which one can refer the intelligibility of the total social world system (p. 15).

So, what we have here is a hierarchical, structural view of social reality. Note, however, tnat once again, the emphasis is on Intelligibility. The irrationality of any particular phenomenon, at whatever level, takes on 'a certain form of intelligibility' if it is viewed in its context. Given a certain level, which, immediately, is phenomenally irrational, it can be made, mediately through examination of its meta-level, to be phenomenally rational and thus intelligible. This process can start at the lowest possible level of intelligibility, the individual, and proceed right up to the level of the total social world, beyond which we cannot take intelligibility. One can place this last level in, say, a planetary, or astronomical context, but this does not, of course, yield intelligibility, as there is no question of rationality, which by definition supposes purpose. Laing notes a paradox here, that the totality appears itself irrational, and thus begs a further meta-context, which would have to be at the level of some cosmic purposefulness, to establish its intelligibility. He does not commit himself on this point.

As an example he gives, predictably, the case of a 'psychotic', who, irrational out of context, can be seen to be quite rational in the context of the family, which then itself appears as irrational. This in turn, requires putting the family as an institution in a broader context, and so on. It should be emphasized that this structuralism is dialectical: as he says, 'these larger contexts do not exist out there on some periphery of social space: they pervade the interstices of all that is comprised by them (p. 15). Thus we can see already, that we are still dealing here with social phenomenology, but with a broader frame of reference. Where before the concern was with the individual, and his immediate context, we now find that, at least in general theoretical terms, meta-, and meta-meta-etc.-contexts are incorporated into the overall schema.

Let us now return to the questions of action. What is at issue here is revolutionary action, but at the level of groups or institutions: 'microrevolutions', as Laing puts it. Laing mentioned examples such as hospitals, universities, in general terms; can we consider any concrete examples?

The first that springs to mind, of course, is the 'anti-hospital' of Kingsley Hall. Kingsley Hall has already been considered in the previous stage; here, we need only note that it does indeed provide an example of an 'Anti-Institution'. Compared to a conventional hospital, it does embody 'sudden, structural radical qualitative changes'. For instance, internal role structures were largely abolished, or 'destructured'; on the other hand, a simultaneous restructuralization took place in that, acting as it did as a focus for numerous counter-cultural events, it led to the formation of other structures, all of which went to make up a higher, meta-level totalized/totalizing structure, namely, the cultural underground. I refer to such things as the Dialectics Conference, which arose largely out of the interaction of the Kingsley Hall residents, notably Cooper, with the political Left Wing; to the Anti-University of London which itself arose out of the Conference, and was, in its turn, a focus for counter-cultural events; to the artistic avant-garde, represented by Cornelius Cardew, Alan Ginsberg, Calvin Hernton and such like, who conducted many experimental music/drama/poetry, etc. events at Kingsley Hall; the brief and somewhat traumatic association of Kingsley Hall with the Sigma Program and the underground press (see Jeff Nuttall, 1970); and so on. Radical structural change, indeed!

It would seem appropriate to consider the institution of 'university' next, in view of the actual historical association.

The Anti-University of London, as far as can be ascertained, opened on 12 February 1968. Information about it (and similar organizations elsewhere) and a 'curriculum' can be found in Berke (1971). Again, we find a concern to break down internal role structures, and to increase the fluidity of its relation to other external structures. Foremost amongst its aims, stated in an article by Roberta Elzey (Joe Berke's wife) which appeared in 'Counter-Culture', were 'a change in the relations among people'. Primary amongst these relations was, of course, that of staff/ student. Although there were lecturers (who were only paid for the first term), the emphasis was on active participation by all. Laing himself gave lectures on Psychology and Religion; specifically, on the accounts of 'inner space' to be found in various mythologies and religions. There were, of course, no exams, and fees were minimal (£8 a quarter plus 10s. per course attended ; goods or services were accepted in lieu of cash, another example of the sort of interactional change envisaged).

A significant feature of the London Anti-University will lead us on to consider the next institution, the household. A household is usually synonymous with a family; the counter-cultural equivalent being the commune. The Anti-University had a commune associated with it; a significant number of the prominent members lived in it, and the two 'institutions' became synonymous. Indeed, it seems to have been one of the major lessons learned from the Anti-University that such enterprises need the domestic stability plus intimacy yet fluidity of a commune to flourish; that if one wishes to found an 'Anti-University', it is best to start with an already existing commune or communal network. (Cf. the study courses now being run by the Philadelphia Association, and the Arbours Association.)

In a debate on the future of hippies at the Dialectics conference, Laing opposed himself to Stokely Carmichael by not condemning hippies and their life style. What particularly excited Laing about the hippie movement was the way they were 'exploring new ways to use architecture'; that is, they were, implicitly at least, recognizing that the divisions of a house made by its occupants, the mapping of physical space into social space, and areas of privacy and communality, even the layout of furniture, possessions, decor, etc; all this leads to characteristic structures of interexperience. By experimenting with the former, the hippes, Laing argued, are discovering new forms of the latter, and that is something worth while in itself. Kingsley Hall, of course, was in part an experiment on these lines; and Morty Schatzman likened it to a hippy commune. The commune would seem to be a very central institution in the counter-culture, as one would expect, from a consideration of the importance of its conventional analogue, the family. In fact, it is perhaps surprising, considering the amount of time Laing has devoted to writing about families, that he has never written anything about their alternative, the commune. It would seem that the social phenomenology of the commune is an unexplored sub-field of crucial importance.

A more obviously political institution that comes in for criticism by Laing is the Police Force. It is interesting to note that when, in an interview in the underground paper 'International Times' in 1968, the final question asked of Laing was what would he recommend that an individual could actually *do*, given the present situation, in the way of political subversion, his answer was 'I think it would be a good idea if some cool heads, and they'd have to be very very cool heads, could infiltrate the police.' I think this example highlights very well the nature of Laing's political thinking.

Laing is clearly dissatisfied with the orthodox Marxist approach. As the initial quote from The Obvious shows, he does not consider that a revolution on the lines of proletarian seizure of state power is a feasible possibility at this historical juncture. His concern, as always, is with individuals; but individuals in their group contexts. One can see the influence of Sartre's criticism of dogmatic Marxism, and its lack of concern with the individual, presented in 'Problem of Method', present here. (Also, of course, Marcuse: this will be considered in chapter 4.) For Laing, like Sartre, is concerned with the relation of individual praxis, and freedom, to groups. That he should find revolutionary potential in sub-class, institutional levels of social reality is, then, significant. If the first feature of this stage can be summarized as 'the revolutionary potential of institutions', the second feature is the concern with the possibilities of individual action, in relation to the above. It is to this that we now turn, starting with the example quoted above, of infiltrating the Police.

Although he never makes it formally, Laing clearly wishes to draw a distinction between those institutions which would have their analogues in the sort of society he would like to see, and those that wouldn't. Examples of the former would be mental hospitals, families, and universities. These have been considered, and the role of the individual in relation to them is not particularly problematic, as such anti-institutions can be set up *within* the existing structure of society, although opposed to it. Witness Kingsley Hall and the Anti-University.

In the case of the latter, those that would not have analogues, the situation is different. No comparable anti-institution can be set up, for the desired end is the total abolition of the institution in question. Individual action must therefore be of a different order. Obvious examples of such institutions would include the Police, the Army, and probably the whole political state machine.

At the Dialectics Conference Laing noted, in discussion with Stokely Carmichael, that we, in the First World, are in a peculiar position in relation to these institutions. Unlike Stokely Carmichael and his people we are not, by and large, in imminent danger of physical violence from them; thus, again unlike him, we have the chance to sit back in relative calm and think about our situation. It is not a matter of sheer survival that we should resort to counter-violence. These facts lead Laing to postulate a basically non-violent form of opposition as being most appropriate. What we should aim to do, he urges, is to peacefully dismantle these institutions, which are not necessary and have irrational and artificial foundations in society. I take it that infiltration of the Police would be an example of this.

I am afraid I cannot entirely agree with Laing here. The social foundations of the Police, etc., may not be necessary in an absolute sense, but they are necessary and entirely rational in relation to the macro-structure of society, i.e. the status quo. As Laing's own theoretical considerations imply, the intelligibility of these institutions requires that they be placed in their own context, that being the class struggle as identified by orthodox Marxism. I believe Laing is quite right in insisting that all levels of social reality should be taken into account; but I cannot escape the conclusion that he himself does not do this, when he considers what the individual can do in relation to groups. Hence, I believe, he arrives at an idealist conception of the possibilities of opposition.

The same point arises in his argument with Carmichael over the hippies. Laing's claim that they are making important discoveries is really irrelevant to Carmichael's assertion that, if the hippies genuinely created their own culture, they too would be suppressed, because bourgeois society could not tolerate it. It would seem, in retrospect, that Carmichael's foresight has been proved; the Underground, after its transformation into a saleable commodity, has, by all appearances, polarized itself into mere decadence on the one hand, and violent political opposition on the other. As Stokely said six years ago (in the Roundhouse, ironically, the focus of the Underground) 'You will have to throw down your flowers and fight.'

I believe that Laing *is* right, however, in his contention that we are privileged by virtue of our comparative safety to sit back and contemplate our reality; and on this point, I think, Laing is also more aware of the difficulties.

The privilege we have is to be more able to form a conception of the 'total social world systems', as Laing puts it. That is, we can, starting with ourselves, work our way up, through the levels and contexts, to form an overall conception of 'what is going on', and our place within it. We can, in the Sartrean idiom, successively totalize-detotalize-retotalize our experience. This idea, introduced in The Obvious, is spelt out in greater detail in Our Present Madness (Laing, 1968b), an interview printed in 'Unit', no. 11. In his words:

> When I go beyond a certain range it's outside of my direct horizon therefore I've got to rely on the writings and personal communications given to me by other people that I know.... I've got to try to piece together some tentative information picture of what the whole thing is like, but I'm aware that it becomes more and more speculative as it becomes more and more second, third, fourth hand. And this applies to absolutely everyone.

Now this is, as he says, fairly obvious. The importance of it lies, however, when it is contemplated in relation to the fact that those who have the power of crucial decisions, i.e. political leaders, are also dependent on second, third, etc. hand information for their picture, *and* these sources are themselves interest groups. He cites the fact that the CIA was known to have withheld important information from Kennedy. The same thing apparently happened in Whitehall when the Civil Service repeatedly failed to inform Labour ministers about committee meetings at which important decisions were to be made. This phenomenon is of course the essence of Watergate.

Asked again what the individual should do in the face of this, Laing replied, 'I think one should endeavour to be uncommitted to any ideological position' in so far as one is dealing with matters which are beyond one's own direct experience. Thus his activism stems directly, and apparently totally, from his experience of the violence perpetrated by mental hospitals and families.

Now while it is obviously reasonable to be most strongly committed to change in those areas about which one is most knowledgeable, it is hard to see, on this basis, how anyone can ever be committed to change on the meta-level, i.e. that identified by orthodox Marxism. Indeed, in the light of Laing's assertions about the speculative nature of knowledge concerning these levels, and his advice to remain ideologically uncommitted beyond the realms of one's own experience, it would seem that he views it as undesirable. Unfortunately, Laing does not comment on this point directly. We may speculate, however, that this may have been in his mind when he said, some time later, that he was 'not an activist in the ordinary sense of the word.' and 'temperamentally not very well suited for it' (quoted in Gordon, 1971). As he said in the 'Unit' interview: 'my temperamental response to (the world situation) is one of extreme pessimism. I get extremely depressed and weighed down by a sense of futility.... I practically never get happy about it.'

Another aspect of what may be called his 'radicalism' concerns his attitude towards psychedelic drugs; a field that went notoriously hand-in-hand with Left Wing political radicalism in the second half of the 1960s.

Looking at the blurb about Laing on the covers of the paperback editions of his books, we find that from 1967 (significantly, perhaps, the year he left the Tavistock Institute?) onwards his 'research' is 'particularly concerned with... varieties of experience including those induced by drugs which expand consciousness, such as mescalin and lysergic acid diethylamide.' And even in 1973 Laing's work was still mentioned in relation to LSD, by Sedgewick (speech, delivered in Stoke, February 1973).

Strangely enough, however, only twice in all his written and published output does Laing mention LSD (Laing, 1968d) - a finding all the more remarkable in the light of the fact that, in interview, he has admitted not only to taking LSD but also to have used it in therapy. Where, then, is the source of information concerning his attitude towards drugs?

The first reference that I can find is a statement by Laing quoted by Alex Trocchi, one of Laing's close associates in the mid-1960s, in an article entitled Why Drugs? (Trocchi, 1965). Trocchi does not give us the source of the statement, but he dates it as written 'about June 1964'. He is presumably referring to Laing's letter to the BMA (which they declined to publish) pointing out the harmless nature of marijuana. Laing wrote: 'I would be far happier if my own teenager children would, *without breaking the law,* smoke marijuana when they wished, rather than start on the road of so many of their elders to nicotine and ethyl alcohol addiction.'

Unfortunately, the article contains no advice as to how to achieve this remarkable feat of smoking marijuana without breaking the law. It does, however, contain a note concerning the author, Trocchi, which states that he 'in collaboration with Dr. R.D. Laing and the writer William Burroughs, is now (May 1965) preparing a general work on the subject of drugs and the creative process'. This potentially remarkable book does not appear to have been published; nor could any comment on it be elicited from Laing's personal assistant.

The next occasion, that I can locate, in which Laing's name is linked with marijuana, was when he (and his colleagues, Cooper and

Esterson, and Sidney Briskin, from the Philadelphia Association) put their signature to the petition, organized by SOMA - Society of Mental Awareness, of which Laing was a committee member - delivered to the Home Office, which was reprinted as a full page advertisement in 'The Times', calling for the legalization of marijuana ('The Times', 24 July 1967). The document, which was financed by those who signed it (notably, the Beatles) presented quotations of medical opinion, a historical survey of the drug's use, and an extensive and convincing argument in favour of its legalization.

Finally, Laing appeared on the BBC TV programme Your Witness: Marijuana (24 August 1967). However, owing to the BBC's refusal to provide a transcript or tape, (for 'contractual reasons) it is not possible to discover what views were expressed during the discussion.

As regards LSD and related psychedelics we have Timothy Leary's and Jeff Nuttall's cryptic comments (Leary, 1970; Nuttall, 1970) which refer back to 1964; but it is not until 1967 that I can find Laing himself mentioning LSD; even though by summer 1968, he talks as if LSD were a thing of the past, at least as far as his use in therapy of it is concerned (interview in 'International Times'). Unpublished interviews aside, his first mention or it occurs in one of the discussion seminars at the Dialectics of Liberation Conference. In his somewhat incoherent reply to a question concerning the origins of violence, Laing discussed the phantasies of one of his patients from his Glasgow days. This patient, who was unable to come to terms with 'who he was' solved his dilemma by being anybody he chose - for instance, Hamlet, which he was able to do, by the ritual act of literally just snapping his fingers. Laing compares this person's action to a possible misuse of LSD. To quote:

...you could say that he, by snapping his fingers and opting out in that way, he's doing what many people may be doing with LSD or with hashish - is a snapping of fingers, or, you can in a phony way use that to simply confuse yourself further by not realizing, or forgetting for a while, not suffering, not experiencing within its own terms, the constrictions and impotence which is imposed on us by the system that we are part of; and in so far as we remain part of it we perpetuate it. On the other hand, LSD and other things like that, needn't be used in that way. They can be used to see through and into the thing further. It doesn't necessarily lead to a cessation of action; it tends to lead to a cessation of action from the ego, and leads to action coming from the self; and that by no means implies that you aren't going to be doing anything. Just remember the Bhagavad Gita! (Dialectics of Liberation record D.L. 14 side 1).

I should like to consider this statement in relation to considerations arising from the Transcendental Experience paper (Laing, 1965e) which was reprinted at the same time as Laing said the above, in 'Politics of Experience'.

I should like to focus on the fact that Laing, in that paper, regards ego loss as characteristic of religious experience, and also of *some* 'psychotic' experience. Our present age, we are told, is 'starving' for the inner, the experience of transcendental, non-egoic realms. For he says 'True Sanity entails in one way or another the dissolution of the normal ego, that false self completely adjusted to our alienated social reality' (p. 15).

In the light of that, the fact that LSD can 'lead to a cessation of action from the ego' takes on both personal and political significance. For Laing argued, in the previous stage, that non-egoic experience, whilst generally invalidated by social reality, is valid on a personal level, and necessary on a social level. Now, however, he seems to be saying more than that: the focus of attention is more on action. Specifically, he implicitly regards non-egoic *action*, i.e. personal praxis deriving from the true self rather than the ego, as a politically desirable thing. LSD, by breaking down the ego, can break down one's ties with the conventional institutions of society, with the 'alienated social reality', thus enabling one to 'see into the thing further', i.e., to take the personal project of the totalization of experience to higher levels. Simultaneously, personally 'deeper' experiences, of the sort described in 'The Politics of Experience', become open to one. The fact that those active in creating new institutions such as Anti-Universities, communes, experimental music groups, etc., tend also to be LSD users further testifies to his claim that '(action coming from the self) by no means implies that you aren't going to be doing anything'.

On the other hand, Laing, unlike so many 'drug radicals', does recognize that LSD can equally well be used as a sort of experiential substitute for the world, a means of escape. Ultimately, with LSD, as with anything else, the final responsibility rests with the individual to ensure his own freedom.

Laing's sole reference to LSD that I could trace that has been published (without his knowledge, apparently) occurs in Metanoia: Some Experiences at Kingsley Hall. The paper, as the title suggests, is about Metanoia, not the LSD trip. Nevertheless, an analogy, he believes, can be drawn:

> LSD 25 was originally regarded as a psychotico-mimetic substance. I propose that this biochemically induced six-to-twelve-hour trip has its natural analogue in what I suggest be called a metanoiac Voyage. The nature of the metanoiac voyage may be 'good' or 'bad', largely depending on the set and setting (Laing, 1968d, p. 12).

This analogy has never, unfortunately, been expanded upon.

In summary of this stage, then, we may say the focus of concern is on the possibilities for action that the individual has, in the context of the institutions of which he is part; in particular, the ways in which an individual, by relinquishing his egoic adjustment to alienated 'reality', and discovering his 'true self', can effect 'microrevolutions' in the institutions of society. Viewed more broadly, such institutional microrevolutions are seen as the way to a more wholesale destructuring (destruction)-restructuring of society, in a gradual, cumulative process of peaceful revolution, not involving the violent seizure of state power by an oppressed class as a whole. We have noted the divergence of this view from orthodox Marxism, and its correspondence, on certain points, with the Marxism of Sartre, and, more extensively, with the hippie Left. We have also noted that this leads to certain problems, practically speaking, in relation to the real possibilities of change in certain institutions; and finally, that these appear to relate, to some extent, to Laing's personal temperament with regard to active radicalism.

STAGE 6: THE POLITICS OF THE FAMILY

> The bourgeois nuclear family unit (to use something like the language of its agents - academic sociologists and political scientists) has become, in this century, the ultimately perfected form of non-meeting, and therefore the ultimate denial of mourning, death, birth and the experiential realm that precedes birth and conception (Cooper, 1971).

> I think that my picture of the family that has been published remains an extremely partial one. Some of the happiest and most fulfilling and rewarding and pleasantly memorable experiences in my life have been in families in which I've lived myself.
> 'Are you abnormal?'
> 'Yes... well, I might be.' (Laing, 1972).

We come now to the last stage of Laing's work *as a psychiatrist;* works subsequent to those included in this stage, such as 'Knots' (Laing, 1970b), and more recently, lectures on meditation and so on, fall outside the continuum here conceived of the theoretical development of concepts relating to human science. Furthermore, it will be recalled that the previous stage was defined not by chronological considerations but by subject matter, namely politics. Many of the sources for this stage were written concurrently with sources for the previous stage. It follows, therefrom, that this stage, too, will be defined, in part, by the consistency of the subject matter of its sources.

What, then, is to be included in this stage?

The first paper here considered is Family and Individual Structure (Laing, 1967j) which was written as a chapter of a book by Lomas (1967) entitled 'The Predicament of the Family'. It was subsequently 'virtually rewritten' as the first chapter of 'The Politics of the Family' (Laing, 1971).

We shall then consider a paper delivered in March 1967 entitled The Study of Family and Social Contexts in the Origin of Schizophrenia (Laing, 1967c), and a lecture given in May 1968 entitled Intervention in Social Situations (Laing, 1969a).

The bulk of this stage comprises the talks given by Laing on Canadian radio, collectively entitled 'The Politics of the Family'. It should be remembered that although the book of that name was not published in this country till 1971, the talks themselves were given in the autumn of 1968, and all the Other Essays date before that.

Other sources will include various comments by Laing on the writings of Reich, prefaces to second editions of earlier books, a report by the Philadelphia Association, and a paper on ritualization delivered to the Royal Society (see Chapter 4).

We start, then, with Family and Individual Structure.

The aim here is clearly stated in the first paragraph:

> I shall try in this chapter to develop theoretical links between our observations of recurrent patterns of individual experience and behaviour in psychoanalysis, and recurrent dramatic patterns *between* people in studying real families as such within their own

social contexts. These two sets of observations tend to be couched in different theoretical and descriptive idioms. It is difficult therefore to put them in ways that are reciprocally enhancing. This is an attempt (p. 107).

I have quoted this introductory paragraph at length as it serves also as an excellent introduction to this stage as a whole. For it defines one of the principal features, as we shall see: namely, the desire to link theories and facts derived from the study of individuals with those derived from the study of familial systems as such. As the reference to psycho-analysis suggests, the former largely consists of the work of Freud and his followers. How does Laing begin this undertaking?

He starts by questioning what a family is, and what we mean by the terms 'family dynamics' and 'the family structure'. A family, he says, is 'a system comprising persons in relationship' (p. 107); as such, the study of it involves not only the patterns of behaviour, but also of experience. A family is a system of interaction *and* interexperience. Understood this way, Laing urges, we must recognize our ignorance concerning the relationship of family dynamics and structure to other sorts of group dynamics and structure. What is at issue, then, is the relation between the structure of the family as observed, and the experiential structures of its members (the focus here is on children), particularly phantasy experience.

Laing notes that it is incorrect to view any group as a set of binary-relations; that is, as a set of relations between individual and the rest of the group. For this is to overlook the observing third party, which must be considered when attempting a phenomenological approach, as Laing is here. Thus, in a family consisting of Father (F), Mother (M), Son (S), and Daughter (D) we have not only son's view of father, mother, etc., i.e. all binary combinations, but also son's view of the relationship between father and mother, between mother and daughter etc.; and yet again, the son's view of the daughter's view of the relationship between father and mother; and so on. Each of these 'views' is termed a synthesis.

Now the interaction within any dyad may be smooth or it may be permeated with strife. The crucial significance of the third party as observer, however, is that the dyad that is observed may differ in its interaction according to who the observer is. For example where *a*, *b*, and *c* are respectively father mother and son, *a* and *b* may interact happily with respect to *c*, that is, when synthesized by *c* as 'parents'; but fail to do so with respect to each other, that is, when synthesized by each other as husband and wife. Or again, sister and brother may get on together, but as daughter and son, they may not.

To achieve a coherent group, each member must perform acts of synthesis whereby members of the group are 'we' and non-members are 'them'; *and* each member must internalize not only his own syntheses but everyone else's also. In other words, each member of the family internalizes a family synthesis for each member of the family. The resulting synthesis of syntheses which each member internalizes is called the internalized family, and is denoted by putting the word in inverted commas, to distinguish it from the family as observed. As Laing says, 'the "family" exists everywhere in each of the people who are in it, *and nowhere else*'.

Now, the 'family' as an internalized system is, on this basis, comprised of internalized *relations,* not isolated objects. As such, it is a space-time system, not merely a space system. It is also, of course, a phantasy system; and Laing suggests that the experience of the 'family' 'may never have become fully differentiated from such fantasy presences as "the womb", "the breast", or "the mother's body"' (p. 112). Hence it comes to be experienced perhaps as an animal, or some sort of protective cocoon, or even a tomb.

Laing next proceeds to examine the notion of internalization more closely, and to focus on one aspect: 'Internalization entails the transference of a pattern of relations from one modality of experience to others: namely from perception to imagination, memory, dreams, fantasy' (p. 113). The 'internalization of the family', then, comes to refer to the process by which perceptual experience of repeated interaction patterns is transformed into other modalities of experience, notably phantasy. Laing notes the discrepancy with the Freudian notion of internalization, which regards the superego as largely built up of parental attitudes. But in Freudian terminology, we speak of 'internal objects', 'introjects', 'part objects'; in other words, internalized *things*. Laing would wish to argue, however, that one internalizes not objects, but relations and structures.

One result of this, Laing claims, is that such an internalized structure can sometimes provide a model for *intra* personal relations. Thus, a child may be engaged in reconciling two 'sides' of himself, without success, if he has internalized a highly disjunctive relation between his parents.

Further, this internalization may be re-externalized, or projected, in Freudian terminology, back onto the world, in which case it forms a model for experiencing the world. But if it is a whole relational system, not a mere collection of objects, that is thus internalized and then projected, it follows that to comprehend this projection one must have access to the original interactional system whence it is derived. This means that when studying the projections of, say, a seriously disturbed person, it is unlikely that sense can be made of these projections without studying the family interaction which, via internalization as 'family', they reflect. As Laing puts it:

> In studying the families of very disturbed people, we have repeatedly been surprised by the extent to which quite delusional structures are recognizably related to family relations. The reprojection of the 'family' is thus not simply a matter of projecting an 'internal' object on to an external person. It is the re-experiencing of the whole system of relations (p. 116).

Laing gives a clinical example to illustrate the point.

The paper proceeds with a consideration of the implication of all this for the psycho-analytic concept of defence. The latter is concerned almost entirely with intrapsychic defences; that is, what a person does to his *own* experience. This Laing regards as insufficient in so far as, in real family life, persons attempt to control or alter the experience of *others*; they also attempt to defend themselves from such attempts by others. Psycho-analysis has no formal concepts for this; yet it needs to be accounted for.

We can begin to do this, Laing thinks, by reflecting on the family as conceived earlier; namely as a system internalized by each member. The experiential reality of the family was the 'family', the shared group presence that exists *only* in so far as each member has it inside them. 'To be in the same family, means having the same "family" inside oneself' (p. 119). In such a situation, the identity of each member depends on all the other members' continued experience of the family as the 'family'.

Consequently, if a child (or any member) attempts to break down this internalized structure, or begins to fail to recognize its validity, this action threatens all the other members, in so far as they depend on his acceptance of it for their own security and identity as members of it. It becomes necessary, therefore, to co-erce the child into experiencing the family in that way, i.e. to set up transpersonal 'defences'.

Such a situation is likely to be extremely problematic for the child, for any acts of spontaneity, or expressions of personal autonomy, are likely to be defined by other members as destructive (of the family), and thus bad or mad. Increasing maturation thus paradoxically becomes viewed as increasing pathology. Again Laing gives a clinical example, and then moves swiftly to conclude the paper by summarizing the points he has made.

The next paper we examine is The Study of Family and Social Contexts in Relation to the Origin of Schizophrenia (Laing, 1967c), which was a paper delivered by Laing at a conference on the 'Origins of Schizophrenia' at Rochester University, USA, held during March 1967. It is reprinted in Romano (1967), and again, somewhat revised, as chapter three of 'The Politics of the Family'. All references here are to the version given in Romano (1967).

In addition to embodying the theoretical approach which, as we shall see, is characteristic of this stage, this paper also expresses ideas which we have met in previous stages; perhaps because the paper was delivered in the USA where Laing's work was probably not as extensively known as over here. At any rate, we are here presented with the by-now familiar account of why Laing does not regard schizophrenia as a disease, the aetiology of which should be 'researched'. It is presented, however, in such a manner as to highlight what is involved in talking of the 'origins' of schizophrenia. For if schizophrenia simply is the socially sanctioned attribution that Laing makes out, we must look to both family contexts and institutional contexts, as they relate to individuals if we wish to discern 'origins'.

Laing refers to Cooper's experiments with his 'anti-hospital', and then to the households set up by the Philadelphia Association, and notes the possibility that 'schizophrenics', placed in sympathetic environments where they are not labelled, tend to have very different experiences to those in conventional hospitals. This leads him onto his 'inner voyage' notion of schizophrenia, which he now terms 'metanoia', a Greek word meaning literally 'change of mind'.

> All life is movement. For instance, one may be high or low, be
> beside oneself... go back or stand still. Of these movements, the
> last two in particular tend to earn the attribution of schizophre-
> nia. Perhaps the most tabooed movement of all is to go back... At
> Cooper's Villa 21 and in our households, this movement has

not been stopped. If allowed to go on, a process unfolds that
appears to have a natural sequence, a beginning, middle and end.
Instead of the pathological connotations around such terms as
'acute schizophrenic breakdown', I suggest as a term for this
whole sequence, metanoia (p. 142).

Metanoic sequences appear to be impossible in families, because
of the knot of mystification that binds the individual. Hospitals,
however, tend to perpetuate the mystification, and with authority
structures analogous to the family, and tranquillizing drugs, manage
to prevent their patients from embarking on this natural voyage of
metanoia. Instead, they turn them into schizophrenics.

So much for the institutional origins, but what of the familial
ones?

Laing considers the case of a young man whose experience was
polarized, so to speak, into left and right. He experienced his
left side, or half, in completely different terms to his right. In
particular, the left side was feminine, and the right masculine, and
both were very old, though not the same age. This apparently extraordinary individual experience begins to make sense when we look at
the family context which this unfortunate man found himself in.

His parents were divorced, and each told him he took after the
other. But each parent accused *the other* of being inadequate;
specifically, the mother called the father 'cissy' and effeminate,
and the father called the mother a 'phoney man'. The child grew up,
then, with a conception of his father as a male lesbian, and his
mother as a female homosexual. Comparable confusions appear to
stretch back as far as the child's great-great-grandparents. In
short, it appeared to him that amongst two parents, four grandparents and eight great-grandparents, there had not been a real man
or woman. Furthermore, he had internalized all these relations, and
relations of relations of relations. The resulting matrix of iden-
tifications foisted upon him defies imagination.

Laing describes this case as 'a paradigm of the internalization
of a multi-generational family situation, such as I have seen in a
number of people whose existential stasis leads to a diagnosis of
schizophrenia' (p. 143). At any rate, methodologically, it is certainly an example of the approach outlined in the previous article,
of rendering individual experience intelligible by seeing it as a
reflected version of internalized family relationships. As before,
Laing describes this theoretical approach as one of social phenomenology.

The next work to examine is a lecture, given to the Association
of Family Caseworkers in May 1968, entitled Intervention in Social
Situations. It is reprinted as chapter two of 'The Politics of the
Family'; references are to that version, although it was first published as a pamphlet (Laing, 1969a). The versions are substantially
similar.

Laing starts by defining the common ground between himself (as a
psychiatrist) and his audience: 'The common ground between social
workers and psychiatrists is the study of and intervention in social
situations' (p. 21). Yet, the psychiatrist normally works within a
medical frame of reference. The consequence of applying such a
frame of reference to social intervention are the objects of Laing's
scrutiny here.

He proceeds by giving an account of a case he was called into, where a young boy was seen as troublesome, at home and at school. His refusal to talk to his psychiatrist had brought about the diagnosis of 'incipient schizophrenia'. Laing investigated the boy's family, and the findings he presents make the child's actions entirely intelligible. The point, however, was that the psychiatrist, who gave the diagnosis, had seen no one from the family but the boy; the PSW had seen only the mother. No one had seen the boy's home, school, or day time haunts. As Laing remarks:
> If we are not lulled by habit into regarding this as normal practice, is it not an odd way to go about things? If one has a 'referee!' say, from a hockey team, because the left back is not playing properly, one wouldn't only think of getting the left back round to one's office, taking a history, and giving a Rorschach. At least I hope not. One would also go to see how the team plays hockey (p. 30).

In other words, the situation, or context, is never known in advance; it has to be discovered. Further, one cannot assume that the people in the situation know what the situation is. This applies just as much to the parents of 'patients' as to the 'patients' themselves. This puts the validity of the vast majority of case histories very much in doubt. The only way to 'diagnose' (literally, 'see through') the situation is to intervene in it. This means interacting with the whole family, at least, but beyond that, particularly on the issue of how to decide whose views about the situation are right, Laing does not here commit herself.

We come now to 'The Politics of The Family' itself, taking as our source the revised versions of the talks as published by Tavistock (Laing, 1971).

As Laing says in the Introduction, he has sketched an outline of an as yet non-existent systematic theory. Judging from other sources, he wishes the theory to be known as that of 'mapping'; at any rate, it employs concepts derived from certain branches of mathematics, notably set theory, which are 'being applied to great effects in linguistics, kinship systems, mythology, and other areas of social science' (p. 66). Laing believes it may be fruitfully applied to the 'psycho-social interior of families in our own society' (ibid.). What is involved, then, in this embryonic theory?

Laing starts by asking the same question: how can the texture of lived experience of family life be related to dramatic structure of the interaction of individuals over generations?

If we call a person's experiential structure A, and the public events which occasion that B, A and B may be said to be in phase or out of phase. For example, if B refers to a wedding, A and B are said to be in phase if the persons getting married experience themselves, 'feel', married after going through B. Such a process, whereby personal experiences match the public events, is said to be 'mapping'. A is mapped onto B.

Now where public event B is held to be sufficiently important, it is regarded as essential that A should be mapped onto B; that is, that the participants in B should experience the 'right' things. If this does not happen, A is disavowed; the person's experience of B is invalidated. So important is it that A should map onto B, that there are a host of mechanisms available to ensure that A is what it should be; in other words, things are done to people's experience to ensure that their experience is the 'right' one. Such actions are termed 'operations', and are considered in detail later. If such operations are not successful, however, A is invalidated, and a psychiatrist is liable to be called in. As Laing puts it:

> If A and B are incongruent, the mind police (psychiatrists) are called in. A crime (illness) is diagnosed. An arrest is made and the patient taken into custody (hospitalization). Interviews and investigations follow. A confession may be obtained (patient admits he is ill, displays insight). He is convicted either way. The sentence is passed (therapy is recommended). He serves his time, comes out, and obeys the law in future (p. 74).

The issue is 'who defines the situation?' Behind that, however, is the issue of what is really going on. As Laing notes, more often than not, what he thinks is going on bears almost no resemblance to what anyone in the family thinks is going on. But one thing is certain: there is often a concerted effort, on the part of the family, to *resist* discovering what is going on. It is to this resistance to discovery that Laing now turns his attention.

Every generation, we are told, projects on to the next, according to (i) what was projected onto it by prior generations, (ii) what was similarly induced, and (iii) its response to such projection and induction.

But what is projected? In his words:

> If I project element x from set A onto element y of set B, and if we call the operation of projection or mapping ϕ, then y is the image of x under ϕ.
>
> As we say, Johnny is the image of his grandfather.
>
> There is always a projection of a mapping of one *set* of relations on to another set of relations. These are relations in time as well as space (pp. 77-8).

In think it should be clear that we are dealing with the same concepts as in the first paper of this stage. But now, they are presented and labelled in a formal and quite explicit manner. Internalization and projection are subsumed under the broader concept of mapping; the inappropriate Freudian term 'defences' is replaced by operations. And it is to operations that we now turn.

Laing quotes, yet again, Hegel's dictum that 'the world is a unity of the given and the constructed', and goes on to examine ways in which we construe the given. 'We construe the given in terms of *distinctions*, according to *rules*. We perform *operations* on our experience, in order to comply with the rules' (p. 90).

Laing supposes that there is 'a set of primitive distinctions' in terms of which we construe the original given. Thus, any experience in which the given is distinguished in any way, is not 'innocent' experience, but is in part a product of our own making. Foremost amongst primitive distinctions, formed by one year from birth, Laing guesses, are:

Inside/Outside
Pleasure/Pain
Real/Not-real
Good/Bad
Me/Not-me
Here/There
Now/Then.

With these, and others, we work on the given, and construct our experience. But there are rules for what distinctions to make in what circumstances; rules are themselves distinctions in action. Our experience is, so to speak, chopped up into inner and outer, me and not-me, and so on. Distinctions go together in one 'slice'; thus 'me - inside - real - good - here' may all refer to the same slice of experience (if one is lucky).

But only certain combinations are allowed; others are forbidden by rules. To enforce these, operations are performed on certain aspects of experience, to make them conform. In some cases, several operations have to be performed. Many of these can be identified with psycho-analytic defences.

For example, a simple operation is denial. x is the case changes to x is not the case. A more complex one is repression, where one first forgets, and then forgets that there was anything to forget.

In fact, complex operations seem to be the rule. Operations are usually themselves operated on to render them 'unconscious'.

The principal function of all these operations is seen to be the 'production and maintenance of E that is at best desired, as least tolerated, in the family by the family' (p. 99).

So far, however, we have only considered operations performed by oneself on one's own experience. But these are only necessary by virtue of transpersonal rules, and do not work without the co-operation of others. Denial is an example of a transpersonal operation; specifically, it is demanded by others and forms a part of what Laing calls a 'transpersonal system of collusion'. Such an operation is at the basis of the Happy Families game, whereby everybody is unhappy, but all deny it to themselves, and deny their denial to themselves and each other. Each colludes in the mutual denial.

Laing next turns to examine rules. It will be recalled that rules, in the first instance, were distinctions in action. As distinctions become finer, so do the rules. One way of producing finer distinctions involves a projection map. This is meant to convey a process whereby certain basic distinctions, say good and bad, are projected onto the world. It is possible to lay out a map of the entire cosmos, in which the good, bad, or indifferent regions, as projected, can be noted. Now if we do this, we find that there are rules as to which areas are to be projected as good, and which as bad. Thus, it is mandatory to project bad on to the Enemy, whoever that may be. Similarly, if one is a Christian, God is good.

But beyond those rules are meta-rules, to the effect that such badness or goodness is *not* to be seen as a projection; that the initial rule does not exist. There are, in fact, rules against seeing rules. A clear example of this is the case of incest. It used to be thought that incest was rare because there was a 'natural' revulsion against it. More recently, people have begun to think in terms of a rule against it. To others however, this is unacceptable, as to *recognize* the existence of a rule is to imply that, were it not for the rule, people would do what the rule prohibits. For such people, it seems necessary to not only have the rule, but further, to have a rule which forbids the first rule to be seen as such.

By way of conclusion, Laing returns to the concept of mapping. Recalling, he says: 'If ϕ is a mapping of A into B, set A is called the domain of ϕ, and set B the range of ϕ' (p. 117).

Families are, as we have seen, particularly significant with respect to mapping. For a family can be both range and domain for mapping to and from the individuals that comprise it, and to and from the world outside the family. As far as the individual is concerned, his body is of unique significance in that it is *the* range for introjective mapping from all domains. Furthermore, his body will in turn be the domain for his future re-projections onto whatever ranges. The family, of course, is the principal domain from which he derives his introjective maps.

Laing moves on now to talk about an interpersonal operation, analogous to projection. He calls it induction. Induction is the operation of inducing another to embody one's projection of them. Induction, therefore, is something one does *to* another's experience. It is very common, indeed, to some degree, universal, in all our interaction; but it can be very pronounced in families. Laing gives a fictitious example, told in the first person, where 'my' father lost his mother early in life, and was brought up by his sister. His wife was big-sister-cum-mother to him, and he never had a daughter, which he wanted. Now I get married, and my father sees in my wife the mother he has lost. This also fits her own image of herself derived from her family. There is thus a convergence of projections upon her, and she moves from being a mere image for them, by induction, to being a genuine embodiment of a woman who died fifty years ago, and about whom she consciously known nothing. But, if she is thus induced into being my father's mother, i.e. grandmother, who am I? My own grandfather? And who is my son? If I am my grandfather, then my son is my father. We may perhaps also speak of holy ghosts!

This concludes our survey of 'The Politics of the Family'. Before we attempt to comment on this stage as a whole, however, we may first consider some other, minor, sources that pertain to this stage.

Shortly after the talks we have been discussing were given, Laing produced a second, revised edition of 'The Self and Others', entitled simply 'Self and Others' (Laing, 1969d). The revision is, in fact, extensive, and although Laing's claim that it has not been 'changed in any fundamental way' is substantially true, one or two changes can be isolated as pointers, so to speak, of his present position.

For example, in the passage where he is talking about a person who is beginning to perceive his position in a social phantasy system (1st edn p. 23; Penguin, 2nd edn p. 39), in the revised edition, not only does the word 'psychotic' appear in inverted commas, unlike before, but the sentence which originally read 'such delusions are derealizations-rerealizations gone wrong' now reads 'such delusions are partially achieved derealizations-rerealizations'. Thus before we had a psychosis... gone wrong; now we have a 'psychosis'... partially achieved. I think we can see Laing's notion of metanoia here; the movement from eknoia (alienation) through paranoia to ennoia, in a process of metanoia. (These terms, and the relations between them, are dealt with in Cooper (1971), 1972 edn, pp. 12-15.)

The first chapter, in particular, is almost totally rewritten. Whereas originally the whole chapter was about phantasy as an unconscious mode of experience, we now find Laing saying, 'I have not used the term unconscious experience, because I cannot resolve satisfactorily in my mind the contradiction between the two words.... Experience, as I want to exploy the term, does not exist without an experiencer' (p. 30). In the absence of any theoretical discussion by Laing of this change of heart, it is difficult to infer what it may mean. One plausible explanation which would seem to be consistent with other changes would be that Laing has foregone his relatively academic stance towards the concept of experience (the term phenomenological is almost entirely missing in the revised version) in favour of what may be called a more personal one. This view would seem to be supported by the following consideration. In the first edition Laing repeatedly emphasizes that another's experience can never be known directly; thus: 'It is important to emphasize that the other person's experience can never be a primary datum of one's own experience' (p. 14). Contrast that to the analogous passage in the second edition:

My impression is that most adult Europeans and North Americans would subscribe to the following: the other person's experience is not directly experienced by self. For the present it does not matter whether this is necessarily so, is so elsewhere on the planet, or has always been the case (pp. 26-7).

Laing's reticence to use the term unconscious experience leads him in difficulties with respect to phantasy. For what now is the nature of phantasy? Is it conscious or unconscious, experience or not? It can hardly be held to be conscious. Yet Laing cannot reject phantasy as a form of experience without rejecting almost the entirety of his work. It really does seem as if he cannot find words to describe phantasy to his own satisfaction. However, in the Preface to the second edition, he makes some interesting remarks:

This formula (of mapping) seems to me to clarify the double usage of phantasy, as in the expressions: the 'contents' of phantasy, and phantasy as a function.

(Before continuing the quote, let us remind ourselves that originally Laing was solely concerned with the 'contents' aspect; the functional aspect was dismissed as 'a problem for physiology and ultimately physics'.) To continue:

As a function, phantasy can be regarded as an operation of mapping, from any domain of experience to any range of experience. It seems to me even possible to conceive of mapping desires (instincts), not experienced in themselves, as it were, on to experience, such that the range of experience so mapped acquires a ϕ (phantasy)-value, and to conceive that a person may not himself recognize that this range of his experience has acquired such a ϕ value usually called the unconscious 'content' of phantasy (pp. 7-8).

This all seems very strange. In the first place, a problem for physiology has become a problem of mathematics applied to experience; though perhaps the oddity here is the *original* definition of the problem.

But it is very hard to see what Laing hopes to achieve by so viewing the contents of phantasy. For this view surely raises more problems than it solves. First, we may ask, what is the phenomenological status of a desire? Is it experiential or not? If it is, it is unconscious. If it is not, as Laing seems to indicate, it is hard to see how it comes to be mapped on to experience. For the function of phantasy is the mapping of *experience* on to *experience*. Finally, even assuming it did somehow get mapped, the resulting range of experience, with its 'ϕ value' is of equally uncertain phenomenological status. It is a range of experience, yet it is not entirely susceptible to 'recognition' by its possessor. To introduce undefined words like 'recognition' can only appear as an attempt to cover over an all-too-vague area of conceptually muddled thinking. To be fair, of course, Laing has no space, in a preface, to elaborate. But, granted that, it would perhaps have been better to wait till a better opportunity arose.

Laing's comments about the individual's body having significance by virtue of being the range for all introjections, the medium, as it were, for the internalization of family patterns, immediately bring to mind the work of Reich, and his concepts of muscular and character armour. This is not the place, unfortunately, to compare the two sets of concepts; though we may be perhaps surprised that Laing nowhere mentions Reich in relation to mapping. It is all the more surprising when we consider that he was interested in Reich's work, at about this time. In an interview in 'International Times', in 1968 Laing spoke with knowledge and sympathy of Reich's theories of sexuality. He also reviewed the paperback edition of 'Function of the Orgasm' in 'New Society', in a brief article entitled Liberation by Orgasm (Laing, 1968c). He bemoans the head-in-the-sand attitude of academics towards Reich, but notes that patients, 'who must be as daft as him', keep on reading his work. For Laing, too, 'The more I know at first hand of what Reich was talking about, the more seriously I take him.' He concludes the article:

> Freud felt there was nothing to be done about it. Our civilization was founded on repression and societal repression was interlocked in alliance with part of the biological constitution of each of us. Reich was more optimistic.... He has left us a vivid record of part of his adventure. We would be wise to study it with care. I, for one, have been instructed.

However, despite his praise, Gordon (1971) reports Laing as saying in reference to Reich that although 'one could work with emotional problems by dealing with their physical manifestations', his own interests were generally 'more verbal and intellectual'.

The final source for this stage is not technically by Laing himself; but I think it can be safely taken to represent his views. It is the Philadelphia Association Report (Philadelphia Association, 1969); a highly abridged version of it appears as an appendix to chapter three of 'The Politics of The Family'. References here are to the original report.

The report contains information about the members of the Association, extracts from the Articles of Association, some statistics relating to the households sponsored and run by them, and a brief account of their 'extra mural' activities. What concerns us, however, is the section which spells out in basic terms, their approach to 'mental illness', so-called.

The notion of rules, as put forward in 'The Politics of the Family', is presented here, and is followed by the following comment:

> All ways of inducing people not to break rules again can be
> classified under two heads: punishment and therapy. If it is
> felt that the person is responsible for his breach of the rules
> (deviant behaviour) he is punished. If it is felt that he is
> not responsible, if he cannot help it, if his mind is 'unsound',
> he is not punished. His behaviour is defined as an 'illness',
> and his 'illness' is 'treated'. But 'treatment' too often, we
> believe, is a concealed form of punishment (pp. 4-5).

There is, so to speak, a meta-rule to the effect that one must not see treatment to make one obey the rules as punishment.

We have the task, now, of summarizing the nature of this stage.

I think it is clear that, although not present in every paper, at least not explicitly, the concept of mapping is the central concept. Closely linked with this concept are the concepts of rules, distinctions, domain and range, and operations.

This stage as a whole, or at least, the theoretical system built within it, can be seen as having a particular relation to the Freudian theory of defences. Specifically, the concept of operation is designed to replace the concept of defence; but also to transcend it, in so far as it is a concept which can just as easily be applied transpersonally as intrapersonally. This was not the case with the psycho-analytic concept.

Still in the realm of Freudian theory, the latter's concept of internal object, and in general, the Freudian theory of object-relations was attacked, and replaced by a system which takes into account not only objects and persons, but relations between them, and whole systems of relations.

Philosophically speaking, the emphasis seems to have shifted from previous stages. The approach taken could be characterized as phenomenological - certainly as far as the earlier papers in this stage are concerned - by virtue of the fact that experience is still focused on as a prerequisite to understanding. The word phenomenological appears very rarely, however, and I think a closer examination of what is being done will indicate other approaches as well.

Harking back to the first paper, which was seen to be paradigmatic for this stage, we recall that what was attempted was to establish a relationship between the 'texture of lived experience', and the *structure* of family interaction. This structure is broadened, temporally speaking, to include as many generations in the 'pattern' as possible, as we progress through the stage, chronologically. By the end, Laing is talking not only of the structure of interactional patterns, but of the structures of experience. This contrasts sharply with, say, stage 3, where it was individual's actions, not the structure of interaction, past and present, that was focused on.

In general, then, I would say that this stage exhibits a large degree of structuralism. We have structuralism on the interactional level, and on the experiential level. The closing example from 'The Politics of the Family' is two hypothetical conversations between mother and daughter. The first, in which the mother attributes evil to the girl, sounds bizarre. The second is identical except that 'evil' is replaced by 'pretty'. And it is the structure, which is identical in both, that Laing urges us to reflect upon.

Granted that this is a structuralism which is interested in

experience, we might expect to find Laing interested in the thought-structuralist schools of anthropology; and indeed he is. For the first time, the name of Lévi-Strauss appears in the bibliography (in 'The Politics of Family'). In January 1970, Gordon (1971) found that Laing's current interests were '(by) attempts to delineate the structures of cultures, (by) the work of the anthropologist Claude Lévi-Strauss, and (by) Michel Foucault's attempt to write a comprehensive intellectual history of the last 300 years in Europe (p. 60).

So much for structuralism. It remains only to be said now that, despite shifts in philosophical position, the primary aim of Laing's work is still, as always, to render intelligible the behaviour and experience of individuals. To summarize very briefly, at this stage, the means for doing that is to establish the texture or structure of the individual's existence in his context, and relate that to patterns of family interaction, which are seen as being 'mapped' on to the individual's experience, or interiorized. This still appears to be the current approach at least of some of Laing's colleagues. It is the approach taken, for instance, throughout the whole of Morton Schatzman's new book (Schatzman, 1973) 'Soul Murder'. One can represent this approach diagrammatically, perhaps, as follows:

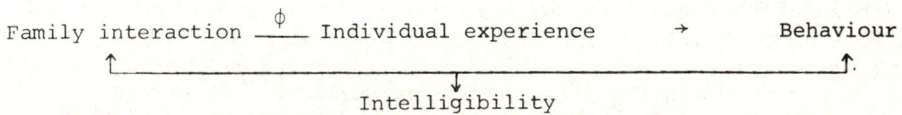

There is a structuralism of interaction, and of inferred experience. Intelligibility resides in the meaning which can be extracted from these structures, by viewing them as *significations*: we are involved with a sub-branch of semiology. But it is an active semiology: the signified is constituted in a dialectic with the signifier; this dialectic appears *in the first instance,* as lived experience: (the meaning of life is the living of it).

On this edifying note, we conclude the review of stage 6.

STAGE 7: RELIGIOUS SENSIBILITY

> Body like dry bone
> Mind like dead ashes;
> This is true knowledge,
> Not to strive after knowing the whence.
> In darkness, in obscurity,
> The mindless cannot plan;
> What manner of man is that?
> (Chuang Tzu)

We come now to the final 'stage' of Laing's development to date - that concerned with, broadly speaking, 'religious' issues. Once again, this stage is hardly a stage at all; like stage 5, the material comprising it runs concurrently with other material which has been deemed to fall in other stages. Again like stage 5, this stage has been defined by a coherence of content, rather than by temporal considerations. The time span runs from 1969 to 1973, and covers a radio broadcast, lectures, articles and Laing's last-written book, 'Knots'.

Once again, this stage is artificial in its isolation as a stage; the documents here presented form the more recent end of a continuum launched at the beginning of stage 4. This continuum will be considered in the next chapter: at present we shall continue, for the sake of consistency, with our method of merely outlining the nature of this 'stage' by itself.

The first text chronologically to be considered, testifies to the arbitrary nature of isolating this 'stage'; namely 'Knots'. For only certain parts, notably section 5 of this book, can really be characterized as 'mystical' or whatever, although the whole book illustrates the degree of abstraction, almost of impersonalism, which is characteristic of this stage. In many respects, much of the book bears close affinities with stage 2: one can certainly see the notion of the 'spiral of reciprocal perspectives' active in the layout of many of the knots. In the Introduction, Laing says, 'I could have remained closer to the "raw" data in which these patterns appear. I could have distilled them further towards an abstract logico-mathematical calculus.' In fact, he has done both elsewhere. For the contents of 'Knots' can be situated, theoretically, mid-way between the extended verbal accounts of binding situations as given in, for example, 'Sanity, Madness and the Family', and the highly abstract calculus which Laing has indeed developed, which is present in the first, but so prominent in the second, edition of 'Self and Others' (which was published at this time), and, of course, 'Interpersonal Perception'.

But the point of locating them at precisely this level of abstraction takes us away from the tone of these earlier works. For Laing writes: 'I hope...(the knots) are sufficiently independent of "content" for one to divine the final formal elegance in these webs of maya' (April 1969).

This quote warrants close scrutiny: its full meaning is by no means obvious. We shall hope to approach this meaning via a consideration of the context from which Laing has drawn the key concept here: maya.

Laing sees patterns of 'human bondage' as 'having' (whatever that means) a *formal* elegance characteristic of maya, that is illusion.

In Buddhism, the term maya applies to the illusory nature of the phenomenal manifest that we call 'reality'. Buddhist texts contain accounts of the illusory nature of many of the Categories central to Western philosophies: space, and time, and the immanent ego, for example.

When one is still veiled in the web of maya, one is in a state which the Buddhists call Sangsara - which means 'wandering' - a state which corresponds quite closely to that earlier identified by Laing as 'normality'. Liberation from this state is the attainment of Nirvana.

In allowing us to perceive this 'formal elegance of maya' by presenting accounts of human interaction and interexperience at an unusually formal level of abstraction, Laing hopes that we can be aware of the Sangsarie quality of our life in the social round.

However, Laing's Buddhism appears to be of the Mahayana or Zen variety; as can be gauged by the more overtly 'mystical' knots. For instance, Laing's assertion that 'although innumerable beings have been led to Nirvana no being has been led to Nirvana' (p. 85) relies on the Zen notion that Sangsara *is* Nirvana, a notion not found in Theravada Buddhism. (Interestingly, it is also implicit in Taoism, and Tantra, these also being branches of oriental 'religion' in which Laing is known to be interested.)

The knot which follows the above quota is typically Mahayana.
Before one goes through the gate
One may not be aware there is a gate.
One may think there is a gate to go through,
and search a long time for it
without finding it
One may find it and
it may not open
If it opens one may be through it
As one goes through it
One sees that the gate one went through
was the self that went through it.
No one went through a gate
there was no gate to go through
no one ever found a gate
no one ever realized there was never a gate.
(This knot in fact dates back to 1967 - see Laing, 1967g.)

The way in and the way out, it seems, are in some respects the same, for knots and for liberation from them - a very Zen idea - both are paradoxical. The difference lies in the fact that paradoxical communication patterns, social phantasy systems, definitions of self, i.e. the genesis of knots, are extended over time; whereas the equally paradoxical, and indeed, strikingly similar, Zen koans which are used to bring about immediately total enlightenment, i.e. liberation from knots are, so to speak, instantaneous.

Laing seems almost reticent to admit the possibility of immediate enlightenment - it conflicts so totally with the Protestant ethic that must have played such a large part in Laing's upbringing. More important, it surely contradicts completely any notion of progressive therapy, not to mention prolonged psycho-analysis. But this may be why he seems even less willing at this stage to discuss therapy; as well he might be, given that he denies the existence of a 'self' that can so to speak 'accumulate' experience, a psychic unity that is sustained over time (Reflections on Meditation, 1973). (In 'The Divided Self', Laing notes this experience, of a lack of continuity of self over time, as characteristic of the schizoid or schizophrenic individual.)

It would be cynical to suggest that Laing's notion of the metanoiac voyage, which with proper guidance is almost always completed within two weeks, is a compromise between the immediate enlightenment of Zen, and the prolonged, gradual progress of conventional psycho-analysis (or conventional Buddhist meditation). Equally, it would be putting words into Laing's mouth, though perhaps ones that he would agree with, to suggest that he considers that prolonged exposure to knot-generating paradoxes leads to not only a 'knotting' of thought (requiring immediate Zen-type thought liberation), but a complex interlocking 'knotting' of many other aspects of the whole person; such as confusion, denial and repression of modes of experience other than the conceptual (dreams, phantasy, transcendental); even down to biological and physical levels (sexual inhibitions, muscular armour, catatonia).

These other systems, especially the physical, are, by virtue of not being formal in the way that conceptual experience is, less amenable to instantaneous restructuration. Hence there is a need for (relatively time-consuming) 'biological' regression.

But let us return to our consideration of 'Knots'.

Now clearly, if viewed as 'statements', the knots presented have no 'logical truth value'; their purpose, it seems to me, is to break down conventional patterns of thinking, which are all-too-solidly rooted in the grammar and syntax of our language, to achieve a form of awareness which is pre-verbal, pre-logical, and simply: 'thus'. One of Laing's favourite phrases is 'as finger pointing to the moon', by which he means that reality is not reducible to statements about reality; that statements about reality merely point to reality 'as finger pointing to the moon'.

Every expression, and every form
is to what is expressionless and formless
what a finger is to the moon
all expressions and all forms
point to the expressionless and formless (p. 87).

But, of course, we, like Laing, must note an ultimate irony here; for he goes on to point out:
the proposition
    'All forms point to the formless'
is itself a formal proposition

To read these knots conjures for me the same uneasy feeling as did reading a passage in 'The Way of Zen' (Watts, 1962) where the Master says:

Those who know do not speak
Those who speak do not know.

By speaking this, does the Master reveal that he knows, or that he does not know? Or perhaps both, or neither? Or even both both and neither. Or neither both nor neither... ad infinitum.

This paradox is clearly insoluble within the realm of language; there is thus nothing to be said about it, which is, of course, precisely the point; though by pointing that out, I have missed the point....

But before I get so dizzy that I no longer feel like writing, I should like to return to that curious phrase in the Introduction, 'the final formal elegance of these webs of maya'.

Many people, notably psychiatrists, appear to have been somewhat offended by this phrase. Some people, like Peter Sedgwick (1971) have taken statements of Laing's such as these (about maya, etc.) and attempted to logically derive contradictory positions from them, in an effort to show, by reductio ad absurdum, that Laing's 'mystical' premises are themselves invalid. Naturally, Sedgwick succeeds brilliantly, but the absurdity to which he reduces everything is his own. For the whole burden of Laing's point, which Sedgwick never even suspects, is that language can be used to *point* to reality; that we can use language to indicate the limits of language; but that when we do this, we should not expect language to conform to the regulative and constitutive principles that operate *within* the sphere of the language system. Quite obviously, Sedgwick has never read - or rather never understood - the ending of Wittgenstein's 'Tractatus'. (Indeed, Laing's position here seems distinctly Wittgensteinian: for not only is there implicit the 'Tractatus' notion that the elements of a [language] system cannot put forward true statements about the system *as a whole;* also present is the Philosophical Investigations notion of the ability of language to *show*, as opposed to talk about, a certain pre-verbal reality. And Wittgenstein's repeated dictum 'Dont think, just look!' is a clear theme of Reflections on Meditation [to be examined shortly]: it also seems to be a necessary conclusion of 'Knots'.)

A more reasonable sort of offence that this has provoked is that which sees any attempt to describe human bondage as 'elegant', which Laing appears to do, as extremely callous.

However, on close examination, we can see this misses the point, too. For Laing is *not* describing these painful situations themselves as possessing elegance. It is the webs of maya, that is, the *illusory forms* which in fact cloak the reality, which possess 'formal elegance'. Expressions point to the expressionless, forms point to the formless. This is what we must realize, to see through the veils of maya. But these are themselves formal propositions. Anything which can be said is. And now, at last, we can come to what I take to be the meaning of Laing's introduction: 'divining' the 'formal elegance' means realizing that the fact that they are 'formal' is precisely that which makes them webs of maya. And any attempt to say anything about them is formal in this sense. *And the relationships depicted, in so far as they are determined by the sort of verbal communications* (i.e. formal propositions) *which, in their typicality, are presented in this book, are similarly formal, illusory, and webbed in maya.*

This insight into the nature of social relations, is a hard one to accept. In our culture, I would think, this insight is particularly dangerous. For it makes sustained social life almost impossible. Our culture, unlike, say, Hindu cultures, does not provide a means whereby one can legitimately leave the normal social round, to pursue experiences which place one in contradiction with sociability. It is significant, I would think, that about a year after 'Knots' was published, Laing left Britain for a Buddhist monastery in Ceylon.

This insight is also a common one for persons under the influence of LSD; it may also account for the otherwise surprising fact that prolonged communal use of LSD is seldom found to be satisfactory by the users. For the LSD experience is such that one feels that everything is beyond words; if one tries to talk, one usually regrets it. Individually, this does not matter, as there is no need to speak. In pairs, a strange sense of mutual non-verbal intuition frequently occurs, so again, the problem of communication usually does not arise. In groups, however, there is very often a sense of mass uncertainty, of high informational entropy, about the feelings, desires, intentions, etc. of the group. This leads to either individual senses of anxiety, or (often disastrous) attempts at communication.

It is perhaps not too speculative to suggest in this context, that, linked to these observations, may be the fact that among the few types of groups who have successfully used LSD communally are those that have used it on the occasion of specifically *non*-verbal communication amongst the group: namely, the playing of music. One thinks of the original 'acid-rock' groups of San Francisco, and more recently, the numerous British groups centred on Ladbrooke Grove, London. One also thinks of certain avant-garde dance troupes and free-theatre groups.

One may wonder, then, in the light of all these considerations and paradoxes, why Laing should have decided to write such things at all, if, as he said, 'all our words are misleading' (Laing, 1969c).

In one sense, obviously, it is not for me or anyone else to say. I suspect, however, that in many respects Laing's dilemma and his solution to it, are analogous to the Buddha's dilemma and his resolution not to finally quit Sangsara till every soul is likewise capable of doing so.

At any rate, paradoxes or not, Laing elected to continue to communicate; it is to texts subsequent to 'Knots' that we now turn.

As far as I am aware, Laing only published one more document before leaving the country, in July 1971, that being the transcript of his radio talk entitled Religious Sensibility (Laing, April 1970).

It is a document that is hard to read, harder to understand, and harder still to write about. The radio version was almost totally incomprehensible. Referring to the text, however, the first step towards making sense of it comes when we take account of the fact that the talk was commissioned by the BBC as a contribution to their series 'Is there a future for religious belief?' Laing's concluding answer is indeed typically Laingian:

If we do not make idols of our own images, will there finally be anything left in any conceivable verbal formula called religious to which we may give our total assent? I've no idea. And I'm not sure that it matters ultimately. For that to which the content of any articulated form of religious belief alludes is certainly not itself a content of any religious belief (p. 537).

How does Laing arrive at this position which seems simultaneously vacuous yet pregnant?

Several themes run, disjointedly, through the text. It will hopefully be less confusing to take each theme separately rather than stick to the order of points of the article.

The bulk of the article is devoted to explaining why Laing is amongst that group of people who 'take religious formulae seriously as worthy of sensible belief' (p. 537) and elucidating the consequences of this fact. We are told more about Laing's personal and intellectual background than, I should think, ever before:

I grew up, theologically speaking, in the 19th century: lower middle-class Lowland Presbyterian, corroded by 19th century materialism, scientific rationalism and humanism.... I listened to and later partook in long arguments on the existence or non-existence of God.... I remember vividly how startled I was to meet for the first time, when I was 18, people of my age who had never opened a Bible.

He describes how his fellow students regarded him with amazement as 'some idealistic barbarian... exhibiting in frayed though still recognizable form the primitive thought-forms of the savage mind (p. 536).

Having established that he had a religious upbringing, he goes on to assert that anyone who has been so brought up, to take religious propositions seriously will *always,* to some extent, seek to discover a way in which these 'formulae' can be said to be true. Furthermore, he claims that if one has not had such an upbringing it is impossible to discover 'what they are about' - unless one experiences 'metanoia', (using the word, presumably, in its more conventional, biblical sense). He does not seem to think it a possibility that a sort of anti-metanoia could occur, in which an equally radical change of mind *away* from the religious could take place; a sort of secular conversion.

He goes on to conclude that the future of religious beliefs depends: 'on whether the human mind will continue to find no other forms in which to express what it regards as a type of truth otherwise incommunicable'. But let us be clear what this is saying. Laing is in fact saying religious beliefs are of a certain form; their future therefore depends on people not being able to replace that form. So much is valid; but only *true* if one accepts, as a further premise, an assertion which Laing has already himself implicitly cast doubt on: namely, that people will continue to imbue these forms with meaning; i.e. continue to take religious propositions seriously; continue to believe in a 'truth otherwise incommunicable'. Laing has already cast doubt on the certainty of this continuance, by linking it to upbringing. He fails to draw the necessary conclusion from his own premises: the future of religious belief depends on the future of child-rearing practices with respect to religious formulae. What Laing does go on to do is to side step this issue, and examine the future of religious beliefs, *given* the conviction that there is a truth to communicate.

This side-stepping is brought about through Laing's confusing *his present*, with the *future* of religious belief on a *mass scale*. Thus he says:

'God is a spirit, and those who worship Him must worship Him in spirit and in Truth.' I believe this to be a verbal formula pointing, as finger to moon, to what I believe is the case. Perhaps I wouldn't if my father hadn't told me; but since I do, I have to allow these words to stand, and find out in what sense I can justify my assent to them.

Thus is Laing's position (the quote is John 4: 24); given his childhood, we can accept and respect that. But then he goes on with what is surely an invalid step:

But until, or if, from a religious point of view, there is a new dispensation giving rise to new forms of revelation, those of us who cannot help ourselves are compelled to continue the impossibly absurd project of keeping these (beliefs) alive.

I find this quite extraordinary. Not only is the tone of it quite unlike, in fact, quite contrary, to what we expect from Laing; but Laing's own implicit assertion that such beliefs are only *born* through childhood training makes an utter mockery of his piety in wishing to keep them alive. In particular, one wonders how Laing stands in respect to his own children over this. Does he bring them up to be 'idealistic barbarians', or does he decide, contrary to what he says here, that he can 'help himself' after all, and allow these beliefs to die out?

The second theme we can trace in this paper concerns Laing's own religious beliefs themselves. Laing has always been reticent to say much about personal matters; and this paper is almost unique in this respect: though even here, we come across Laing's disarming ability to couch what he is saying in terms which render it powerful on impact, but vague and insubstantial on close scrutiny; an ability he seems to share with the European phenomenologists who inspired him. (This is not necessarily a criticism: the status of these writings is similar to that discussed in stage 4 as 'poetry': the 'impact' is the whole of the point, phenomenologically speaking.)

We have already quoted Laing's use of the verbal formula about 'God is a spirit...' he goes on to develop this notion. He notes that spiritual sensibility, in general derives its form, but not contents, by mapping social forms on to spiritual metaphors. Thus we get, in Feudal Europe, God the King ruling, through his Angel/Princess over his Kingdom, and so on. But now we can see through all that; we can recognize that these things that are ascribed to God are merely metaphors, verbal formulae. In a nutshell, we realize that 'God is not anything that can be said about him.' Laing alludes to Huxley with a reference to 'perennial philosophy'; indeed, he seems much influenced by Huxley's approach (1946) when he says: 'And so it's no longer a question of comparative religion, but a question of a comparison of the forms that religious sensibility clothes itself' (p. 537). It is only when we have broadened our religious horizons *beyond* that within which we have been brought up that we can hope to:

> realize that the forms in which we all cast distinctions between inner and outer, heaven, earth, and hell, righteousness and evil, gods, archangels, angels, man, the creator and the created, are distinctions which just possibly have the very faintest claim to convey to us some fleeting shadow of that which is not contained in any one of the images we use in our attempts to allude thereto, but itself contains them all.

I shall leave the reader to translate this masterpiece of meiosis into comprehensible English: it seems to me to be saying much the same as the opening article of stage 4, where Laing talks of there being 'no better word for this experiential domain... than the spiritual world - or the domain of spirits, Powers, Thrones, Principalities, Seraphim, Cherubim, the Light' (1964b, p. 191). The point is not that there *are*, there *exist*, 'spirits, Powers' etc., or 'heaven, earth and hell... gods, archangels, angels' etc., in the same way as desks, trees, or Wimpole Street exist; simply that there is an 'experiential domain', a 'type of truth' which, so far in history, man has found no way of talking about - it is 'otherwise incommunicable' - other than that known as religious or metaphysical.

Laing employs the same tantalizing approach; of saying something apparently startling and then failing to make its implications explicit, when he says:

> Some of us have a sense of ourselves and of the world as we perceive it, as not derived ultimately from any of the things we can

sense. Myths give expression to this. Myths are essentially
dramatic. And we haven't come across any better way: as far as
I know, human spiritual sensibility has not yet found another
form to clothe itself. It may do.

And he goes on to talk about the future of religious forms, but
gives no clue as to what he does 'sense' himself to be 'ultimately
derived from'.

The third theme that runs through the paper is the theme of the
Radio 3 series: whether there is a future for religious beliefs.
Laing does not, however, ever examine the question in precisely
those terms. He does not talk so much of belief, but rather draws
a distinction between experience, and verbal expression, as he did
in stage 4. The former he clearly regards as a human universal;
though he never does much to defend this thesis except to state it.
The latter, religious expression, he regards as culturally and
historically relative, and thus liable to unpredictable change; but
also, and for that reason, not really worth worrying about. For
here, as throughout his writing, Laing is asserting the primacy of
experience. The only difference now is that the experience which
is primary is also a form of experience which is ultimately not
accountable in verbal terms: we have reached the limits of what can
be said; now there is only showing and experiencing.

Laing appears to have reached the same conclusion with respect to
his profession: for in July 1971 Laing left the country to retire to
a Buddhist monastery in Kandubodda, Central Ceylon, to practise
meditation. He stayed for over a year; needless to say, he published nothing during that time. Sedgwick (1971) quotes a letter
from someone who met him, however, who reported that:
> he does (Theravada Buddhist meditation) for seventeen hours a
> day... (and) has been doing better, much better, than long-time
> time meditation experts, Sinhalese Buddhists as well as foreign...
> (Laing) is serious, dead serious about it... he does not have any
> plans whatever to return to Europe... nor to write again (p. 46).

His first public appearance in Britain, as far as I can gather,
since his return, was the lecture he gave on 10 October, entitled
Reflections on Psychiatry (Laing, 1972a). Before returning to
Britain, Laing had given a lecture tour in the USA.) After a tirade
against mental hospitals, and the training systems for doctors and
psychiatrists, he spoke more constructively of a new scheme he has
that genuine asylums should be set up, all over the world, run by
people who know themselves, their bodies, their emotions, etc. He
laid great emphasis on the harmonious unity of four interdependent
systems: the physical, the mental, the emotional, and the social.
His particular emphasis, in this lecture, was on the physical subsystem; it thus falls outside of our immediate direct interest here.
But he spoke still in June 1973 of international asylums, in places
where one is free from the police - these being taken as the real and
symbolic presence of state control over individual life and experience.

It will be recalled, from stage 4, that the first occasion for
religious writing of any depth in Laing was his notion of schizophrenia as an 'Inner Voyage', with its possibility (no more) of
transcendental experience. It is a view which Laing still holds, as
came out in the ITV discussion programme Something to Say (21

December 1972). Partly reprinted in 'The Guardian' (27 December) in which John Morgan and Professor C.M. Carstairs discussed Laing's views with him. Laing admitted that many people called mentally ill suffer deeply, but reaffirmed that some, not all, were paradoxically open to heightened awareness 'almost to an exquisite degree'. Carstairs accused Laing of a 'curious retreat' from both the horrors and the triumphs of progress in the material world, which Laing denied, asserting merely that he has 'more sympathy than you (Carstairs) have to those people who find... complete immersion in that space-time box'. Carstairs replied that whilst he recognized the existence of transcendental experience he denied that it occurred more than extremely rarely in schizophrenics; apparently failing to see that this is precisely Laing's point and complaint. As Laing went on to say:

> I think it would be less rare if (the 'schizophrenic') was in the company of psychiatrists who could act as guides to him in what he has found himself to be in.... I think the mind needs to breathe out like lungs do, and there's a time for moving in the external world, and there's a time for moving back....

The concept of metanoia seems here to have reached a balanced maturity: for it is a natural process, and now the context of its occurrence or absence is natural. The last phrase quoted above particularly brings to mind the passage from Ecclesiastes - popularized by Pete Seeger and the Byrds:

> To every thing, there is a season
> and a time to every purpose under heaven:
> A time to be born,
> a time to die;
> A time to plant
> and a time to pluck up that which is planted;
> A time to kill,
> A time to heal;
> A time to break down
> and a time to build up.
> (Eccles. 3:1-3)

The phrase that Bateson (1972) uses to describe his own work also seems applicable to Laing at this point: 'an ecology of mind'. For Laing now sees the various divergent, even polar, needs and propensities of the mind as governed by a higher unity: an ecology of consciousness which mirrors the structuralism of social relations that Laing proposes (as in the 'previous' stage).

This notion comes out more strongly in the fascinating lecture Laing gave in January 1973 entitled Reflections on Meditation (Laing, 1973). It is this lecture which gives us the most detailed and articulate source of information concerning Laing's most recent views; we shall examine it in some depth.

Laing noted that in recent years there appears to have been a considerable social/cultural movement that has expressed critical interest in the nature of everyday consciousness; a movement that is one of: 'allowing oneself to find a greater period of time for not thinking, or doing anything, and not feeling guilty about it, or worrying about it in one way or another.'

He does not speak of the Protestant ethic by name, but it is clearly the more or less conscious rejection of that ethic that this movement is concerned with. He recalls moments in childhood when he 'floated into a completely empty, limitless space... (a) very blissful state of complete quiet', suggesting that many children and adults have such experiences.

But such experiences can become objects of addiction, Laing warns, as they can be deliberately cultivated, by a variety of means. One of these is Transcendental Meditation, as taught by the Maharishi of Beatle fame; and Laing recounts a story of a friend of his who, after practising this sort of meditation could 'put himself into a state which he could only describe, or convey to my imagination, as more than 500 of acid'. This sort of comparison seems quite common; the popularity of such movements as the Maharishi's ISKON and Divine Light with ex-LSD users further testifies to this.

Laing says he 'often felt a bit uncertain about how much to cultivate that sort of meditation:... too much of it is an indulgence, too little of it is extremely unbalanced.' He speaks with admiration of people 'who had refined this polarity of the mind. I take it to be a perfectly natural component of the mind, "breathing" in a balanced way, in and out, sometimes being in a state of activity, and sometimes resting.'

So here again we see this notion of the mind more as an organism: a being that 'breathes', is 'natural' and, it seems, is capable of being healthy or unhealthy. But how is this state of healthy natural balance to be achieved.

The solution Laing offers is to balance the above sorts of meditation with a different sort which 'looks at the phenomena before one, just as they are, wherever one is, and does not make any particular thing out of them: but simply pays attention to whatever it is.' This was the sort of meditation he was engaged in in Ceylon, and he recognizes that it is one that is particularly difficult to communicate about. Nevertheless, he has undertaken to do just that - as, indeed, I have by writing about what Laing says; I would ask, however, that the reader bear in mind Laing's reservations which I reiterate on his behalf.

The starting point in the exposition of this meditation may be taken as the following question: 'How, in general, could one hope to have access to anything that one could approximately call Reality, or Realization, or anything else, if all one's perception's are shrouded in superimposition?'

The immediate answer is given: 'So this is the thing to do, then: to drop the mirror between, and just look at what are the various impositions upon it.'

Laing is dealing here, of course, with an age-old philosophical problem; it is, in its generality, the so-called Problem of Knowledge. But it is the problem as the phenomenologist sees it, not as the empiricist sees it. (Only phenomenologists ever see anything - empiricists merely look.) We will go into the philosophy of this in a while: for the moment, let us continue with the practice.

As far as I can make out, what is involved is the prolonged observation of some phenomenon (by prolonged I mean several hours a day for several days or weeks) till a breakthrough occurs in which one is 'able to look at, for a flash, or a twentieth of a second to see, the phenomenon just as it comes up and as it goes down, without any haze.' Having thus spotted the pure phenomenon, without any mental constructs superimposed on them, one 'places on that some identification marker' which acts as an index, or reference point, thus allowing one to actively distinguish, in a normally perceived phenomenon, which is the pure phenomenon, and which (presumably by elimination) is the mental construct superimposed thereon.

Laing himself apparently chose the sensation of the tip of his own nose as his phenomenon: he had to do it 'unremittingly for several days' before he felt he had 'got anywhere', being amazed, and appalled, at how difficult it was. How, he asks, if it takes days of arduous work even to 'see' the tip of one's nose as it really is, can one feel in any way confident about, for example, talking to someone?

His success in these matters he considers small, and irregular: which makes one wonder how it is for the average devotee, since Laing was reported to be 'doing much better than long-time meditation experts' (Sedgwick).

Laing carries on to examine some of the pitfalls involved in these deliberate attempts to control one's own consciousness. Taking Bion's practice of 'no-recall' and 'no-desire', he shows that there are many and varied states of mind which can be cultivated, some of which appear to possess the quality of being 'interestingly self-validating' when one is in them. So the dilemma is: if one has a choice of type of consciousness, (as does the meditator, the drug user, and so on) which ones are the 'best' to cultivate? And by what criteria?

Laing does not adequately answer this question, admitting he has no answer - even for himself. But then, he goes on to add, seemingly in contradiction, that he sometimes regards one's endless attempts to question or justify, one's state of mind, as 'simply another illustration of the mind worrying about something; a restlessness which has got no validity insofar as the category in which it is placed.' He then goes on to say, significantly: 'It is simply regarded as ipso facto of interest to have a mind that is clear and quiet.'

This, then, is Laing's 'answer' - if it can be called that. In many ways, I feel, it cannot; for it in no way follows from the question; it is merely a blunt assertion: 'ipso facto'. It is more an assertion about Laing's personality; and it is certainly one that ties in with his description of himself as 'temperamentally not very suited to... radical activism' (Gordon, 1971).

It is not an answer because the question itself is not answerable purely in terms of consciousness: to talk about 'the most desirable states of mind' is ultimately meaningless unless one recognizes (as Laing, a phenomenologist, certainly should) that consciousness is always consciousness *for*; and, therefore, useless unless one takes into account the nature and significance of the *object* for consciousness.

In other words, it is at least irrational not to take into account the nature of the demands that are likely to be made upon one's consciousness before one takes the plunge and chooses one's 'state of mind'. Eternal bliss consciousness may be fine for the Tibetan monk, but it is unlikely to help the Vietnamese peasant while the napalm rains down. LSD may throw its taker into glorious 'realms imaginal', but it will hardly help him to cope with a judge and jury who tell him he is a criminal for letting himself be so thrown.

Laing, then, advocates 'a mind that is clear and quiet': an advocacy which is either vague and trivial to the point of saying nothing; or, more likely, it is one which says nothing about the fact that such an consciousness is only a viable proposition given a certain form of social being (Laing seems to have forgotten Marx's extraordinary insight, so crucial in earlier stages, that was summarized in the Preface to the 'Critique of Political Economy'.) To be fair, Laing has mentioned the necessary connection between states of mind and social being before - particularly the social conditions necessary for radical activism; and he also concludes that, having done the meditation thing, 'I do not know whether I can recommend this sort of procedure to anyone else.' As always, the existentialist ethic that it is you and I that must take responsibility for the Path that you and I choose, is predominant. What is lacking, surely, is the explicit statement that certain states of mind are only 'viable', i.e. only present themselves as a real *choice*, given certain social conditions. (Perhaps we may look forward, however, to such statements, partially implicit, partially conspicuous by their absence, when Laing has the time to *write* about these things, rather than give lectures around them.) As Engels put it, 'men make their history themselves but in a given environment which conditions them.'

What I fear in the things Laing says here is that he has somehow forgotten this all-important dialectic - or at least, that he has forgotten to express it, which, in view of the likely misinterpretations, is almost as bad. In the light of the totality of Laing's work, this lecture does not convince me, (any more than 'Politics of Experience' did) that he is *irrevocably* slipping (or 'ideologically back-tracking', as Tyson (1971), puts it) into idealism and metaphysics. Given this lecture alone, however, one might quite forgivably form that impression.

Talking about his own experiences with meditation, and what it has done for him, Laing paints a picture that is by no means entirely blissful. He claims to have achieved ecstatic peaks, certainly; but also, and indeed probably by comparison, he has realized that

> what goes on, as far as I could identify it, in my mind, is much more boring and trivial and apparently not worth the attention that I give to it. But then I wonder [he continues] is that true for everyone? Is everybody's mind made up of all that slush, and dirty bits and pieces, and terribly boring redundancies and repetitions, and a few faded images that one is attached to, and all that, you know, worrying about money, and if one is not hungry now, then one is going to get hungry....

Indeed, he goes so far as to describe meditation as 'the practice of looking at my own mental numbers without stopping (which), for me, has been one of the most appalling experiences of my life.' One would imagine a person such as Laing would not make statements like that lightly.

At any rate, he sums his feelings up with the most delightful of the countless stories for which Laing is renowned. I quote in full:

> There is a story told by a group of people going round Edinburgh, of a little girl, who was asked by her teacher to read a book on penguins, and then write an essay on them. Her essay consisted

of one line, in which she said: 'This book tells me more about penguins than I really wanted to know.'

After looking so closely at himself; his mind, his body, his emotions, and so on, Laing says he feels rather like this little girl. Yet he also says

> I felt quite glad if I had to read the book (i.e. which tells him more about himself than he wanted to know) to the extent that having done so,... I do not know whether I can recommend this sort of procedure to anyone else.... I don't know, I really don't. I think maybe I have said enough.

I interpret this as saying that, like the little girl, Laing found moments of illumination, interest etc., in reading the book; but when it comes to writing essays, or giving lectures, *i.e. to communicating,* then to have read the book is to know too much. It is also to know that each person's life is a totally new book, not simply a revised edition: hence Laing cannot advocate it, or discourage it. One must simply do it, or not.

So far as I know, Laing has never publicly aligned himself with any particular religious position explicitly - his position within the religious world appears to mirror his erstwhile position in the Left-political world - but further clues can be picked up from interviews.

Far and away the most illuminating in this respect is Mezan's article (1972) in 'Esquire'. Here we learn that Laing's oriental sabbatical took him first to Ceylon, where he studied meditation, then India, to study yoga, and finally Japan, 'to have a look into Zen'.

Mezan apparently quizzed Laing quite pressingly as to 'who he was', how he had made himself of his influences. Laing's response, it seems, after a bit of dodging was as follows: 'I'll read you something that will tell you exactly where I am', the something being a fairly lengthy quote from the Brahma-Sutra-Bhasya, of Sri Sankaracarya. The gist of the quote is that subject and object, or consciousness and matter generally, have totally different beings and attributes. The superimposition of attributes of one onto the other, although logically impossible, occurs in human experience because of the inveterate human tendency towards self-identification and attachment. It is towards overcoming these that Laing is trying to head. In his words:

> It's a renunciation - a ridding yourself of attachments until you are maintaining yourself in a minimal fashion: you eat just enough, breathe just enough, to stay alive, to continue. The only guidelines for behaviour are not to hurt anyone, meaning not to cause harm to any part of the cosmos, and not to lie. Which you recognize is a very very subtle thing. I don't think I lie or do anyone any harm.

And then later, discussing politics he says, 'I engage in no strictly political actions - except in the sense of following the Tao.' And finally Mezan describes Laing's exposition at an informal meeting, of the Diamond Sutra, a central document in Mahayana Buddhism generally, and specifically in Vajrayana and Tantric schools.

In July 1973, Laing gave a highly informative interview with the French cultural weekly, 'L'Express'. Asked why he went to the East, Laing replied:

It was a project I had had for several years. I didn't want to take off until the experience started at Kingsley Hall was on a good footing. I spent six months in Ceylon, seven in India, with my family, just relaxing.... There I was able simply to practise specific disciplines of meditation. I spent most of my time doing nothing in particular.... The East for me, I repeat, was the best place to get away from it all, not simply in the physical sense, but also in the spiritual sense. I found it very restful to be in a place where I could escape from my own social system into a system where I didn't have to shoulder any responsibility, where my involvement was minimal. But these are not tranquil places for everyone - not for those who live there. Whilst I was there, there was an uprising and 6,000 people were killed with 12,000 imprisoned in detention camps. (Laing, 1973b. Translated by John Tillisch).

Such forthrightness and honesty appears to upset some people. Sedgwick seems to be particularly intolerant of Laing's wishes for peace and quiet, calling it a 'betrayal'. Sedgwick's 'case' seems to rest, however, more on his physical presence in Ceylon than on *what* Laing actually did, in Ceylon, England or anywhere else. But is Laing (or Sedgwick) any the less (or more) responsible for the oppression in Ceylon through being in England? It seems insensitive - to put it mildly - to attack a person for wanting to 'escape responsibility' for a few months, after the pressures of five years at the focus of Kingsley Hall programme. And as Laing says, elsewhere in the same interview: 'It is people's privilege to see in me whatever they want. They are free to do so. It is also mine never to take or to have taken any particular stand.... I only write about the truths I discover.'

This completes our review of the texts of this stage. Our last task in this chapter is thus to attempt a summary of this, the last stage.

We have seen that Laing's position, and his interests, can be, at least loosely, identified with the doctrines of Tao and Zen, and perhaps to a lesser extent Tantra. Particularly apparent was his rejection of the typically Western notion of selfhood (of the non-transcendental variety), and by implication its religious analogue, the Soul, and his espousal of the Buddhist conception of personal identity as a cosmic illusion.

But we also noted that on 'religious' issues, like all others, Laing asserts the primacy of experience. Thus, in general in this stage, Laing's aim is through an analysis of the *forms* of religious expression, to come to an appreciation of the way in which religious formulae convey some semblance of truth. That there is a truth to convey is assured by his insistence on the primacy of experience, and his (unverified) conviction that religious experience is a human universal.

It is apparent that there is a focus on the formal: this is visible not only in the passages where he explicitly discusses 'form', but also in his very mode of presentation, as in 'Knots', where the level of abstraction all but obliterates content.

In this somewhat tenuous sense, then, the formalism of Laing's religious writing mirrors the structuralism of his more empirical writings of the 'previous' stage.

However, this is something of a one-way mirror: for whilst structuralism is capable of synthesizing formalism with empirical considerations, the converse is not true. The formalistic approach Laing takes towards the issue here discussed has an innate tendency to divorce itself from the empirical foundations which alone can give it meaning and validity. As usual, we shall merely note this at this point; in the next two chapters we shall be looking at this as a contradiction, and one that is specifically, i.e. historically, situated in Laing's career; in particular, we shall be considering its *political* implications.

At this point, we have only to say that the initial, analytical moment of the review of Laing's work is now complete.

Chapter 3

THE REVIEW, PART TWO: SYNTHETIC

> To grasp the meaning of any human performance we must employ what German psychiatrists and historians have called 'comprehension'. But this involves neither a particular talent nor a special faculty of intuition; it is simply the dialectical movement which explains the act by arriving at its terminal signification from its starting conditions (Sartre, 1960).

We now proceed to examine the transition from the first to the second stage. What contradictions do we find, within stage 1 itself, that can illuminate this motion?

It will be recalled that the form of conceptualization present in stage 1 was characterized as intra-individual. That is, all the theoretical schemata developed relate to the individual qua individual; or, more precisely, they relate either to structures internally differentiated within the individual (true self-false self systems, etc.) or to the individual in relation to an undifferentiated other, i.e. the world. Implicit in this form of conceptualization are a number of contradictions, which we shall now examine.

In so far as the world is taken as undifferentiated other, to that extent a distinction is *not* made between other persons and other things. The act of globally grasping the world (i.e. the totality of not-self), as 'other' thus apprehends other persons in the same terms as inanimate objects. It thus commits the very act of reification which Laing bemoans of psychiatry.

The origin of this error is, of course, close at hand; psycho-analytic theory. As Laing was himself later to point out, psycho-analytic theory has no formal concept of 'the other', of 'you', as opposed to me. In the realm of this theory, two persons can never meet. The point is made nowhere more forceably than in the terminology of psycho-analytic theory itself. That branch of this theory that deals with the relevance of other people for the self is termed, significantly '*object* relation theory'; and with respect to the nature of this theory, it is an accurate label. Unfortunately, with respect to what is actually the case, it is a misnomer in the most radical sense. (For refined accounts of the errors of psycho-analytic theory in this respect, see Laing, 1975j, and Schatzman, 1973.)

Bringing this contradiction into somewhat sharper focus, we may say what is *presented* here is subjectivity-as-against-undifferentiated-objectivity; whereas what *is the case* is subjectivity-as-amongst differentiated-subjectivity i.e. intersubjectivity. The interpersonal nature of the human world stands in contradiction to Laing's schema, regardless of whether it is the individual-versus-the world, or intra-individual-structures aspect that is focused on. For these two aspects collapse into each other: if the world itself is undifferentiated, the differentiation implicit in there being a schema must be wholly within the individual. Similarly, if differentiation is exhausted *within* the individual, the world, against which individual qua whole individual is defined, must be undifferentiated.

This particular contradiction becomes especially problematical in one critical instance. For one crucial person in the human world, implicitly reified and negated by Laing's undifferentiated conception of the world, is Laing himself; or, more generally, the therapist/researcher who is in relation to the patient. By virtue of the undifferentiated world given for the patient, the intentional act by the therapist of recognizing the patient, is itself negated. The therapist is conceptualizing the patient in a schema which prevents the patient from recognizing the existence of the person presenting the schema, i.e. the therapist. The schema is thus undialectical (in contradiction to the innately dialectical nature of the human world) in so far as it has no place within it for the person presenting it. We may state this contradiction succinctly by saying that the intrapersonal nature of the schema is in contradiction with the interpersonal nature of the situation where one person applies a schema to another person, i.e. the therapeutic/research situation.

Let us look at the implications of this. In accordance with this schema, Laing states that understanding the patient entails becoming aware of the nature of the patient's being-in-the-world. But, concretely, in the therapy/research situation, the patient's being-in-the world is being-with-Laing; i.e. a form of being which is in its essence interpersonal. This contradiction thus strikes at the very heart of the enterprise as conceived by Laing.

Laing appears to partially realize this; that is, he realizes it as a situation, but not as a contradiction. Thus he says 'in the therapeutic relationship, the focus may be on the patient's way of being-with-me' (1967j, p. 25). What he does not say, or appear to realize, is that his schema has no way of conceptualizing what being-with-me is.

We have seen that Laing's schema posits (though not explicitly) subjectivity within the patient and *objectivity everywhere else* (i.e. the subjectivity of the patient vis-à-vis his being-in-the-*objective*-world). Everywhere, that is, including the observer. This is contrasted with the natural scientific approach which sees objectivity everywhere, and most of all in the patient; though just as Laing's approach does not realize the objectification of the observer, similarly, this approach, the natural scientific, does not realize that it implicitly assumes the subjectivity of the observer.

Laing notes the contradiction inherent in the 'objective' approach of natural science, when applied to persons; he does not note the contradiction inherent in his subjective approach. But it is, as we have seen, nevertheless present. In consequence we have, on a broader level, another contradiction, that between the objective and subjective approaches per se. Strictly, this contradiction is not intrinsically present *within* this stage; it appears here only in so far as the subjective approach, manifest in this stage, constitutes itself as one moment of this contradiction. The objective approach is brought in by Laing only (so he thinks) to be knocked down and thrown out; he does not see it as impinging on the subjective approach. Their relation he sees as one of absolute negation, and thus no relation at all. The subjective, for Laing, unilaterally negates and rejects the objective. We have seen, however, by virtue of contradictions within the subjective analogous to those within the objective, that such a unilateral negation is not feasible. Rather, both must, in some dialectical way, be transcended.

Every contradiction mentioned relates to what we are taking as the central issue: Understanding. Before we can let these contradictions free to their own movement, we must relate them to that which gives them their significance: the aims that Laing has in mind. Thus we may see in their motion the unfolding of Laing's theoretical praxis, which, in its turn, is the constitution of the ends which define and are defined by his project: the Understanding of Persons. In this way we hope to render intelligible Laing's work (which is itself the quest for intelligibility).

It is to Understanding, then, as conceived here, that we must now turn explicitly.

We noted earlier (Chapter 2) that Laing seems clearer about *what* understanding is than *how* it is to be achieved. Specifically, 'what' it is, is the empathic grasping, on the part of the therapist of the nature of the patient's being-in-the-world. Yet, as we have seen, so long as the focus is merely on being-in-the-world, it is impossible to come to grips with the patient's being-for-others, and thus, crucially, his being-for-the-therapist. And as, in fact, the being which the therapist is confronted with is, at least in part, the patient's being-for-the-therapist this approach precludes the possibility of its own success. Hence we can see that our, or rather Laing's, distinction between the 'what' and the 'how' of understanding is not valid. The nature of the 'what' affects - specifically, precludes - the realization of the 'how'. Or, in other words, through exposing the self-contradiction of the 'what' we can see the very impossibility of the 'how'.

It follows, therefore, that progress from this situation cannot be forthcoming in purely methodological terms. It is not a matter, we could say, of finding a more efficient 'how' which will enable us to achieve the original 'what'. For the 'how' and the 'what' are intimately connected, and cannot stand apart from one another. This is as much as to say that not only must Laing's conception of how to attain understanding change, but also, and with that, his conception of what understanding *is* must change.

We may already state some of the properties which will of necessity be found in a progression from this stance.

First, and most important, we require a form of conceptualization that places the individual, not in a world which is an inert monolithic objective totality, but in the world as it is; that is, in a world populated by other persons, who exist in relation to him inasmuch as he exists in relation to them. Put simply, we require a theory that gives us a subjective self *and* a subjective other *and* a means by which the two can meet. In a word, we require a theory that incorporates the notion of *intersubjectivity*. That is to say, a theory whose epistemological foundations recognize and assert that the individual experiences other individuals as experiencing him; without, of course, implying that the individual does not experience himself. Thus, in this motion (i.e. progression), the focus diffuses itself in a process of becoming sharper: by splitting its object of being-in-the-world into being-for-others and being-for-self, only to bring them together again as a now internally illuminated being-in-the-world.

Second, we require that the notion of understanding changes so as to keep up with this change. That this notion be defined not as the grasping of the other's being-in-the-world (which in itself, i.e. as a pure object of undialectical understanding, is inaccessible subjectivity), but as a grasping of the other's being-for-self in relation to his being-for-other (including his being-for-me) *and* in relation to what his others are for him.

Implicit in this is that we require, third, a knowledge of *how* this is possible. We require, then, to know the canons of the form of intersubjective knowledge.

But enough of requirements. We should rather be looking at what we *have*, as given by stage 2.

What we have, at least as an aim, is as follows. Let it be considered in relation to the requirements noted.

> This book ('The Self and Others', i.e. stage 2) attempts to depict the own person within a social system or 'nexus' of other persons; it attempts to understand the way in which the others affect his experience of himself and of them, and how accordingly, his actions take shape (Laing, 1960, p. ix).

Do we have anything here but a pledge to fulfil our first requirement? And again, in the following quote, do we have anything but the recognition of the failings of the prior approach?

> In a previous study (i.e. 'Divided Self')... it was often necessary to extend our account... to a whole 'nexus' of other selves, 'real', or conjured up. We shall now try to bring 'the others' and the 'interactions' that occur between 'self' and 'other' into sharper relief (Ibid. p. 69).

As we have seen (Chapter 2) this book presents many examples of being-in-the-world as relation between being-for-self and being-for-others. Witness, for example, chapters ten and eleven which deal explicitly with 'existential position' (i.e. being-in-the-world) as a function of the action of the self and of others; or chapter two which deals with what it is to be a member of a social phantasy system. The whole of Part One of the book deals with 'modes of interpersonal experience', a term which is synonymous with intersubjectivity.

So it appears, initially at least, that Laing has fulfilled the *first* set of requirements necessary for a transcendence of the contradictions of stage 1. Note that it is a genuine transcendence, not an absolute negation. The notion of being-in-the-world has not been rejected, in favour of a different mutually exclusive, notion.

Rather, it has, through a *bringing out* of its inner distinctions, been allowed to return to itself, but taking with it an awareness of its own inner nature, which is now equally its outer appearance.

But what of the other requirements? What, particularly, of the concept of understanding? Once again, it appears, initially, that Laing has fulfilled the requirements. For he does try to understand a person's being-in-the-world in terms of his being-for-self and being-for-others. Bearing in mind that the symmetry here demanded between self and other entails that a person's being-for-others exists in relation to the others' being-for-him, let us consider the following quotes:

> To understand fully the one person's experience of his 'position' obviously one would require a knowledge of the actions of the others, as well as of his actions... and phantasy... (A person's) sense of place will have been developed partly in terms of what place he will have been given in the first instance by the 'nexus' of original others (pp. 126-7).

As we shall see shortly, the notion of understanding, crudely developed here, more rigorously later in this stage, does not, in fact, resolve our dilemmas, despite appearances, except in one special case: Namely, when self and other are therapist and patient respectively. That is to say, granted that self and other form a dyad, the notion of understanding presented here is only applicable when one element of the dyad is the person who is doing the understanding. It follows, therefore, that this form of understanding is still only applicable to *one* person, in isolation (from everyone but the therapist). This point will be argued at length shortly. For the moment, however, we turn our attention to the only part of this stage in which this patient-therapist relation constitutes the dyad; namely, chapter one of 'The Self and Others'.

The chapter deals predominantly with the notion of phantasy. Vis-à-vis this notion itself, it will be discussed fully in a subsequent chapter. What concerns us here are the passages where Laing discusses the epistemological status of phenomenology as deployed by him. The issue is all the more delicate because of the fact that phantasy is an *unconscious* mode of experience.

> Psycho-analytic theory is largely based on attributions by *P* (analyst) about *O*'s (analysand's) experiences, which *O* says he is not aware of having.... Now in doing this (act of attribution) the psychoanalyst is taking the basic phenomenological step, which is both necessary and hazardous. He has to step beyond his own experience of the patient, into the patient's experience of him.... It is necessary, if one is to begin to understand the patient.... It is important to emphasize that the other's experience can never be a primary datum of one's own experience.... The phenomenology of the existential analytic method has not been sufficiently studied. At present, one can provisionally refer to 'empathy' or 'intuitive understanding'.... The logic of inference implied in such phenomenological attributions is a matter for separate investigation (pp. 12-14).

So, *even* when dealing with one person, the analyst who attempts to understand his patient can only 'provisionally refer to empathy', etc.; and the logic (i.e. the theory of verification) of any attributions made on the basis of these, is recognized as being unknown.

What we seem to have here, then, is not so much a concrete advance in methodology and theory, but a greater theoretical awareness of the problems, which are begging for advancement. Our third requirement, then, is not fulfilled but rather, and as yet only, realized, in the fullness of its implications, as a problem.

At any rate, philosophical problems or not, Laing's concern is to understand the behaviour and experience of any individual in his social context. As we saw in Chapter 2, this leads him to rely on research which utilizes an entirely different paradigm to his own; namely the so-called Newtonian paradigm of cause and effect. This was seen to be particularly embarrassing in connection with the concept of communication, which was thus replaced by Laing with the concept of 'perspective'. We may say, then, that, purely *within* stage 2 a contradiction was generated and resolved: between Laing's aim to *understand*, and the *causal* nature of Communication Theory. That there should be such contradictory development *within* one stage, which was, we said, the site of theoretical stasis, illustrates the somewhat arbitrary nature of including 'Interpersonal Perception' in stage 2. As we are about to see, however, it also shares, with 'The Self and Others', a much more basic contradiction, which more than justifies its inclusion. But first we must return once again to 'The Self and Others'.

The review in Chapter 2 revealed a contradiction in 'The Self and Others' that we must now focus on. The aim was to depict the individual in a nexus, and, on the basis of this, we thought, earlier in this chapter, that we had found a true intersubjectivity in the realization of that aim. Yet, as the review showed, the nexus was polarized around merely *two* concepts, self and others. That is, when there is more than one other, they are merely grouped together as 'others', and apprehended, once again, as a totality. Any individuality in this multiplicity of others is thus negated, and so too is their individual subjectivity; and hence, alas, the truth of this schema as intersubjective, in the full sense, likewise vanishes. It is only in the case where 'other' is a single person that the schema can be said to be intersubjective; i.e. where one is dealing with a simple dyad. So already we have lost the nexus. (Which is not to deny that Laing can, and does, talk in nexual terms; simply that in so far as he does, he is talking either outside the terms of his own conceptualization, or, as is usually the case, the nexus is taken undifferentiatedly, i.e. *not* intersubjectively.)

But the loss goes deeper. For unless Laing is to conceptualize himself out of existence, by failing to include himself in his theoretical totalization, as he did in stage 1; unless, that is, he is to make the same mistakes and generate the same contradictions all over again, he must constitute himself (or more generally, the observer) as one element of the dyad. This, of course, leaves us high and dry with an individual again; albeit one who is at least conceived as being in relation to the person observing him, which he was not in stage 1. Such is explicitly the situation in chapter one, of 'The Self and Others'. The situation there, although not particularly fruitful, by virtue of the limitations at that juncture of Laing's phenomenology, was at least not contradictory.

This cannot be said of the rest of the book. For we can now formulate the principal contradiction of this stage as being that between the need for a multivalent theoretical formation in which to conceptualize the multiplicity of persons, and their relations, that comprise a nexus; and the purely binary formation that is feasible using the concepts of 'self' and 'others', which reduces to an effectively monadic formation as soon as the observer constitutes himself as an element in the theoretical field.

In fact, Laing as observer fails in every chapter except the first, to constitute the observer as such an element. The bulk of the book is concerned with an observed agent (self) in relation to a single other or generalized others, with the observer *outside* the field he is observing, despite the fact that, as we have just shown, this is theoretically contradictory. Thus the bulk of the book may be characterized, strictly speaking, as contradictory; only chapter One escapes this charge. Thus, chapter One and the rest of the book exists in a relation of contradiction, that can certainly not find its resolution in their own terms.

As our brief account of the first chapter showed, the concept of Understanding so far developed in this stage is too vague to allow a particularly meaningful relation of the contradictions established to be made to it. It will be remembered, however, that 'Interpersonal Perception' gave us a strictly formal definition of Understanding. To recall, it was defined as the conjunction of one person's meta-perspective with the other person's direct perspective on the same issue.

Now this definition circumscribes the scope, and thus illuminates the transgressions, of this stage admirably. Note, initially, that understanding is *absolutely* confined to two people. p understands o when p guesses correctly what o is thinking (concerning issue X). There is no way, within this schema, that p can understand o's relation to q. That is, no way that Laing can understand his patient's relation to his mother taken as a relation, for example. The virtue of this explicit formulation, which becomes even more apparent when written using their symbolic algebra, is that the fallacies of talking about understanding without theoretically including the understander are that much more obvious. Similarly, the fallacy of attempting to include more than two agents. (It is perhaps worth pointing out that the term 'agent' simply refers to the unit responsible for action. This is usually, of course, the individual; but there is nothing in this scheme to prevent it being taken as a group, or even a country, provided *no internal discrimination* within the unit is permitted.)

Thus, the situation now vis-à-vis Understanding is basically that it 'happens' 'in' one person, but refers to a dyadic relation, where one half of that dyad is the person who understands. We should note, however, that such Understanding may occur in two significantly different contexts. First, it may occur in respect of the therapist's relation to his patient, i.e. when the therapist understands him. Here, the observer completely co-incides with the understander.

Second, however, understanding may occur between a dyad that is undergoing therapy; as when a husband understands his wife over some issue, when they are having marital therapy. Now it may be possible that the therapist, who is external to this dyad, *knows* that the husband understands: as, for example, he would do examining the results of the application of the IPM tests to the couple. However, it is essential to stress that this knowledge is epistemologically identical to objective natural scientific knowledge. It is emphatically *not* 'understanding' on the part of the therapist with respect to the couple or to either of them as individuals. Of course, the therapist and the husband may constitute themselves as a dyad and achieve understanding as defined here - but it will be to the exclusion of the wife.

Thus, somewhat paradoxically, the definition of Understanding given by the IPM method does *not* allow the administrators of the tests to 'understand' the data that the method yields; it allows it merely to be *known*. By virtue of its inability to understand more than one individual at a time, this method transforms the meaningful relationships *between* people into meaningless forms of abstract objective knowledge. *The interactional system as such remains irrevocably incomprehensible.*

It would be appropriate at this juncture to relate the motion we have so far observed to certain aspects of biographical information. For it is not being suggested that these theoretical developments find their motive force *purely* in the airy regions of theory itself. Of course, any precise attempt to relate a *given* observed development to a specific practical difficulty or theoretical contradiction must remain speculative; Laing himself is the only person even in principle who could do that. I accept therefore, that the connections I shall suggest between theory and practice are no more than plausible, and in principle, unverifiable. (Not being a logical positivist I do not regard them as meaningless!)

From 1951 to 1956 Laing worked as a doctor, a psychiatrist, in an Army Psychiatrist Centre and then Glasgow City Hospital. Despite any personal idiosyncracies of his approach (which we have already noted - see Chapter 2, stage 1) the *structure* of his relation to his patients was, therefore, the 'orthodox' one of doctor-patient *qua isolated patient*. Despite, again, any leanings towards a communal context for patients (see Cameron, Laing, McGhie, 1955) we may safely assume that the overriding status of his patients, *for him*, was that of 'individual'. Granted, then, that the *entire* clinical material of 'The Divided Self' was drawn from these years, and that the initial draft of the book was *completed* in 1957, we may reasonably read into these facts a plausible connection between the theoretical orientation of 'The Divided Self', and the nature of Laing's involvement with and perception of those patients whose lives form the prima materia for that book.

Laing moved to the Tavistock Clinic in 1956, and by 1958 had begun research into the families of schizophrenics (the results being published in part in 'Sanity, Madness and The Family'). Also dating from this time was his research into marital couples, later published in 'Interpersonal Perception'.

Now, assuming Laing did not commence intensive work on 'The Self and Others' till 'The Divided Self' was complete (i.e. 1957-8), this gives us the fact that work on 'The Self and Others' ran concurrently with his research into marital couples and families of schizophrenics, i.e. dyads and nexi. Once again, a plausible connection is fairly apparent.

It should also be borne in mind that from the early 1950s at least Laing had been reading continental philosophy. Thus already in 1955 (op. cit.) we find Laing and his colleagues commenting on the 'presentation of phenomenological evidence' by nurses in a ward experiment conducted by them.

The next major change in Laing's theoretical position (i.e. the transition from stage 2 → 3) cannot, however, be related to biographical details. For the research context remains unchanged. The catalyzing event was rather the publication by Sartre of his monumental 'Critique de la raison dialectique', and it is towards the relevance of this forbidding tome for Laing that we must soon begin to turn.

Returning first, however, to stage 2, we recall the two related principal contradictions of this stage: the need for multivalent theory versus the binary nature of self-other theory; and the need to understand relationships as well as individuals versus the inability of 'understanding' as here defined to do so.

As before, we may state in advance some of the properties which will be necessarily found in the transcendence of these basic, and other secondary, contradictions.

First, we require a theory which can give us individuals: in relation to themselves, qua individuals; in relation to each other two at a time, qua dyads; in relation to relations of other individuals, i.e. p in relation to (o's relation with q) that is, qua *thirds*; and finally, in relation to the entire nexus, qua part of whole.

Second, we require a theory which can conceptualize the observer as a third in relation to any or all of these relations. That is, a theory which posits the observer as an element, essential yet distinct, in the field he observes.

Third, we require a theory which understands all these relations *as relations*, not merely as multiplicity of individuals; in particular, it must understand the relation of the observer to these relations.

Finally, it must give us the criteria for its own truth. That is, it must give us already a logic of its own epistemology.

It is important to note that these requirements are not the phantasy of a latter-day Hegel: they are all direct real practical issues for Laing and his colleagues - notably Esterson - at this stage in their career. The first set of requirements relates directly to their research with families. When faced, as they were every day, with the bewildering confusion of perspectives and relationships that characterize a 'normal' family let alone a 'schizogenic' one, some sort of *theory* for the grasping of this *reality* is a *practical* necessity. Their experience with the radically different forms of relation between them and their subjects, according to who of the family was present, testifies to the necessity of the second requirement. A theoretical scheme in which the observer cannot 'understand' with certainty more than one person at a time is hardly likely to prove efficient in the practical study of families; which amounts to saying, nor is one in which there are no formal criteria for assessing the validity of 'understanding' if it *is* attempted in relation to more than one person at a time.

They are, or better, they 'reflect' practical problems; but these can only be solved in theory. For what the real issue here is concerns the correspondence of the nature of real, human, day-to-day existence with theoretical attempts to grasp it in thought, i.e. to understand it. What is required is a form of knowledge which, like human existence, is *dialectical*. No purely *practical* reorientation could be sufficient, for what is problematic here is the *mode of thinking human reality*. No mere technical refinement in research methodology could suffice.

As we know, the initial moment of this radical change was purely theoretical: the publication by Sartre of the 'Critique', in 1960, and Laing's reading of it. It is not surprising, therefore, that the first manifestation of the change was also theoretical: the publication, in May 1962, of Laing's article Series and Nexus in the Family (Laing, 1962).

Now, we noted that in stage 2 the notion of nexus was 'polarised around merely two concepts, self and other'. This may be rephrased by saying that this approach, by defining a 'self' by distinction from 'others', accords theoretical priority to the individual, who is only *subsequently* 'framed' in his interactional context. As we have seen, this leads to problems; and our requirements demand an approach that sees an individual always in terms of logically prior relations. Consider, then, the opening paragraph of the first text of stage 3, in relation to these points:

> Persons are not separate objects in space. They are centres of orientation to the world. These different centres and their worlds are not islands, but the nature of their reciprocal influence and interaction has always been difficult to incorporate adequately into interpersonal theory. By considering the person from the beginning in terms of one of his group metamorphoses, without according any theoretical or methodological priority to the person as an abstracted ego extrapolated from his interhuman context, there is some hope that a radical advance... is possible. This is what Sartre in his... Critique de la Raison Dialectique seems to me to have already begun to achieve (Laing, 1962, p. 7).

'Group metamorphoses': that is to say, the viewing of the *same* individual in relation to y; in relation to the group, and so on. Laing is demanding, then, the viewing of the individual in relation to a variety of relations, or 'alterations', as Sartre terms it. He is demanding, in fact, the meeting of our first requirement for this new transition.

Similarly in the Introduction to 'Sanity, Madness and the Family':

> Each person does not occupy a single definable position in relation to other members of his or her own family. The one person may be a daughter and a sister, a wife and a mother. There is no means of knowing a priori the relation between: the dyadic set of reciprocals she has with her father,... her mother, and the triadic set she has in the trio of them all together.... People have identities. But they may also change quite remarkably as they become different others-to-others. *It is arbitrary to regard any one of these transformations or alterations as basic, and the others as variations*.... We have tried to develop a method, therefore, that enables us to study, at one and the same time, (i) each person in the family; (ii) the relationships between persons in the family; (iii) the family itself as a system (Laing and Esterson, 1964, pp. 20, 23).

I think we can see in these quotes (and many more could be given) a pledge to fulfil at least the first and third of our requirements.

But what of the second requirement, that of the constitution of the observer as an element in the field he observes? Laing and Esterson do not refer to this point explicitly; rather, they make the following strange comment: 'Our interest is in persons always in relation either with us, or with each other, and always in the light of their group context' (p. 21).

Either with us, *or* with each other. This seems odd: for in so far as Laing and Esterson are 'interested' in these persons (and do anything about that interest) they are, ipso factor, in some sort of relation with them. It is not a question of either/or, but of what *sort* of both/and. This point, as we shall see, is almost a theoretical dead-end for Laing; not so for Esterson. In his follow up to this book, 'Leaves of Spring', Esterson takes the implications of these requirements to their limits, and likewise, the realization of them. This is particularly so with this issue. For instance:

> But the way a person relates is not simply a function of himself; it is a function, too, of the way the others, *for instance the observer*, relates to him. And so, the observer must be aware of his own pattern of response if he is to evaluate the behaviour and experience of the person he is studying. The investigator must become himself a person for study.... The observer, with the co-operation of the other, constitutes himself as part of the field of study, while studying the field he and the other constitute (Esterson, 1970, pp. 217-18).

All this is to say that the relationship between the observer and the observed must be a dialectical one: one cannot escape the conclusion that, in 'Sanity, Madness and the Family' at least, Laing is undialectical in this respect. Nor is this oversight ever brought out explicitly by Laing anywhere else in this stage: the problem seems rather to be *implicitly assumed to be resolved* - a stance remarkably similar to that described by Laing as 'mystification'. For instance, in another text of this stage (Laing, 1965a), Laing writes:

> We have to ask how we decide what to us is the central issue, if our perception of the central issue is disjunctive with perceptions of the family members themselves. The only safeguard here is to present the perspectives of everyone in turn (including our own) on '*the shared situation*', and then to compare the evidence for the validity of different points of view (op. cit., p. 347).

Now what exactly is meant by 'the shared situation'? Shared by whom? Does it include, critically, the family members' view of Laing, and Laing's view of himself in relation to them? He does not say, in abstract terms; nor is it possible to infer it from the examples concretely given, as they are taken from 'Sanity, Madness and the Family'. And as far as the latter is concerned, there is no systematic attempt to constitute the observers as part of the observed field.

It is perhaps also possible, retrospectively, to see an awareness of this need - for a real dialectic between therapist and therapand - in Laing's decision to set up the Kingsley Hall community. That is, to live the dialectic first, rather than to think it. We shall be discussing later the problems inherent in this move (which are still utterly unresolved).

There is, of course, a reason, or at least an excuse, for this oversight. The research reported was conducted between 1958 and 1962; Sartre's book, which points out the necessity of a dialectical approach, was not even published till 1960. We do not know exactly when Laing read it, but whenever it was, *at least* half the research period was over. Sartre's dialectical insight could not, therefore, have been a guiding light for more than a small part of their research.

Finally, we must examine the fourth requirement, that of the criteria for the truth and validity of the method.

Sartre's theory does indeed provide such a set of criteria; and we know that Laing himself was aware of these, and had grasped them, by virtue of the account of them he presents in 'Reason and Violence.' To quote:

> By what specific set of operations do we hope to manifest and prove the reality of the dialectical process?.... The problem is to give a critique of the instruments of thought whereby history is conceptualized intelligibly. If such a critique is itself a valid undertaking, what will be the criterion of the vailidity of our procedure?.... The validity of dialectical reason rests on its own translucency.... If dialectical reason exists, it can only be, from the ontological point of view,... a totalization: and from the epistemological point of view, the permeability of this totalization to knowledge, where the act of knowing is itself totalizing.... Thus it is not only a sector of reality characterized by totalization (i.e. human history) that must always be everywhere intelligible, but the totalizing movement itself. Herein consists the translucency of dialectical reason: its second intelligibility (Laing and Cooper, 1964, pp. 102-4).

The validity of dialectical reason (i.e. the approach taken by Sartre and, apparently, by Laing and Esterson) then, rests on its double intelligibility. However, we must recall that such intelligibility, for Sartre, depends on the dialectical variant of what Husserl called 'the phenomenological reduction'; that is, here, the retracing of human action to praxis, *and beyond,* to individual project. In the light of this, the reservations of Laing and Esterson, already noted, become critical. To refresh our memory:

> Within the terms of phenomenology itself, this study is limited methodology and heuristically.... Inferences about experiences that the experiencers themselves deny, and about motives and intentions that the agent himself disavows, present difficulties of validation that do not arise at that phenomenological level to which we have restricted ourselves (Laing and Esterson, 1964, pp. 25-6).

Let us be clear what is going on here. The validity of dialectical reason rests on its intelligibility, which in turn rests on a complete phenomenological reduction from observed behaviour to personal project. Laing and Esterson are dealing with social situations which are characterized by alienated praxis; that is to say, the phantasy components of experience and interexperience are presumed to be intensive and possibly predominant. Thus, a complete phenomenological reduction here would require discovering the full intelligibility of the phantasies involved; and as they say, this does indeed 'present difficulties'. Their approach, therefore, has been to leave the reduction incomplete; specifically to stop at the level of praxis (free or alienated) without descending to the level of project. In view of the practical exigencies of their research this is entirely understandable. The point, however is that this limitation *precludes the possibility of using the criteria of validity established by Sartre.*

We have already seen that Laing identifies his, admittedly limited, procedure of reducing apparent process to praxis but no further, with the production of intelligibility, which conflicts, strictly speaking, with Sartre's use. It now seems that they adopt the same tactic towards the criteria of validity: as when they speak of an 'undeniable bedrock', and 'quite manifest contradictions'.

This, it must be emphasized, is *not* to say their approach is invalid. It is valid: *as far as it goes*. More to the point, however, is that it is also extremely limited; at least in respect of what could, theoretically, be achieved using this theoretical approach. This point comes out in the extremely reserved preface to the second edition; it also explains the 'sense of anticlimax' experienced by many critics of this book.

For example, Tyson (1971) concludes that Laing and Esterson 'have been forced into a partial retreat' (p. 4), by having to admit that they have not explained anything, but merely made something more intelligible than supposed. Like many other critics, Tyson seems incapable of believing that they did not really want to explain anything, causally, despite their repeated assertions of this. Tyson, and others, assume that unless something is causally explained, nothing is achieved: at most, intelligibility is a poor substitute for 'real' social science, which, they think, involves the discernment of causal connections. But regardless of what real social science is, this point of view betrays the most abysmal lack of fundamental understanding of what Laing and his colleagues are about. The rigidity, in critics like Tyson, of what may be called the 'causal dogma' does nothing but add to the strength of Laing's case against the orthodox view. So monolithic is this view, it cannot even see opposition to it as opposition, but merely as a failed attempt to be such orthodoxy itself.

To say what Laing and Esterson have said repeatedly, but which apparently needs to be repeated yet again: they were *not* attempting to explain anything, if explanation is taken to involve causality. They were attempting to render certain behaviours and experiences intelligible, but they recognize that they have been able, by virtue of an incomplete phenomenological reduction, to achieve this only partially.

We are now wholeheartedly in the realm of stage 3: we would be wise to see exactly where we stand in relation to where we have been, in stage 2.

We have seen that the main contradictions of stage 2 were solved, immediately in theory, by the alignment with Sartre's views. In theoretical practice, however, the solution is nothing like so total. What we see now is not, as before, a theoretical system the nature of which is in contradiction to the nature of human reality. For, as Sartre has shown, dialectical reason has the form of *totalization,* which characterizes both human reality, and human knowledge of that reality. Rather, we have a situation where Laing's theoretical practice falls short of that insisted upon by Sartre as necessary and sufficient. We have seen that, in a later work, Esterson (1970) catches up on that falling short; but that is, strictly speaking, outside our scope.

The transition from stage 2 to stage 3 can be characterized, in very abstract terms, as a paradigmatic change of basic philosophical orientation: from existential to social phenomenological. No longer, in stage 3, do we find being-in-the-world, even the internally differentiated variety of the 'Self and Others'. No longer a static being, but a dynamic becoming, through alterations, group metamorphoses and totalizations. The individual is no longer a passive (albeit conscious) being, but an active source of dialectical praxis. With symbolic significance, 'Sanity, Madness and the Family' is not a member of the series Studies in Existentialism and Phenomenology, but of a new series, The World of Man; as indeed, are all of Laing's books hereafter (except 'Politics of Experience').

It appears also that Laing and Esterson themselves would wish to emphasize the importance of this transition; for their position vis-à-vis orthodox clinical psychiatry appears to have changed. In the original preface to 'The Divided Self', Laing gives the impression that his new approach is to be regarded as an alternative to run alongside the more conventional view. He asks that he be not judged by the aims of orthodoxy; but he does not appear to reject those aims *in themselves*; merely to challenge their *sufficiency* as an adequate approach to the whole problem.

Similarly, in 'The Self and Others', Laing says 'no aetiological theory that I subscribe to is stated in this book' (p. ix); we do not get extended arguments against the validity of aetiological theories as such.

Now, no doubt Laing believes that his alternative is the superior one - and no doubt, he is correct. The point, however, is that we are not given a feeling of immanent apocalypse; a feeling that orthodoxy itself will begin to smolder and eventually burn away under the scorching rays of Laing's existential illuminations.

Contrast, then, Laing and Esterson's reflections on what they see as the historical status of their new approach, of social phenomenology (from the Introduction to 'Sanity, Madness and the Family'):

...the transition from a clinical to a social phenomenological perspective.... That this study is transitional is both its weakness and its strength, in that we hope it will constitute a bridge between past and future efforts in the understanding of madness.... We believe that the shift of point of view that these descriptions (i.e. the case studies of 'Sanity, Madness and the Family') both embody and demand has a historical significance no less radical than the shift from a demonological to a clinical viewpoint three hundred years ago (pp. 25-7).

No longer, then, a mere alternative, but the beginning of what Kuhn (1970) has described as a 'paradigm change'.

Major paradigm changes do not, or rather, have not in the past, occurred in isolation from other sorts of historical change; indeed, it is mistaken - as Marx's insights have shown - to regard changes in, paraphrasing Foucault, the 'architecture' of knowledge as being primary: they have tended to be parasitic upon changes more fundamentally rooted in the structural relations of society; 'in the last instance' (as Althusser would say), economic changes. Now the changes focused upon by Laing are basically changes in the architecture of knowledge; but with immanent implications for changes in other spheres. The most immediate of these, of course, concerns the *practice* of 'curing' the 'mentally ill': but one would anticipate ramifications through the entire structure of 'the human scene', if, indeed, what we have here is a major paradigmatic change. As we shall see some, at least, of these broader ramifications are to be found in the transition from stage 3 to subsequent stages.

As we have noted, Laing characterizes his new philosophical orientations as 'social phenomenological'; yet he does not specifically offer a definition of 'social phenomenology' as such. It is simply repeatedly identified as that approach which Laing and Esterson take. Examining the introductions and conclusions to the case histories, one by one, we find that, in practice, social phenomenology thus entails, for Laing and Esterson, the following.

We shall not be able to compartmentalize our inquiry in terms of clinical categories. Clinical signs and symptoms will become dissolved in the social intelligibility... (of the girl's experience and actions), as they are seen in the light... of the praxis and process of her family (p. 32).

We shall have to begin once more at the beginning, and explore afresh, without presuppositions, whether these schizophrenic signs and symptoms are intelligible in terms of the praxis and process of her family nexus (p. 76).

... the necessity for a variety of 'sightings' (i.e. totalizing perspectives) of the family in action is revealed particularly clearly (p. 110).

Once more we have set ourselves a *limited* aim and in our view we have now achieved it. More evidence could have been presented, many more apsects of this family could be discussed, but we have, we believe, adduced sufficient evidence that two particular symptoms that are usually taken to be primary symptoms of an organic schizophrenic *process*... are here intelligible as social *praxis* (p. 106).

The question is: Has what is usually called her 'sense of reality' been torn in shreds by the others?.... How socially intelligible are her areas of confusion and her mode of communication? (p. 132).

Her parent's view of this girl as 'ill' was essentially congruent with the clinical psychiatric gestalt. We shall here present a radically different gestalt, in which the *attribution* of illness becomes socially intelligible.... We shall review the experiences and behaviour of (this girl) as seen through the eyes of her mother, father, older sister, psychiatrists, nurses, and ourselves; and, finally, as seen through the eyes of Mary herself (pp. 203-4).

Only when the maternal grandparents and a maternal aunt and her husband were seen, did an intelligible picture of the whole family situation, constellated around Hazel, come into focus.... The following is our synthesis of the multiple perspectives before us (p. 222).

By seeing Agnes's situation simultaneously from our point of view and hers, we can now begin to make sense of what psychiatrists still by and large regard as nonsense (p. 265).

I have quoted at length here, as it is apparent, from the quotes, that there are several things supposedly being made intelligible. In the first place, and indeed throughout, the patient's experience and action is rendered intelligible as 'social praxis' - in particular those that are seen as 'symptoms'.

In the second place, it is the whole system of family-in-action that is made intelligible, via a synthesis of 'multiple perspectives'.

And finally, it is the act of attribution of illness as such - i.e. the action of psychiatrists - that is rendered intelligible.

Now these are clearly three very different things; yet, they are intimately related, as Laing and Esterson themselves show by their examples. The fact that their method, social phenomenology, should find it both desirable and possible to operate successfully on these three different levels of intelligibility, testifies the degree that this method does indeed meet the requirements we noted for an adequate transcendence of the contradictions of the previous stage. But, as they note, this success is limited:

> our totalization of the family itself as a system is incomplete. Our account of each family is to a considerable degree polarised around the intelligibility of... the person who has already begun a career as a schizophrenic. As such, the focus remains somewhat on the identified patient,... rather than the nexus itself. This we believe to be historically unavoidable (p. 26).

In other words, they focus on the individual 'patient': her views on the others, and the others' views on her, rather than 'the nexus itself'. The second level of intelligibility, that of the system per se, is thus incompletely realized, even in the limited sense of intelligibility employed by Laing. To that extent, the transcendence of 'stages' is still not fully achieved.

The intelligibility of the attributive act is even less fully achieved; for attribution of illness is a form of alienated praxis that is, properly speaking, external to the family system altogether. That is to say, this act is either carried out by psychiatrists, who are, in an obvious way, external to the family; or by the family members in *imitation* of psychiatrists. We can see here a tortuous series of alienations and reflections: for the psychiatrists, and the whole mental hospital set up, are as Foucault (1967) and others have shown, a reflection of the paradigmatic authority/morality structures found in the bourgeois family. In a process of double alienation, the family regrasps its authoritarian essence, now fortified with 'psychiatric technology' (the 'Technology of Consent' as Eysenck has so insightfully called it) and 'scientific objectivity', by applying psychiatric criteria and notions to itself - or rather, to its progeny.

The act of attribution is thus external *and* internal: the moments of its intelligibility range from the dyadic interpersonal to the historical-political-ideological. At any rate, a totalization which is polarized, as Laing and Esterson's is, simply around the 'patient', cannot hope to render intelligible the act of labelling that person a patient.

As already implied, these three levels of intelligibility a themselves mutually interdependent. For strictly speaking, the intelligibility of the individual (patient) is not available in abstraction from the intelligibility of the family system as such. And the family system, in particular its action of defining its offspring as bad or mad, can only find its intelligibility in its relation to other institutions in society - schools, hospitals, prisons, churches, factories, etc.; and *these* relations require to be further related to the broad economic and ideological structures of modern capitalist society as an internally differentiated whole.

We can see here already the latent contradictions of this stage. As we have seen, we do not have a fundamental contradiction between the nature of the theoretical formations drawn upon (Sartre) and the nature of the reality to be accounted for; both are now capable of realization as embodiments of dialectical reason. Rather, we have here a number of more specific contradictions in the realm of practice. Some, locatable in the field of theoretical practice, have already been alluded to; others, in this and other fields have yet to be considered. At any rate, it is to the elucidation of the contradictions inherent in Laing's position in stage 3 that we now turn.

If we conceive of a vertical continuum of totalizations, starting, at the 'bottom', with individual project, moving up (via successive totalizations) through individual praxis, social praxis, to institutions, and then to the highest level of meaningful social abstraction, relations of production, class systems etc.; then, we may locate Laing's position in stage 3 as being that of individual praxis, occasionally moving up to social praxis.

We have seen, however, that full dialectical intelligibility will not rest content with being restricted to one or two levels of this continuum. For the being of intelligibility is the translucency of totalization to itself. Each totalization requires to be detotalized and retotalized; nothing short of a complete totalization of all these levels of totalization is required for a full intelligibility. But such a totalization would be a totality; and there are no totalities in history. Such a notion remains, then, an abstract ideal; but it is one towards which we must move if we are to grasp the human world in its intelligibility, which is to say, in its humanity.

Thus, we find the necessity for Laing to move both up and down in this continuum - in other words, to expand the 'horizons', as Merleau-Ponty would say, of his knowledge. Specifically, he must *descend*, phenomenologically, to the level of project, which, as we have seen, involves the comprehension of others' projects; and he must *ascend*, similarly, to discover the intelligibility of ever higher, more complexly structured sectors of human reality. We may, then, formulate this as a contradiction, locatable at this stage, between the breadth of totalizations necessary for a grasping of human reality, and the narrowness of Laing's totalizations to date. This principal contradiction is manifest in two principal aspects: the reductive, to the level of project; and the constructive, to the level of total human reality, or, anticipating for the sake of clarity Laing's future terminology, the 'total world system'.

Let us consider the reductive aspect first. The rendering

...xis, Sartre tells us, requires the re-discovery
...he individual, and, (by interposing this with a
...aterial objective conditions, 'the field of the
...athetic grasping in the flux of consciousness, the
...erience of the other's praxis, which is the syn-
...oject and his given field.
..., for us, not only a therapist, or a researcher, but,
...riter. It is through the medium of his writing that
he i...   / this intelligibility. His writing itself must therefore come   be capable of inducing in its readers this sort of sympathetic re-discovery of the experience of those who are to be understood. This point of view, unfamiliar for empiricism to the point of heresy, is nothing new to phenomenology; what is new is merely the rigour with which the requirements of a scientific, that is, dialectical, that is, social, phenomenology are spelt out - as they are by Sartre. The phenomenological tradition even has a term for it: Passion.

Dr John Heaton, now a colleague of Laing's, and a director of the Philadelphia Association, has written an excellent article (Heaton, 1972) which deals with these notions; although he uses more philosophically conventional terms. In particular, he traces the connections between the phenomenological reduction applied to oneself, i.e. phenomenological reflection, and the psycho-analytic notion of 'insight', which in Heaton's context appears to parallel Sartre's notion of 'comprehension'. Heaton produces a quote from Husserl, concerning the desired impact of phenomenology, which certainly seems to anticipate the apocalyptic tone that we find in Laing's writing in the next stage:

> ...the total phenomenological attitude and the corresponding epoché is called upon to bring about a *complete personal transformation* which might be compared to a religious conversion (sic), but which even beyond it has the significance of the greatest existential conversion that is expected of mankind (Husserl, 'Gesammelte Werke: Husserliana', vol. VI, p. 140).

Metanoia? Perhaps; thought it will be argued that it is Laing's most recent pronouncements, concerned with meditation, that bear the closest resemblance to the Husserl-Heidegger tradition of phenomenology.

Considering the constructive aspect next, social phenomenology requires successive totalizations; given a totalization to the level of a family as a system, we must go beyond this, and replace the family in society. We must, as it says in 'La Critique', move from Group to History. To say the same thing a different way: if we wish to understand the experience and behaviour of the individual, to discover the rationality of his Weltanschauung, we must place him in his nexual context. But the nexus, i.e. the family, then itself appears incomprehensible, irrational; so it too must be placed in a meta-context, and so on. Quite obviously, these higher contexts, which it seems Laing must turn to if he is to continue his Quest for Understanding, are, at least implicitly, political domains. Furthermore, it is a form of Marxism which Laing is now professing to be employing in theory: we need not be surprised, then, to find forms of radical activism emerging in association with Laing, to find practical problems overcome by the creation of radical alternative structures for whatever is problematic. It should be noted, however, that Laing has nowhere ever stated, to the best of my knowledge, that he is 'a Marxist', but it does seem implicit, in the Introduction to 'Reason and Violence', when it is said: 'Sartre affirms and strongly supports by impressive argument the view that Marxism is the only possible philosophy for our age' (p. 25). (Despite tha claim six pages later: 'Philosophy does not exist.') Even this is not conclusive, however, as the Introduction was written by Laing *and Cooper*, the latter being much more politically conscious, by all appearances, and certainly a Marxist of sorts.

We have, so far, elucidated two principal contradictions at this stage. It would be as well to examine the motion of these, in fairly general terms, before turning to the more specific contradictions.

The task is made difficult by virtue of the fact that Laing's theoretical progress appears to be following a 'law of uneven development'; by which I mean to say that although the contradictions here arise together, their transcendences occur at different times - in our terms, in different stages.

Thus, the phenomenological descent, the reduction to the level of individual experiences, is attempted in stage 4. The subject matter is largely concerned with experiences which are essentially private; Laing's own writing sets off on an 'inner voyage' which speaks directly to the reader: he wants to 'turn you on,... drive you out of your wretched mind' and thus into your true self. The topics of discussion are transcendental religious experience, inner voyages, personal alienation, and so on; and the style of writing is poetic, apocalyptic, passionate; it employs (as Heaton tells us phenomenology should) 'concepts which cannot be grasped, which can never reach the level of thematic clarity, whose purpose is to 'turn you on' (Heaton, 1972, p. 145). Or, as Desan (1966) has said in reference to Sartre:

> When we say that man is project, we imply that in his continual act of existing he 1 cannot be conceptualized, that is, understood by clear concepts, but 2 he can be comprehended.... Comprehension is not knowledge... it is nothing but that movement of the human consciousness by which it reproduces the project of the Other (Desan, p. 66, referring to Sartre, 1960, p. 105).

Thus the critics of 'The Politics of Experience', with their positivism, logical or otherwise, have typically missed the point again when they bemoan the 'psychedelic imagery with its voyages and trips' (Clare, 1973), the 'schizoid and love-denying philosophy (which) seeks to involve us in the destruction of personality, the logic of death' (Holbrook, 1968, p. 47), its lack of 'development of a continuous argument' (Tyson, 1971), and even, amazingly, its 'intemperance' (ibid.). One detects a sense of outrage; as if to say: 'This is going too far! Describe these experiences, by all means, induce them in me? No thank you!' Which, of course, simply testifies to the validity of Laing's assertions concerning the degree of alienation entailed by 'normality'.

This style of writing did not, of course, develop over-night. The papers written in 1964 bear the initial marks of the change: and we can detect considerable differences, even, in the April and November versions of the same paper (Is Schizophrenia a Disease/What is

Schizophrenia). The papers of 1965 (A Ten-Day Voyage, Violence and Love, Transcendental Experience, etc.) continue the trend, (1966 sees *no* significant publications, except 'Interpersonal Perception', which was completed in 1965) till we reach the climax, in 1967, with the publication of 'The Politics of Experience'. The latter appears, not surprisingly, to be as far as Laing wishes and/or is able to go in the emotive direction. For sources subsequent to that, whilst still presenting a similar position in most respects, do so in a less psychedelic (to use the term in its proper sense, i.e. consciousness-expanding) fashion, being more concerned with a definition of that position than a magical invocation of it. As is implicit in what Sartre says about the total process of understanding, *both* are necessary (which is not to say that Sartre would necessarily approve of Laing's methods of invocation). It is not, as Anthony Clare (1973) seems to think, a matter of Laing'returning to the fold'.

The ascending moment, of increasing levels of totalization, finds its realization in what we have termed stage 5. The schema outlined in 'The Obvious'(Laing, 1967) (see chapter 2) is explicitly an attempt to provide a more complete totalization. It is, however, a schema, and very little more. We have already noted that, as far as published work is concerned, Laing fails to develop this schema through application; indeed, over the question of violence and political opposition, we found no attempt to apply it, despite its obvious applicability.

Nevertheless, Laing praises those that do attempt these high level syntheses, stressing their difficulty; as when he commends certain unspecified talks (probably Paul Sweezy's: see Cooper, 1968) at the Dialectics Conference during a summing up speech (Laing, 1967, D.L. 13 Liberation Records).

Two points need to be made about this apparently simply theoretical ascension. First, we must note, as Laing does, that at the last level of totalization, that of the Total World System, the whole itself appears irrational. Every sub-system has found its rationality in its context, its place in next level of the system; but the whole by definition has no further human context. Yet it begs one. To be more precise, certain levels of the system beg a meta-context for the whole: hence one gets the mythical cosmologies of religion, which (we would say) anthropomorphize the cosmos, thus rendering the total world system at least potentially rational. Religions as such can be viewed as coherent sub-systems of the totality, at a relatively 'high' level; 'lower' sub-systems - political parties, status groups, families, individuals - may then 'beg' *and find* the rationality of the whole, (and thus their part in it) through adherence to religions.

It is tempting to imagine that such is the position of Laing: that after failing to find ultimate justification for his existence in political terms, because of the irrationality of the whole, he turned to religion and found such justification by positing a transcendental agency, a 'cosmic pattern' as he puts it, to make sense out of the whole. Tempting, but, at very best, misleading. But we are anticipating too far: Laing's so-called 'mysticism' will be examined later. Meanwhile, we have a second point to make concerning these progressive totalizations.

It will be recalled that, at the end of stage 3, Laing's totalization of the family as a system was by his admission incomplete. This 'historically inevitable' contradiction was not, however, to be transcended in stages 4 or 5; neither of these take clinical material from families. Rather, where there is any 'clinical' material at all, it concerns specifically individual experiences: Jesse Watkins' Ten-Day Voyage, for instance.

It is not until 1967 then, with the first paper of stage 6 (Family and Individual Structure), that we find Laing dealing specifically with this (Laing, 1967j). We have already examined the way Laing spells out how the members of a family come to be a 'family', which is, in effect, a fully totalized nexus. Only now can Laing begin to answer adequately the question: 'what is the phenomenological reality of the family?', for only now can Laing begin to formulate what the 'family' is for its members. It is, perhaps, surprising that it has taken so long; four years earlier Laing had spelt out, in painstaking rigour, the theory he is only now applying:

> The third (i.e. the observer of a dyad relation) is not the totality he totalizes, but... he realizes himself as integrated in the totality he totalizes. Each person as third is absorbed into the totality.... *The central problem* is the whirling unity of the various syntheses, of the multiplicity of unifications. Do these syntheses make *the* synthesis?
>
> At the moment when the multiplicities of serial syntheses fuse into an overall synthesis... it has been easy for some sociologists to lapse into idealism - to postulate a new transcendant being. But at this moment it is each third... who operates the syntheses, totalizations, and any unification of them *by interiorizing the totalizing designations in and through which other groups treat his group as a totality* (Laing and Cooper, 1964, pp. 131-2).

The language, in 1967, is less academic, but the points are undeniably the same: we can recognize these 'multiplicities of unifications' as the 'elementary acts of group synthesis' of Family and Individual Structure. What is particularly interesting is that not only does Laing make full use of Sartre's formulation, but he goes on to examine, in practice, empirically, the mode of the solution of the 'central problem'.

The 'central problem' is how is the synthesis of syntheses possible: how do members of the family as individuals become the 'family'? And the solution was by each member *interiorizing* the totalizations (of others) of his group (family) as a totality ('family'). The *mode* of the solution, then, concerns *how* individuals interiorize the views of other people concerning themselves (among others).

Laing attempts to answer these matters, in 'The Politics of the Family', by his theory of mapping, whereby interiorized relations exist as unconscious phantasy. But unlike the somewhat nebulous concept of phantasy employed in 'The Self and Others', phantasy here is conceived of as implicitly structured. In the words of a writer who is obviously influential for Laing at this stage, namely, Jacques Lacan, 'The discourse of the unconscious is structured like a language.'

We can describe Laing's efforts here, then, as an attempt to learn this language by investigating the *external* structures (i.e. family structures), which, Laing supposes, give rise to these internal structures, and thus to be able to understand the 'discourse of the unconscious', i.e. to carry out a phenomenological analysis of 'unconscious phantasy'.

Once again, these practical achievements of stage 6 have been anticipated: I quote again from 'Reason and Violence' (Introduction). 'There *is* plenty of room for a phenomenological examination of "unconscious phantasy"... insofar as the latter is conceived in its reality as experience and not as a series of mechanisms to be imposed upon a subject' (p. 26). By the 2nd edition (1971) Laing is able to add that a 'marriage' between existential analysis and the world of Lacan would be in order here.

I would wish to argue, therefore, that as far as theory is concerned, stage 6 represents an entirely logical and consistent extension of stage 3. Despite a reduced use of Sartrean terminology (most notably, the virtual omission of praxis and process), the overall scheme would appear to be a highly fruitful mingling of social phenomenology and structuralism. (As such, it would appear to be something of an achievement, intellectually. For the two originators of these approaches, Sartre and Lévi-Strauss, appear to find progressively less in common. See, for example Lévi-Strauss's 'The Savage Mind', chapter Nine. I take this also to be the meaning behind the otherwise peculiar sarcastic comment in the 1971 preface to 'Reason and Violence': 'Petty disputation regarding "history" or "History" should not delay the ceremony' (i.e. the marriage between existentialism and structuralism.)

The concepts of group synthesis, totalization, interiorization, series, nexus, alterity, and so on are all present, even if they are given different names. Furthermore, the positive theoretical contents of stages 4 and 5 - limited though it is - appear to have been conserved. Thus, we find in stage 6 references to 'metanoia' (Laing, 1967c, p. 142), and 'Total World System' (ibid., p. 141, and 1971, p. 48).

But if, as we have argued, there is a theoretical contiguity between stage 3 and stage 6, then we must ask why there is a gap, temporally, of virtually four years. Or, to put the same question in a different way, what is the relation between the developments of stages 4 and 5 to the continuous theoretical stream of stages 3 and 6? To answer this, we must return to the specific detailed contradictions of stage 3, as promised earlier. For, let us not forget, we have been engaged so far only in tracing the motion of the *principal* contradictions of stage 3.

Stages 4 and 5, relative to stage 3, can be characterized as ones of broadness of outlook and concern; such, indeed, was the essence of their transcendence of stage 3. We may rephrase this conclusion by saying that Laing, and his colleagues, took steps to alter not merely their theorizing, nor even just their practical research/therapy 'methodology', but rather their whole relationship to their profession, their patients, and ultimately, to society as a whole. It is therefore to practical, ultimately *political*, contradictions that we must now look as if we are to grasp the motion of the stages in their intelligibility.

We may conveniently take as a starting point the notion of schizophrenia as presented at the end of stage 3. The issue is merely described as a 'social event' in 'Sanity, Madness and the Family' - any other comment on the nature of schizophrenia is 'put in parentheses'.

An article published in April 1964 (Laing, 1964a) in 'New Society', however, says this:

> Since 1958 Dr. Esterson and I have been engaged in studying the actual circumstances around the social event when one person comes to be regarded as schizophrenic. We have studied over 50 cases, and *without exception* it seems to us that the experience and behaviour that gets labelled schizophrenic is *a special strategy that a person invents in order to live in an unlivable situation* (p. 17. Emphasis in original).

Now there are a number of consequences of this view. First, and most obvious, it puts Laing and Esterson in direct opposition to orthodox psychiatry. For the latter 'treats' the person, whereas it is his *situation* that is unlivable. In other words, a psychiatric ward, by insisting that there is something wrong with *the person* is in that respect identical to the person's original situation, which defined him as bad or mad: *both* are thus 'unlivable' situations, to that extent (which may be more or less considerable). The hospital ward is thus itself a mystifying context, in that it refuses to see the person's prior (family) context as mystifying but sees it simply as 'family life'. It thus perpetuates mystification by denying it in the first place.

However, as Laing (1965a) has shown, in the last text of stage 3, successful therapy is largely dependent on a demystified context. THis is precisely what is denied, he claims, in the orthodox mental hospital. So we have, for Laing, a practical contradiction: the objective need for a demystified context for therapy, as against the innately mystified contexts of hospitals and families.

Laing's colleague, David Cooper, had been conducting an experiment in a mental hospital since 1962 (see Cooper, 1967 and Chapter 2) where it was hoped to provide such a demystified context. Accounts of the experiment vary, but it seems to be a universal conclusion that, ultimately, any ward within a mental hospital, no matter how 'liberal', is beset by contradictions. Yet the need for a genuine 'asylum' was being felt more than ever.

At the same time, Laing's views on the nature of schizophrenia changed. We noted in the previous chapter the first account of his new 'inner voyage' notion; but it was not possible to specify how Laing came to the idea. He subsequently (1967c) stated that such metanoic sequences occurred in Cooper's experimental Villa 21, and refers to Bateson's (1961) account of such a voyage. Laing also claims to have been 'particularly concerned with unpublished protocols sent me by people who have managed to negotiate a sort of "voyage" without however being labelled, hospitalised or in any way treated' (ibid., p. 142). One such protocol, subsequently published, was presumably A Ten-Day Voyage (Laing, 1965).

The relation of the Inner Voyage theory to Laing's *personal* experience is paradoxical. I imagine that most readers of 'The Bird of Paradise', especially, assume that Laing has himself gone through such a voyage. ('I have seen the Bird of Paradise, she has spread herself before me, and I shall never be the same again.')

However, in December 1968, in a speech to a Conference, apparently held in France (Laing, 1968d) he talked of Mary Barnes' and others' experiences at Kingsley Hall: 'They are making the voyage. *I have never made that voyage myself,* and possibly none of us here have.... None of us is in a position to do more than trust this process' (p. 19).

By his insistence on drawing an analogy between this sort of voyage, and an LSD trip, one might imagine that 'The Bird of Paradise' refers to the latter. Yet Laing has denied this (Gordon, 1971) insisting that it was merely events from his 'inner life'. I am unable to resolve this paradox: but I cannot avoid the conclusion that LSD was highly instrumental in the genesis of this theory. After all, we know that Laing was in contact with Leary's League for Spiritual Discovery, which emphasized 'spiritual rebirth' through LSD-produced ego loss. Also, metanoia was not the only experience typical of Kingsley Hall; LSD was apparently used there, under Laing's supervision.

The setting up of Kingsley Hall, which provided the resolution of the contradiction concerning demystified contexts, and also provided a medium for the testing of Laing's new views, effectively cut the bridges between Laing and orthodox psychiatry. But it also built many more bridges in their place, and Kingsley Hall became, as we saw in the previous chapter, a sort of counter-cultural focus. At any rate, it appears to have been the occasion for Laing's short-lived political activism. But even before Kingsley Hall, we find Laing asking, in the highly programmatic What is Schizophrenia (Laing, 1964g) in what way invalidation of a hospitalized schizophrenic 'serves for the maintenance of the civic order'. He goes on to say: 'Socially, this work (on families) must now move to further understanding..., to the meaning of all this (personal mystification) within the larger context of the civic order of Society - that is, of the political order, of the way persons exercise control and power over one another.'

And indeed, Laing's writings over the next three years live up to this programme; they are truly concerned with the politics of experience; and thus, with alienation.

Alienation, of course, is a universal feature of humanity in this day and age, and as such, it includes Laing himself in its grasp. He avoids, narrowly, the charge of elitism - such as has been levelled at Marcuse in respect of 'One-Dimensional Man' - by insisting that 'we who are still half alive', must, like anyone else 'begin to think, feel or act... from the starting point of his or her own alienation' ('Politics of Experience', p. 11). In such a situation, everyday conceptions of madness and sanity are as good as useless. In particular, the 'sanity' of Laing and his colleagues automatically becomes problematic on this view.

I think we can find, in the comments Laing makes on this problem, the recognition of a contradiction that has been running throughout the whole development, but which has never been made *explicit in its generality.*

The absolute basic minimum for any form of social encounter, of which psychotherapy is an example, is two persons, a dyad. Now Laing has written much on dyads; particularly, the need for absolute mutuality or reciprocity between the two members if the dyad is to be a genuine social encounter. The contradiction to which I refer is that between the integration of the dyad through reciprocal encounter, and its disintegration through the polarization of the two members into therapist and therapand (or similar role duality). Such a contradiction can be manifest at a number of degrees of intensity. Behaviour therapy, for instance, described by Laing as 'schizoid', apparently without irony, must be the most extreme manifestation of it in a supposedly therapeutic context (excluding Nazi euthanasia).

Laing has always had a sensitivity towards this contradiction. In his first ever publication, in fact, the closing sentences are: 'the barrier between patients and staff is not erected solely by the patients but is a mutual construction. The removal of this barrier is a mutual activity' (Cameron, Laing and McGhie, 1955, p. 1386).

Or, a few years later, in his first book:
The personalities of doctor and psychotic... do not stand opposed to each other as two external facts that do not meet and cannot be compared.... THe therapist must have the plasticity to transpose himself into another strange and even alien view of the world. In this act, he draws on his own psychotic possibilities, without foregoing his sanity' (Laing, 1960, p. 34).

'His sanity' is assumed; it is the rock, which is somehow also plastic, upon which a therapeutic relation is built. It is this, we can now see, that prevents the transcendence of this duality. (As Laing himself commented on 'The Divided Self', in 1964: 'I am still writing in this book too much about Them, and too little of Us.' (Laing, 1964e).) But now, things are different:
We psychotherapists are specialists, as they say, in human relations. But the Dreadful has already happened... to us as well as to our patients.... *We* have to discover our 'inner' world.... We are all implicated in this state of affairs of alienation. To me this context is decisive... for psychotherapy.... Under these circumstances, our relationships with our patients are our re-search.

A re-search, a search, constantly reasserted and reconstituted for what we have *all* lost.... Our research is validated by the shared experience of experience regained in and through the therapeutic relationship in the here and now (Laing, 1965b, pp. 64-5).

Therapy is now, it seems, a dialectical process, in which both 'moments' aim for the *'wholeness of being human'* (p. 63). But such is an ideal, obtainable only, if at all, under very specific social conditions. For, ultimately, a therapist *is* a therapist (and thus his partner is a therapand), if only in so far as he is *paid* to be a therapist. This contradiction would seem impossible to transcend entirely, then, whilst our alienation is still objectified by money.

We spoke of 'very special social conditions'; and now perhaps we can see what they might be. Kingsley Hall was a start, but even there, there were 'money hang-ups'. The residents still had to pay for their private analysis, just as the professional analysts had to charge: *given* that they intended to have money at all and thus, in Laing's words 'be a part of the system, and insofar as one is part of it, *one perpetuates it*' (Dialectics of Liberation Conference).

One can only conclude, then, that real multivalent encounter is only possible to the extent that one is outside the system *all together*; i.e. to the extent that one has formed a commune that is totally self-supporting. Only then can one *start* to attempt a truly genuine, mutual, social encounter.

For practical purposes, the above criteria are, no doubt, impossible. The point then becomes to realize, as fully as one can, exactly what the bounds of possibility are: freedom as the recognition of necessity. The point is emphatically *not* to fool oneself into thinking one has achieved the impossible simply by thinking one has achieved it.

As far as Laing is concerned, then, I cannot escape the conclusion that he is presenting a very idealist conception of what it is possible to achieve *within* existing social structures, just as he reached idealist conceptions of political opposition (see Chapter 2, stage 5); and in both cases, for the same reason. Namely, his failure to abide by his own dictum of placing any institution - be it the Police, Kingsley Hall or his own consulting room - in its meta-context, in order to perceive its rationality, and its structural determinations. This, I hasten to add, is *not* to deny the reality of Laing's 'really decisive moments in psychotherapy which... are unpredictable, unique, unforgettable... etc.'; nor to deny that Laing's methods may be infinitely superior to orthodox approaches (as he refuses to give an account of the actual practice of therapy, it is hard to say); simply to assert that when the ideal is impossible, any account which does *not* specify those impossibilities but *does* posit the ideal, is itself idealistic.

Laing himself certainly experienced the contradictions of counter-culture within proto-culture. Berke (1971) describes Laing's typical day whilst living at Kingsley Hall (which he did for over a year): the late hours typical of communes, the early mornings in which he did his writing, and his ordinary working day as a therapist, not to mention the resulting lack of communication with his family; all led to a state of physical and mental exhaustion. His split with Esterson, in the summer of 1966, appears to have been the last straw, and he moved out, but continued to visit frequently.

It is also significant that Laing himself defines the aim of therapy as the meeting of only *two* people. We could perhaps say that his therapeutic practice is lagging behind his theory: we have already noted his theoretical development beyond dyadic perspectives; but these theoretical advances appear to be negated in his consulting room. (We are here referring to Laing as a therapist rather than a research worker.) We should, however, not forget Kingsley Hall; but the relationship between the Kingsley Hall community and Laing's consulting room has never been made clear.

It is interesting to note that Laing's therapy is considered to be extremely conservative, if not outright reactionary, by many commentators in America. Ruitenbeek's (1972) introduction to 'what Radical Therapy is all about' is one of the more coherent comparisons of British and American approaches:

> Radical therapy distinguishes four kinds of psychoanalysts and
> psychiatrists.... Gamma psychoanalysts or psychiatrists, the
> third category, like Laing and Szasz, are radical in their poli-
> tics but conservative in their practice, since they still
> adhere to Freudian and neo-Freudian methods of psychotherapy and
> place an emphasis on individually oriented psychotherapy. They
> stress... psychoanalytic concepts (pp. 4-5).

(For an account of radical therapy, see Agel, 1971, and Ruiten-beek 1970, 1972.)

We are in agreement, then, with Laing, that the removal of interpersonal barriers, the recovery of 'the wholeness of being human' is at least in part, a *political* problem. It is fitting, therefore, that we should now turn to the difficult task of assessing the rise and fall of Laing's political activism.

The rise of Laing's activism coincided, as we saw, with the rise of the British Underground Movement (Nuttall, 1970); Laing's part in it was not that exceptional. Of course, one is hampered by a severe lack of biographical information about Laing's activity; but as far as can be gathered, he did very little if anything in the way of overt political action: nothing comparable, at any rate, to the activities attributed to his mentor, Sartre. And in retrospect, it is hard to see what could have been done on those lines. At any rate, Laing's interests, as he himself has put it, are more 'verbal', which is fair enough, as I suspect that his words, spoken and written, have done more to raise the level of 'political' awareness in this country than a few well-placed bombs would have done.

We do know that Laing reacted to the political scene in a way scarcely conducive to practical action: he notes that he is not himself physically threatened by the violence of society; yet he speaks of extreme depression, a sense of being weighed down, when he contemplates the world situation. It is impossible to find a hint, especially in the 1967-8 period, of the optimism which I imagine is a prerequisite for being a successful 'revolutionary'. And as we have already noted, Laing attributes his stepping down from radical activism to the nature of his personality.

From there, Laing returned to more academic matters - notably, the incorporation of structuralist thinking - and to 'spiritual' matters. Is this a legitimate step? - it is certainly not without precedent - or is it, as Sedgwick (1971) claims a matter of 'betrayal'? I do not presume to judge, though I have my private opinions, which appear to coincide neither with Laing's nor with Sedgwick's. Where I think Sedgwick is wrong is when he says the following:

> The social and the religious trends in Laing's philosophy
> appeared to be held in a tension which, if not dialectical (be-
> cause of its total lack of integration), nevertheless held the
> promise of a more definite political evolution. It now seems
> that Laing has resolved the inconsistencies of his position by
> yielding to the mystical, anti-political (and surely anti-
> human) current in the chaos of the sensibilities (p. 46).

Now even granted that this was written whilst Laing was in Ceylon, it is still inexcusable. To say that the relationship between the social and the religious is undialectical, i.e. no relationship at all, in Laing, is to betray an almost total lack of understanding of 'The Politics of Experience', and of 'Knots'. It is precisely the undialectical relation between social experience and religious experience that is prevalent today that Laing is bemoaning! And even if Sedgwick's information, that Laing intended to remain in Ceylon indefinitely, had been correct, that still does not give him the right to accuse Laing of 'betraying' the 'International Left'. Laing's position in this respect reminds me of Bob Dylan's position: sudden fame had made them both into a myth on to which various groups, sub-groups and individuals grafted their own fantasies - with little regard for what was actually the case. Their positions are remarkably parallel, in fact: Dylan became famous as a protest singer, and the Civil Rights people claimed him for their own. Whereupon he moved to San Francisco, dropped protest songs, and more or less single-handed invented a new style of music, based on and inspired by, the use of psychedelic drugs. Needless to say, he was branded a traitor, booed off stage and so on, till the public caught up. And when, some time later, he retreated from the West Coast drug scene, to spend more time in private contemplation, the hippies then yelled 'traitor'! And so, I think, with Laing, too many people are too eager to say, yes, Laing is one of us, therefore Laing is such-and-such; and when they discover he is not entirely such-and-such, there is such righteous indignation. And the irony of it is that no one has spelt out so well as Laing the absurdity, the violence, and the tragedy of the 'One of Us, one of Them' game.

Sedgwick's rejection of Laing appears to be based on two assumptions: that mysticism and politics are mutually incompatible; and that Laing is, now, also totally mystical. Now whilst it may be the case that certain sorts of mystical states *cannot* be conducive to any sort of political commitment, it is not *obvious* that Laing is mystical in that sense. For Sedgwick originally criticized Laing's mysticism *before* his retreat to Ceylon.

I think perhaps one suffers from a lack of adequate vocabulary at this point: for there is a vital distinction to be made between that sort of 'mysticism' which is indeed a-political and potentially reactionary; and a different sort, which is by no means necessarily so. Now this second sense of 'mystical' refers simply to experience which is non-egoic, which as Laing himself has stressed is a form of experience which does not necessarily lead to a cessation of action. Personally, I am convinced that there is nothing 'mystical' about this sort of experience, in that it is no 'mystery', no miracle, but a natural occurrence to be expected, given certain circumstances, and welcomed accordingly. It is not so much mysterious as mystified, as Laing tries to show in the 'Politics of Experience'. And it is precisely this mystification which such experience is subject to that leads to mysticism in the first sense, where the 'mysticality' of the experience appears to be pursued in its own right. This sort of mysticism usually seeks to clothe itself in incomprehensible metaphysics, and to incorporate large quantities of myth and ritual, and thus all too often to lose sight of the original *experience*, whose fate was to be mystified. A complete inversion may occur, such that what was once sought, is now prohibited. (The history of the Agape in the early Christian church offers an excellent example of this degenerative process.)

So in what sense *is* Laing 'mystical'? I think without doubt Laing is 'mystical' in the sense of advocating non-egoic experience -- but there is nothing a-political about that; on the contrary, the 'Politics of Experience' is precisely about why it *is* political.

Is he mystical in the further sense? All I can say here is that I do not find him so. I cannot find in Laing's supposed 'mysticism' anything that is *innately* anti-political.

But that is not to assert that Laing himself is consistent over 'political' matters. It does seem beyond doubt that Laing has retracted his position politically. What I am denying is that this is inevitably, or even in fact, due to his 'mysticism'. I believe the reasons are much more mundane: like a big house in the country, for instance.

In what way, we must ask, has Laing retracted?

We begin to get intimations that his scepticism extends to *all* political positions in the interviews in 1968; though retrospectively, Laing has claimed that this began as early as the Dialectics Conference: 'I guess I identified myself with the Left by being there, but even at the time I made it clear that I really had no idea what could come of such an extraordinary conglomeration of people' (Laing, 1972a).

It is not quite so clear exactly *whom* he made this clear to.

Laing regards himself as a neutral: 'Politically, I think I'm neutral, really' (ibid.).

And however much these (positions) seem to offer a solution in the fervour with which they're adopted by their proponents, they are all answers to questions that I would say that my main stance has been, in what I've written, one of scepticism, to all the answers that have been proposed (Laing, 1972b).

(Interviewer): 'Do you, for example, take the view that really profound radical change in society would transform the individual personality and psyche....?' (Laing): '...I don't see how that change is likely to be effected' (1972b).

I am afraid that all of this talk about 'political neutrality' rather reminds me of Mick Jagger's pitiful statement: 'I am an anarchist, really.' Jagger may be an anarchist in the sense that he leads an 'anarchical' life, i.e. there is no one (no 'arche') to tell him what to do - and doubtless he has a pretty wild time. And no doubt, Laing is 'politically neutral' in the sense that he does not generate by his own will, political actions.

But surely terms like anarchy and neutralism convey more than this? How, for example, would Jagger react to anarchy *in other people?* To people pointing out that if all property is theft, they might as well 'liberate' Jagger's property? Not too well, I suspect.

And how, indeed, would Laing react to genuine political neutrality in other people? For, *precisely as his own work has shown*, day-to-day interaction, normal social life is 'political'. Political neutrality means nothing less than a cessation of *all* interpersonal activity (and if 'The Politics of Experience' is to be believed, all *intra*personal activity, too!). Now this may be a very comfortable position: for Laing. But how would he react if other people were to become politically neutral? Be they ever so political, I think it likely that one would soon miss the life support systems (food, clothing, heating, shelter, as *absolute* basics) if they fell apart *as systems* owing to mass political neutrality.

Obviously, no revolution ever occurred through political neutrality. The appalling irony of Laing's present position is that he has shown, in the past, more forcefully than anyone, that everyday social life is just as 'political' as a revolution: *yet it masquerades precisely as neutrality ('normality')*. Could Laing quote today the saying of Péguy, as he did in 1965f: 'Everything begins in mysticism, and ends in politics'? I doubt it. (It is perhaps significant that already in the rewritten 1967 version of this paper, this quote is omitted!)

Just one of the ironies in all this is that Sartre, one-time Marxist influence on Laing, seems to be increasingly identifying himself with the sort of political stances that Laing was identified with in the 1960s. Consider, for example, Sartre's comments on the politics of drug use:

> What do you think of the increasingly widespread use of marijuana?
>
> Sartre: On the individual level it appears to me to have no great importance, I have smoked it.... Similarly in the case of heroin... in the name of what will the law prevent people from committing suicide? For me, the problem here is also to determine if their use of hallucinogens demobilizes militants.... When I see that some consider recourse to hallucinogens a sufficient affirmation of their freedom, and excuse themselves from action, I wonder (Sartre, 1973).

Or again, Sartre's concern for spontaneity and freedom in politics, and his rejection of party politics - 'The Communist Party and Freedom, they don't mix' (Sartre, 1974a), as he puts it - the global concerns (Ecology, Sexual Liberation), all remind one of Laing in the mid-late 1960s. And finally, one is reminded of Laing's statements about 'so long as one remains part of the system, one perpetuates it', when Sartre says

> I won't vote.... It is not necessary to enter the system. A vote, whatever the ballot, is a vote for the vote, an acceptance of the institutions. How can legal action overthrow the law?.... This is one reason I am drawn to the Maoists. I believe in illegality (1973).

One could multiply examples of previous statements, exhorting political action, that are now implicitly contradicted; it would serve little purpose. For surely we must allow the arch-exponent of metanoia to 'change his mind'? But as Roberta Elzey Berke pointed out, vis-à-vis Laing's present position, rebirth is one thing; but one has also to grow up again. I cannot help feeling that Laing's present position reflects a political naivety that is 'childish' (though without the sense implied by 'unless ye become as little children, ye cannot enter the Kingdom of Heaven.' If we are to be biblical about this, I would think first of the eye of a needle).

This is simply another way of expressing the idealism which, in specific instances, we have spotted already. For it is an idealist dialectic that can see in the (political) opposition of contradictory 'positions' *only* the mutual opposition, *only* the 'contradiction' pure and simple. We shall be examining this assertion in the next chapter, when we look at the degeneration to which Laing submit's Sartre's dialectic. For the time being, we shall conclude by saying that there is very little if anything, in Laing's supposed 'mysticism' which is innately contradictory to a revolutionary or radical position. (For an exposition of why and how Buddhism, which is substantially Laing's 'mystical' stance, is *not* incompatible with revolution, see Snyder (1968).)

What I do find contradictory, and frankly hypocritical, are Laing's assertions that his political position has always been what it is now. Personally, I find his present position unacceptable (or at least, not commendable); that is my opinion. What is doubly unacceptable is that he should make this out to be the position he has taken all along - critically, in the years 1964-8. This second unacceptability is, I suggest, a fact, not an opinion. (One can only, of course, base all this on what Laing actually said and wrote; what he felt about it at the time, and feels now, i.e. the question of his inner sincerity; this is a question that on principle cannot even be raised in the writing of a thesis. And it is, after all, available to anyone, on the Dialectics of Liberation recording of 'The Obvious', to hear Laing denying the possibility of political neutrality.)

Having thus concluded the review of Laing's present position, and its history, we move on to attempt to grasp Laing's work as a 'totality' - or to be more precise, as an arrested totalization-in-progress.

Chapter 4

LAING'S WORK AS A TOTALITY

> When I go beyond a certain range it's outside of my direct horizon, therefore I've got to rely on the writings and personal communications given to me by other people. Then like everyone else I've got to try to piece together some tentative information-picture of what the whole thing is like (Laing, 1968).

THE TOTALIZATION

We must now face up to the hardest task: the attempt to grasp Laing's work as a 'totality'; in using this term, we do not wish to reify Laing's work, to say it comprises merely *this* insight, *that* fact, and *the other* opinion. Yet, we wish to be able to grasp it in some sense as a whole. What we shall attempt to do, then, is demonstrate and render 'graspable' the overall coherence of his work as a dynamic system of psychiatric, political and theoretical practice. This is not an exercise in inventing non-existent self-consistency. Rather, it is a specific recognition that any river, for all its waterfalls, rapids, whirlpools - in a word, its fluidity - has a source, banks on either side, and a general direction of flow towards the sea. (A sea, however, is not definable in these terms.)

It will be recalled that the central issue that we have discovered in Laing's work is that of Intelligibility (using the word in its everyday as well as Sartrean sense). Specifically, we found that each stage that we isolated was in some way concerned with the problem of understanding, or rendering intelligible, some aspect or level of the 'human scene'. This is what we refer to when talking of the 'heuristic consistency' of Laing's work. Furthermore, we found when examining the transitions from stage to stage, that such transitions were usually, though not solely, motivated by inadequacies in hitherto existing means of rendering intelligibility.

It would be a mistake, however, to consider Laing's theoretical development as purely linear; to imagine, simplistically, that stage 1 represents the crudest, and stage 7 the subtlest, schema for producing intelligibility. The theoretical structure of Laing's career is not, vis-à-vis temporality, one-dimensional.

Let us recapitulate. Stage 1 led on, irrevocably to stage 2, and stage 2 to stage 3. At stage 3, however, we found a theoretical schema - Sartrean Marxism -, *the potency of which was not exhausted by Laing's practical application of it*. This was not true of stage 2, for instance. For at the end of stage 2, Laing had gone as far as he could with that theoretical schema. At the end of stage 3, this was emphatically not the case. Now one aspect of the reason for this is that the Schema of stage 3 is dialectical: it denies the self-sufficiency of any one level of conceptualization. Thus, dialectically, to understand the individual requires studying his own family context. But to understand the Family as a phenomenon, apparently irrational, requires studying *its* context; and so on. The nature of the theoretical stance of stage 3, then, has sweeping implications which I would summarize as follows: *to adopt a truly dialectical stance vis-à-vis the human world commits one to study and action on a number of discrete yet related levels of reality.*

Let us see exactly what this has meant in the case of Laing.

Stages 1 to 3 dealt primarily, if not exclusively, with the question of understanding people supposed to be mentally ill. We have seen how the achievement of this, to the level attained in stage 3, required more and more attention being paid to the nature of the human context. But the end of stage 3 shows us, suddenly, the hitherto unexpectedly vast deficiency of contextual location. Hence, in stage 4, initially, we do not find attempts to take individuals' experiences and render them intelligible: we find a stepping-back, as it were, to view the whole context of what psychiatric diagnosis means in our society.

There have been many interpretations of 'Politics of Experience' which say that whilst Laing used to think it was the family which drove people mad, he now thinks it is Society which does so. I trust this view, which may be conveniently labelled 'the Ever-Expanding Scapegoat Theory', has been revealed as the simple-minded naivety that it is.

Similarly, the *practice* of stage 3 was recognized by Laing to be limited, not only in the direction of further, broader, totalization, but also in terms of phenomenological reduction. He was, as he said in the Introduction to 'Sanity, Madness and the Family', reluctant to talk about, say, the phantasy modes of experiences of his subjects.

In stage 4, although he no longer uses the clinical context, he *does* descend to this level; and indeed, beyond, arguing for the existence of modes or realms of experience frequently denied altogether. But his aim is not now to render intelligible a given piece of clinical material: it is to invoke *in you and me,* experiences in these modes; for we are dealing with things innately non-observable, non-verifiable, even perhaps, non-describable.

Can we, therefore, in the light of this 'descent' in level, still maintain our thesis of heuristic consistency? I think so. I have already argued that, in principle, Laing's use of what may be called 'poetry' (i.e. not strictly logical propositions) can be seen as an attempt to bring about what Sartre calls 'comprehension', (i.e. the re-living of the project of the other) in the instance where what is to be comprehended occurs in those experiential realms best described as 'spiritual'.

I say 'in principle'. The point is, does it work? There is no one answer, of course: there are as many answers as there are people who have read 'Politics of Experience'. For the answer 'yes' conveys that the reading of the book invokes in the reader those experiences, and 'no' the converse. All I can say is that repeated extensive study of the book, in a variety of moods and states of mind, has brought me as close as I ever want to get to being mad; or at least, mad without a guide. Obviously, I cannot speak for anyone else on this point.

As one would imagine, this 'descent' altered Laing's notion of what 'schizophrenia' is. I have already demonstrated that, despite subtle modifications and qualifications, his notion of schizophrenia has not *fundamentally* changed since 1964. What has happened, and what constitutes stage 6, is that Laing has found a way of incorporating the essentially personal insights of stage 4 into a theoretically coherent context. (I should point out that I am here referring to one of the two major aspects of stage 4: the Inner Voyage. The other aspect, of normality as alienation will be considered subsequently.) He has done this, as we have seen, by the incorporation of a structuralist viewpoint, in addition to the dialectical/phenomenological viewpoint of earlier stages.

Despite their very different tones, then, I do not believe that 'The Politics of the Family' in any way repudiates or contradicts 'The Politics of Experience'. Rather, we should see in the former, and indeed in stage 6 in general, *a return to the clinical*.

If the position is theoretically more coherent, it is also - practically, that is, therapeutically, more coherent. For though Kingsley Hall is no longer running, numerous households are. Not that these are without their contradictions. As I have argued elsewhere, so long as Laing or whoever in practice runs these places remain *professional* psychiatrists (or even professional anti-psychiatrists), then insurmountable contradictions will arise. It does indeed come down to politics in the end: we have had the Politics of Experience and of the Family; there will be no further real progress till we have the Politics of the Commune. And as David Cooper (1971) said, in the future, books will not be written, they will be done. (For Cooper's stand on the issue of 'professionalism', see Cooper, 1967b.)

Summarizing, then, I see a continuity, as far as 'schizophrenia' - its meaning, implications and 'treatment' - is concerned from stage 4 to stage 7. This continuity embraces both theoretical and practical issues.

But there is more to stage 4 than the Inner Voyage; in particular, we must consider the issue of 'normality' as a state of alienation.

We saw that Laing's analysis of this alienation involved, at stage 4, an account of this state as an immediate phenomenon (chapters one and four of 'Politics of Experience' for example) and an account of how and why this state arises (Violence and Love, 1965c, for example). Implicit (dialectically) in all this, then, is the issue of how to get *out* of this state. This, as we have seen, is overridingly a *political* problem. And once again, there is a continuity to be found: and not merely from stage 4 to stage 5. That stage 5, that of political activism, follows from stage 4 has already been argued; but is it a coincidence that stage 3, which provided the theoretical occasion for the blossoming out into stage 4, (and thus into stage 5) should have been that stage at which *Marxist* concepts should have been introduced, for the first time? I think not. When Laing and Esterson talk, in the Introduction to 'Sanity, Madness and the Family', of a 'historical significance no less radical...' they were correct: more so than they could, perhaps, have envisaged. And the final paper of stage 3 (Laing, 1965a) which begins with a discussion of Marx's concept of mystification, was this not bound to lead them to the realization of the need for political action? The Dialectics Conference, after all, was dedicated to the 'demystification of violence of all sorts'.

It is another question, of course, what the future of political activism is. That is, for our purposes, what are we to make of the relative decline of political activism in Laing after 1968? He speaks of his continuing desire to promote 'microrevolutions', at a face-to-face level. Is this a valid, even heroic stance, *the* way for Laing to best deploy his undoubted talents. Or is it a matter of Bad Faith, a typically bourgeois 'cop-out'? I do not know. The issue is connected, obviously, to the one considered above, of being a 'professional'. At times I feel that *anything* short of totally dropping out of the money cycle is bad faith, if one professes revolutionary intentions. Yet I am prepared to accept a grant to write this thesis, because I have something to say, and because I am simply too scared to drop out. Who am I, then, to criticize a man who quite obviously has so much to say; and so on. One could argue the point all night and frequently does.

At any rate, it is possible to consider stage 5, then, as another natural outgrowth of stage 4, with its roots in stage 3. That stage 6 should have chronologically followed stage 5 (in fact, to a large extent, it does not; the temporal overlap is considerable) is, I propose, beside the point. For it is profitable, as implied above, to regard stage 4 as nodal: stage 5 is a branch, in one direction; stage 6 is a branch in a different *but not contradictory* direction.

Nor is it true, I would argue, that there are merely two branches on this Tree of Knowledge. For we must not forget stage 7.

I think it will be readily admitted that the continuity here is even more apparent. The first writings of Laing of a religious flavour occur at the beginning of stage 4, dating 1964, and continue, through 1965-6 to 1967 with 'Politics of Experience' and of course, the 'Bird of Paradise'. It is difficult, I admit, to find 'religious' writings in 1968 (although, see 1968d); that being the year of Laing's political commitment - and, indeed, a year of political awareness in general (Paris in May, American and British universities, etc.). It could be argued, perhaps, that Laing rejected 'religion' in 1968 for politics, became disillusioned with it, and returned to religion thereafter. I do not believe this is the case. For throughout Laing has stressed the dialectic of the political and the spiritual; it was Laing who amazed the political underground, (in 1964, during the first meeting of the Philadelphia Association with them) by saying 'the only way we can define our aim is as this: to reveal the greater glory of God' (quoted in

Nuttall, 1970). We have already discussed the issue of political action vis-à-vis non-egoic experience and LSD.

At any rate, although 'Knots' was not published till 1970, the first Knot, i.e. the first occasion that Laing chose that extraordinary *style*, dates from July 1967, with Appearances and Disappearances (Laing, 1967g). Perhaps significantly, this first Knot was the most mystical of all those in 'Knots', the one concerning Dharmas and the Gate. Work on 'Knots' must have continued through 1968, as it was completed early in 1969.

So all this, plus, obviously, his year in Ceylon, constitute merely another branch which, once again, is first visible at the beginning of stage 4. As to the question of roots, in this case we clearly have to look further back. There are indeed few occasions prior to 1964 on which Laing has exhibited religious knowledge, let alone experience: a rare example might be in 'The Divided Self', when he says, with astonishing foresight: 'the cracked mind of the schizophrenic may *let in* light which does not enter the intact minds of many sane people whose minds are closed. Ezekiel, in Jaspers opinion, was a schizophrenic' (p. 67).

That the roots *were* there, of course, we now know well, since Laing has spoken of his Presbyterian upbringing. How much this has affected what he feels and says, as well as how he says it, is, as he admits, impossible to gauge. I would imagine it to be considerable.

So, the image that I wish to convey of Laing's development involves a stepping-back, at stage 4, and a subsequent branching out of interest. It can perhaps best be illustrated diagrammatically as in Figure 1.

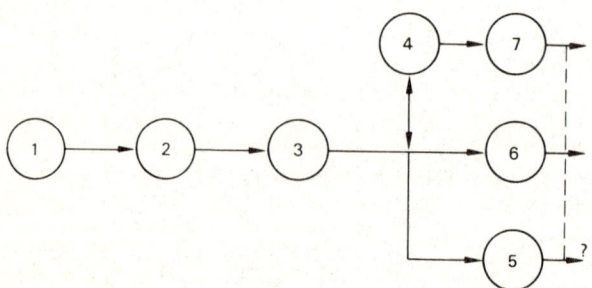

FIGURE 1

Up to stage 3 is, so to speak straightforward. Stage 4, set back from the main stream (1 - 6) of basically 'clinically' or 'psychiatric' writing, leads on to stage 7; but also, *via the main stream* (see 'The Obvious', p. 7), i.e. picking up again the Sartrean/ Marxist influence of stage 3, to stage 5. Connections between stages 5, 6 and 7, are shown dotted to indicate, on the one hand, that they are *not* mutually exclusive; and, on the other hand, have not been adequately synthesized by Laing (or, to my knowledge, by anybody else).

This brings us up to the present time. It is my opinion that
stages 5, 6 and 7 are all still 'open'; in a way that stage 2, for
example, is not. That stage 7, the quest for adequate ways to talk
about the 'spiritual realm', is still on-going is, I think, fairly
obvious. Nor are there signs that stage 6 is closed: for Laing is
still active in the Philadelphia Association. He conducts seminars,
visits the communities, and discusses plans for future communities.
He is, in a word, still committed to the question of therapy, and
theoretical bases for the same.

Whether stage 5, that of radicalism, is closed is really a matter
of opinion, according to what one is prepared to accept as counting
as political radicalism. That his personal politics are still Left-
Wing is hardly in doubt; the question is simply what is he doing
about it. If one takes the orthodox view of radicalism (so to
speak!) then it must be agreed, stage 5 is over for Laing. If, on
the other hand, one allows a more individualistic, liberal, perhaps
even utopian, notion of radicalism, then the question cannot be
fully answered, for want of information; but it is certainly possible that radicalism of this sort *is* continuing in Laing today.

So much, then, for the structure of Laing's career vis-à-vis
theoretical stages. It is time now to turn from this structure,
this chronological skeleton, to look again at the contents; the
flesh, so to speak, which our knowledge of the 'bone structure' on
which it hangs allows to grasp, not amorphously, but as an overdetermined totalization.

We will do this by considering, in relation to a field of unified temporality, two issues, which can be identified throughout
Laing's career.

First, in broad terms, we will look at the philosophical influences on Laing's career. The emphasis, however, will be as much on
what Laing does with them, as on what they have done to Laing, by
way of direct influence.

Second, we will examine, more specifically, the development of
Laing's notions of the nature of psychosis. This is a task of
synthesis and clarification; and a much needed one, in view of the
prevalence of misunderstanding on this issue.

In examining these two, almost polar, aspects - one broad, one
specific - we will discover, in both cases, that we are led back,
time and again, to the organizing theoretical principle of the
totality of Laing's work: Intelligibility. What follows, then,
will hopefully form some sort of basis for the last chapter, where
we attempt to branch out with this concept, into broader, sociological realms.

PHILOSOPHICAL INFLUENCES

Being and nonbeing is the central theme of all philosophy, East
and West. These words are not harmless and innocent verbal ara-
besques, except in the professional philosophism of decadence
(Laing, 1967a).

It is to the question of philosophical influences that we now turn.
At the outset (which is to say, in 'The Divided Self') there is

no doubt as to the predominant influence: existentialism. As Laing himself says:

> The reader versed in existential and phenomenological literature will quickly see that this study is not a direct application of any established existential philosophy. There are important points of divergence from the work of Kierkegaard, Jaspers, Heidegger, Sartre, Binswanger and Tillich, for instance. (With a list like that, there would have to be!)
>
> To discuss points of convergence and divergence in any detail would have taken me away from the immediate task. Such a discussion belongs to another place. It is to the existentialist tradition, however, that I acknowledge my main intellectual indebtedness (p. 10).

Of these sources, it appears that Kierkegaard and Heidegger have been the most influential. Unfortunately, I do not feel qualified to talk about Kierkegaard at any length; nevertheless, it is obvious that he had a deep impact on Laing, if only because of the repeated references to 'The Sickness unto Death' (Kierkegaard, 1946). This book Laing considers highly relevant to the issue of inauthenticity, of not being oneself. However, the same issue is also focused upon by Heidegger; and in view of the apparently more lasting and pervasive influence of Heidegger on Laing, it is his views on the matter that we shall be concerned with. For if Laing 'embodies' any philosophical position, it is that of Heidegger.

In *very* general terms, however, we may say that there is apparent in 'The Divided Self', and in all of Laing's career (except possibly stage 3) the influence of Kierkegaard's distaste for science: in particular, for attempts to impose natural scientific paradigms onto a consideration of the human scene. Although Laing never mentions it, one may suspect that Kierkegaard's 'Concluding Unscientific Postscript' (1941) was in some way influential. Indeed, to take a whole-hearted leap into philosophical speculation (if not 'speculative philosophy'), can we perhaps see in Laing's endeavour for 'a science of persons', some sort of synthesis between Kierkegaard's Romantic Existentialism and Hegel's Systematic Rationalism, expressed in and through Heidegger's Phenomenological Ontology?

Laing's relationship to Sartre, at this juncture, is of an altogether different order. Of the half-dozen or so references to Sartre in 'The Divided Self', all are references which invoke *example* not *principle*. His use of Sartre is much more superficial than his use of Heidegger. For instance he quotes and praises Sartre's discussion of Bad Faith; but because it describes, or points to, a particular phenomenon, not because it embodies a philosophical method or position to which Laing particularly adheres. The Sartrean distinction between the pour-soi and the en-soi (that is, the crux of 'Being and Nothingness') is referred to, admittedly, and Part 3 (of 'Being and Nothingness') Being-for-Others, is described as 'brilliant'. But as we have seen, Laing was not really able to employ these concepts fully at this stage: his use of the notion being-for-the-other does take him outside of the context of his own conceptualization.

In my opinion, Heidegger's 'Being and Time' (1962) is the most influential book, philosophically at any rate, for this stage; and indeed, for a very large part of Laing's career. It is not possible, unfortunately, to summarize this monumental work of genius in the present context; it is essential, however, to have some idea of its aims and achievements, to appreciate its immense importance for Laing.

Basically, it is an enquiry into the nature of Being; but as Heidegger notes at the outset:

> To work out the question of Being adequately, we must make an entity - the inquirer - transparent in his own Being. The very asking of this question is an entity's mode of 'Being'; and as such it gets its essential character from what is inquired about - namely, Being. This entity which each of us is himself and which includes inquiring as one of the possibilities of its Being, we shall denote by the term 'Dasein' (p. 27).

Dasein (which literally means 'being-there') is Heidegger's term for what we may roughly call personal being. The book thereafter falls into two divisions, an analysis of the nature of Dasein, and the analysis of Dasein's relation to temporality. I have neither found nor been able to formulate a more succinct summary of the book than that given by William Nicholls (1969) in his 'Systematic and Philosophical Theology'. Thus he says:

> In (Being and Time) man's existence (i.e. Dasein) is described as 'fallenness', 'being-towards-death'. The ground of his being is thus said to be anxiety (or dread). Man is pre-eminently a *historical* being, who achieves authentic existence only in the courageous resolve to accept his situation in the world and his coming death, and so is freed for life in the world with others (p. 171).

To expand for our immediate purposes: the fundamental structure of Dasein is being-in-the-world; and this resolves into Being-with, and Being-one's-self. Now, the importance of 'Being and Time', for 'The Divided Self', lies in these two features: first, the most important thing, (the 'fundamental structure') about a human being's existence (Dasein) is the nature of his being-in-the-world. That is to say, if we wish to grasp, or come to terms with, another human being (as psychiatrists do or rather should), we should look not only to his actions, his behaviour, but to the meaning of his being-in-the-world, to what it means for him to be here.

Second, this being-in-the-world resolves into being-with, and being-one's self: that is, to understand the former involves grasping the impact and relevance of other people's existence for him; and grasping the way in which a person is, or is not, himself.

It should already be obvious, I think, that it is precisely these issues that Laing is involved with in 'The Divided Self'. Did Laing not himself summarize the situation: 'Existential phenomenology attempts to... set all particular experiences with the context of (a person's) whole being-in-his-world' (p. 17). Throughout 'The Divided Self', we find Laing utilizing Heideggerian concepts and distinctions always with a view to understanding a person's being-in-the-world.

The theologian Francis MacNab has noted the influence of Heidegger on existential psychotherapy, and on Laing particularly. Thus he says:

> The existentialist influence in psychotherapy has been most pronounced in that form... known as 'existential analysis'....

Existential analysis, like phenomenology, attempts to appreciate and reconstruct the patient's inner world of experience; but it does so in a more comprehensive and distinctive manner, for in addition to representing a wide blend of phenomenology, existentialism, and psycho-analysis it adopts as its central framework the overall ontology of Martin Heidegger. It is thus distinguished from all other forms of existential psychotherapy (MacNab, 1965, p. 139).

Reviewing the situation of existentialist psychotherapy in Britain and the Commonwealth, he notes that 'published works in this field are limited virtually to those by R.D. Laing' (p. 130). Happily, this statement is no longer true; but we should remember that the influence of Laing in rendering it false has been immense.

Laing himself gave a lecture in 1960, entitled The Development of Existential Analysis in which he pointed out that existentialism is not the *whole* of psychotherapy; it is primarily a means of research. Unfortunately, the lecture was never published; we would undoubtedly know more about Laing's relation to Heidegger if it has been.

But to return to Heidegger: a large part of 'Being and Time' is concerned with the possibilities, for Dasein, of 'authenticity', or authentic being. So too, in 'The Divided Self', Laing deals repeatedly with this question, which appears as a dilemma, if not an insurmountable tragedy, for the schizoid or schizophrenic person.

Chapter Eight of 'The Divided Self', entitled The Case of Peter, brings out these points. Peter was a man who lacked a sense of authentic being:

> he was nobody 'really'.... He had felt all along that he was, in his own words (which incidentally are also Heidegger's) 'on the fringe of being', with only one foot in life and with no right even to that (p. 125).

Of course Laing draws heavily on the notion of ontological security here as well; this notion will be considered shortly, in relation to Tillich. But the above passage also brings into question the issue of Truth. What does it mean when Peter says he is nobody 'really'. The question of truth arises, indeed, throughout this book: for Laing is insistent that, as we are dealing with persons, not objects, we must employ a personal conception of truth rather than an objective scientific conception. *Adequatio intellectus et rei* is emphatically not sufficient. We must look to 'existential truth'.

Now this again is evidence for Heidegger's influence. 'Being and Time' involves a distinction between scientific truth and another sort, which Heidegger refers to by its Greek name aletheia; a distinction expanded upon greatly in his On the Essence of Truth (in 'Existence and Being', 1949). Now aletheia means in Greek, not-covered, or revealed. It in no way incorporates the notion of agreement, or consensus that is so integral in our usual sense of truth as *adequatio*. It is intimately linked with the concept of logos, which has a subtle meaning somewhere in between 'discourse' and 'manifestation'; perhaps 'revelation' sums it up best. Thus, the truth (aletheia) of the logos (revelation) lies precisely in its being-revealed, in its nakedness. It is this kind of truth that Laing refers to later, in 'The Politics of Experience' and elsewhere, as a 'self-validating datum'. But in 'The Divided Self', Laing merely talks about existential truth, and the understanding of it; but tells us little about how to grasp it. However, with a reading of Heidegger, we can begin to see what is involved. For Heidegger shows that 'disclosedness' is an aspect of Dasein's authentic possibility for being-in-the-world. Thus, inauthenticity, the plight of the schizoid person, involves a refusal of disclosedness, a denial of his personal truth.

The situation becomes clearer in 'The Self and Others', where Laing first makes explicit reference to aletheia. To quote:

> When one sees actions of the other in the light of this latter form of truth or falsehood (i.e. aletheia), one says that a man is truthful, or 'true to himself' when one 'feels' that he means what he says, or is saying what he means. That is to say, his words, or for that matter his other ways of expressing himself, are 'true' expressions of his 'real' experience or intentions ('The Self and Others', p. 120).

As far as I can see, this is nothing more than a rephrasing of Heidegger's assertions that Dasein's authenticity lies in its 'thrownness-towards-the-world', its 'disclosedness'. Thus:

> Being-true as Being-uncovering, is a way of Being for Dasein. What makes this very uncovering possible must necessarily be called 'true' in a still more primordial sense. The most primordial phenomenon of truth is first shown by the existential-ontological foundation of uncovering. Uncovering is a way of Being for Being-in-the-world.... To Dasein's state of Being, *disclosedness in general* essentially belongs.... To Dasein's state of Being belongs *thrownness*; indeed, it is constitutive for Dasein's disclosedness. (Heidegger, 1962, pp. 263-4).

To give Laing the final word on this: 'One of the central issues in an existential analysis of action is to what extent and in what ways the agent is *disclosed*... in and through his actions' (op.cit., p. 117, my emphasis).

The critical reader cannot have failed to notice the preponderance of words such as 'grasp', 'feel', 'Understand': all of which point to a highly intuitive, non-positivistic conception of knowledge. That this is both inevitable and, so far, non-rigorous, should be apparent. Heidegger, of course, is aware of this; more so than Laing appeared to be in 'The Divided Self', though by the time of 'The Self and Others' we do find a cry for 'the security and assurance of well-worked-out criteria of verifiability' (p. 13-14).

Heidegger's awareness of this can be gauged by his insistence on establishing the 'transparency' of the being that is inquiring into being; but he seems to have immobilized this dialectic. Indeed, the accusation of representing statically an innately dynamic field is one of the more frequent ones levelled against Heidegger. At any rate, Laing does not seem to have been impressed by Heidegger's attempts at elucidating the epistemology of Verstehen; and he has by and large abandoned Heidegger as a guiding light for his more rigorous scientific formulations.

But this is by no means to say that he has abandoned Heidegger altogether: for it will be recalled that we felt compelled to regard much of Laing's later writings, especially stage 4, as 'poetry'. And as Colin Wilson, in his 'Beyond the Outsider', has argued, we would be wise to regard Heidegger in much the same light. Much of Heidegger's writing, especially his later work, is virtually incomprehensible if viewed as 'philosophy', in the sense of systematic, rigorous logically consistent propositions; but comprehensible, illuminating, indeed beautiful, if viewed as 'poetry' in the broadest sense; i.e. as emotive, 'pointing-towards' language, rather than analytic-descriptive, representational language. This view, I would argue, is supported by the clear evidence for Heidegger's passionate interest in poetry, and especially the poetry of Hölderlin (who, incidentally, is referred to by Laing as one of the many artists who have 'shipwrecked on these reefs' of the Inner World. Whether his interest in Hölderlin is through Heidegger's writing or not is unknown). See, for example, his Hölderlin and the Essence of Poetry (in Heidegger, 1949).

What role, then, does Heidegger play after the period in which the theoretical pivot of Laing's work was the notion of being-in-the-world as it appears in 'Being and Time'. In stage 3, he plays no role at all. The only references to him occur in 'Reason and Violence', and there merely by virtue of Sartre's occasional comment on him.

The situation in stage 4 is entirely different. We may already suspect this, from the discussion above of Laing's and Heidegger's employment of 'poetic' techniques. But one fact alone should alert us to a renewed significance of Heidegger for Laing: his repeated quotation of Heidegger's phrase 'The Dreadful has already Happened.' (For the record: it appears at least seven times, viz. Laing, 1964c, f, 1965b, c, and d, and 1967a, b.)

Unfortunately, I have not been able to locate the exact source of this quotation. (Laing himself never even indicates which book it is from.) The situation is confounded by the problem which is perennial when dealing with Heidegger: translation. Heidegger makes extensive use, particularly in 'What is Metaphysics' (1949) and 'Being and Time' (1962), of the word 'Angst'. This word has been variously translated as Anxiety, Uneasiness, Dread - or simply left untranslated. My interpretation of the quote rests on the assumption, therefore, that 'Dreadful' is a translation of an adjective derived from Angst.

What does Heidegger mean by Anxiety? By a remarkable display of etymological juggling, he extracts the meaning of 'not-at-home-in-the-world-ness'. Dasein's mode of being, we have seen, is being-in-the-world. But in-so-far as Dasein is not the world in which it is in, there is involved a 'fallingness' of Dasein into the world. Dasein 'flees', therefore, in the face of itself, into the world. It is in this falling-into-the-world that Dasein comes across, phenomenally, the state of mind of Anxiety - that is, of 'not-at-home-in-the-world-ness', or 'uncanniness'.

But it is not possible, Heidegger continues, to specify what it is that one is anxious of, in particular terms. On the contrary, it is generality itself which is the source of anxiety. In his own words:

> That in the face of which one has anxiety is characterized by the fact that what threatens is *nowhere*.... The obstinacy of the 'nothing and nowhere within-the-world' means as a phenomenon that the *world as such is that in the face of which one has*

> *anxiety*.... What oppresses us is the *possibility* of the ready-to-hand in general; that is to say, the world itself. When anxiety has subsided... we are accustomed to say that 'it was really nothing'.... *Being-in-the-world itself is that in the face of which anxiety is anxious* ('Being and Time', pp. 231-2, emphasis in original).

To summarize: Dasein (Human Being) does not feel at home in the world; not because of any specific threat, but precisely because of the 'nothingness' of the world. This comes about ontologically, through Dasein's fallingness into the world. But, it is precisely in this falling into the world that Dasein is fleeing from its own nothingness. In falling into the world, Dasein is seeking familiarity, reassurance, 'everydayness' as Heidegger puts it. In a word, Dasein is plagued by nothingness: the nothingness of the world, and the nothingness of its own core.

This, incidentally, is what I take to be - certainly how I experience - the meaning of Laing's statement ('Politics of Experience', p. 33) 'There's nothing to be afraid of. The ultimate reassurance and the ultimate terror.'

Now, the above quote comes from one of the most powerful sections of 'Politics of Experience': chapter one, part VI, the Experience of Negation. Philosophically, this is the crux of the book. For the politics of experience are, quite simply, who negates whose experience? When we look, then, to what is *positively* experienced, what is it but: the experience of negation?

The influence of Heidegger is highly pervasive here. When Laing writes 'Being and Non-being is the central theme of all philosophy, East and West,' he is really giving us *the* central theme of the first thirty odd introductory pages of 'Being and Time' and thus its raison d'être. His method of treating this central theme, however, does not coincide directly with Heidegger's: it is nearer, I think, to Hegel's. But more of that later.

To return to the quotation concerning the Dreadful: the most expanded reference to this by Laing is to be found in Practice and Theory: The Present Situation (Laing, 1965b). It will be necessary to quote at length:

> Experience is not 'subjective' rather than 'objective', not 'inner' rather than 'outer'.... Least of all is experience 'intrapsychic process'. Such transactions, object-relations, interpersonal relations, transference, counter-transference, that we suppose go on are not the interplay merely of two objects in space, each with his or her ongoing intra-psychic processes. But if we do not know this already, how can we realise it?
>
> I suggest the reason for this confusion lies in the meaning of Heidegger's phrase, *the Dreadful has already happened*.
>
> We psychotherapists are specialists, as they say, in human relations. But the Dreadful has already happened. It has happened to us as well as to our patients. We, the therapists, are in a world in which the inner is already split from the outer, and before the inner can become outer, and the outer become inner, we have to re-discover our 'inner' world. As a whole generation of men, we are so estranged from the inner world that there are many arguing that it does not exist.... When the Dreadful has already happened, we can hardly expect other than that the Thing will

echo externally the destruction already wrought internally (pp. 64-5).

The Dreadful has happened, to all of us. That is, referring back to our account of Anxiety, the ground of our inner being is Anxiety: because the inner world is split from the outer, and denied. Dasein thus finds itself a stranger in an (even stranger) world. Not-at-home-in-the-world-ness. The Thing, (i.e. the Being of the World, its 'Worldhood', as Heidegger puts it) 'echoes' externally our inner devastation.

I think we may summarize Laing's achievement here by saying that he is synthesizing numerous accounts, originally presented from a host of different intellectual traditions, of what is basically a single phenomenon: the nature of being human in the world. More specifically, he is bringing together a historical, political notion of alienation, with a philosophical account of human ontology, the dynamics of the process being described in psycho-analytic terms (splitting denial, and so on). Finally, he establishes a dialectic between this, and religious expression, such that both moments are illuminated and illuminating. For example, his citation of the Gospel according to St Thomas both takes from, and gives to, the account of the human situation, an added significance:

Jesus said to them:
When you make the two one, and
When you make the inner as the outer,
and the outer as the inner
and the above as the below...
then shall you enter the Kingdom (quoted in 'Politics of Experience', p. 140).

So what are we to make of Laing's relationship to Heidegger?

In his early works, he adopted, through his espousal of existential analysis, the Heideggerian ontology as a means of conceptualizing human Being. Later, he found this inadequate; specifically, on account of its inability to account for the interactional/intersubjective aspects of human reality. Later still, however, with his awareness of our historically conditional state of alienation as a denial of interaction and intersubjectivity, he again had recourse to Heidegger: not as a rigorous system, but as a powerful form of expression of this state. One might say, the Dreadful has already happened, even in Heidegger's philosophy. The truth of the being of Heidegger's philosophy is its expression of the denial of Being. Its untruth lies in the impression it gives that authentic being is possible - just like that. The reason why 'Politics of Experience' is not *purely* Heideggerian is the meaning of this lie: that authentic being is a *political* problem.

In fact, a political consideration of Heidegger can be very illuminating. (That is, of Heidegger's *writing;* I am not referring to Heidegger's personal involvement, if it was such, with Nazism.)

Authentic being, which is for Heidegger, the summum bonum, the moral goal, is conceived as possible under certain conditions. We must examine these conditions politically. They are basically twofold, one general, and one more specific.

Generally, authentic being is only possible if man makes a decision: to accept the nature of his being-in-the-world. It requires the courage to accept the groundlessness of his being (anxiety).

The most important particular instance of this being is man's being-towards-death. Authentic being requires the acceptance of the inevitability of one's own death.

Now this does appear somewhat fatalistic, if not downright reactionary. Yet, it is undeniable, as Laing shows in the 'Politics of Experience', that we *are*, in actual fact, confronted with a terrifying groundlessness, the void, nothingness, the Pit, the Absurd, (and so on through all the myriad cultural manifestations of this one primal phenomenon). It is equally undeniable that we are all going to die.

What Laing has done, then, is to put this in a historico-political context, and thus inevitably also a religious context; and has shown that this inner devastation, whilst currently 'true', is by no means humanly essential. And, of course, the awareness that this is a historically contingent state points to that which Heidegger never could (at least not explicitly): the objective political need for revolutionary praxis; the imperative to *do something* about the world, inner *and* outer; to be mother, father, child and even midwife in the birth of the (Guevarist?) New Man.

At this point, we may see some of the philosophical background to what I consider to be Laing's major 'psychiatric' discovery (though this word needs qualification): the paradigm of death-rebirth.

Laing does not discuss Heidegger's concept of being-towards-death. Nevertheless, in the context, it is an interesting one. Let us remember, its acceptance, ontologically, was regarded by Heidegger as a prerequisite for authentic being.

Laing, I would say, goes further than this: he insists that we must not merely live towards death; *we must die and go through death*. Laing, of course, is talking of existential death; it seems strange that Heidegger should perceive this being-towards-death so acutely in its importance, and then still identify existential death with biological death. Here, of course, we can understand the rigidity, the tension, of Heidegger's writing: he is thrown towards death, but cannot welcome death with open arms and go through it, as he thinks it is biological death. Hence he must remain poised over death.

For Laing the situation is much more fluid. For he knows that life, authentic being, is on the other side of death. But he also knows of the vast interlinking system of levels, sub-levels, meta-levels. And through this knowledge we can see, I think, that the death-rebirth paradigm has a multilevel applicability. We have the death and rebirth of the individual (which, of course, splits up, or rather, breaks *down*, to its phenomenal appearance in a multitide of experiential realms: the Christ archetype, in the 'spiritual' realm, the death wish in the phantasy realm, and so on).

But paradigmatically, we have the same phenomenon at an institutional level: an institution approaches a critical point; its infrastructure is unable to cope with the context in which the institution as a whole has to operate; inefficiency, decadence, chaos, replace the internal/external order; the entropy level exceeds that compatible with institutional 'life', and the institution 'dies'. But order proceeds again out of chaos, and a new institution is born. (See, for example Cooper's 'Death of the Family'.)

The same process can be imagined to operate on even broader, cultural levels.

Of course, we should bear in mind that these are merely analogies: no one is suggesting that an institution has a 'life' apart from the real concrete lives of those that comprise the institution. Nor is it even to suggest that such an analogy can or should take the place of a concrete dialectical study of the institution in its own terms. It is to insist, however, that by showing (a) the heuristic, analogic, metaphorical, multilevel applicability of this paradigm, and (b) the multilevel interaction, the 'structuration' of the total social whole, we may perhaps come to perceive the nature of the problem of authentic being. For it is a problem which has ramifications on *all* levels of the total social system: as such, it *must* be of concern to sociologists, as well as existential psychiatrists, be they physicians or metaphysicians. The relevant questions, here, for the sociologist would be situated by the limits posed by: what sorts of institutional structures are conducive to authentic being? and: what are the conditions for the possibility for the emergence of such institutions? However, these questions are taking us away from our immediate concern: the question of Laing's philosophical influences.

We shall turn now from Heidegger to a brief consideration of Paul Tillich.

The crux of Tillich's theology is that of the New Being in Jesus the Christ. But what does Tillich mean by Being? For Tillich, God is identified with being-itself, 'the ground of being'. Being is that which resists non-being or nothingness.

In his 'Courage to Be' (1952), Tillich talks of anxiety, in a way which recalls Heidegger's use of the term, but differs fundamentally in the role it plays in his philosophy. Tillich distinguishes three forms of anxiety: the anxiety of fate and death, the anxiety of guilt, and the anxiety of meaninglessness. This three-fold anxiety is viewed, by Tillich, as no mere neurotic superficiality: it stems from the very nature of human being, which is perched, so to speak, 'on the boundary' of being and non-being. Faith is the answer to anxiety for Tillich: faith being found through contact with the being-in-itself (i.e. God) which lies 'behind' all merely phenomenal manifestations of finite being, including one's own individual being.

If one ignores the highly dubious Kantian implications of this position, then it would seem that Tillich's position boils down to this, empirically speaking: anxiety occurs in the state of ontological insecurity, faith occurs in the state of ontological security. Laing in the 'Divided Self', by linking ontological security to empirical contingencies rather than a priori human conditions, immediately casts doubts on the validity of Tillich's position.

Nicholls (1969) has commented that 'the Gospel for Tillich is concerned with what R.D. Laing has called "ontological insecurity"' (p. 236), but he does not note this contradiction: that Laing is talking empirically (in 'The Divided Self') whereas Tillich is talking philosophically, and a priori. It is a condition of Tillich's position, I imagine, that all men have 'ontological security' in the sense of a grounded Being, i.e. God is within all men. Can this be said of Laing's use of the term? I do not think so. Yet many people (Nicholls is by no means alone in this) continue to identify Tillich and Laing in this respect. (There is even a tendency amongst 'avant garde' Christians to call on Laing for empirical support for their philosophical positions!)

I suspect that Laing himself was aware of the *danger* of this confusion; and that his awareness was expressed in the footnote which occurs under the first reference to ontological security ('The Divided Self', p. 39). '*Despite* the philosophical use of "ontology" (by Heidegger, Sartre, Tillich, especially), I have used the term in its *present empirical sense* because it appears to be the best adverbial or adjectival derivative of "being",' (my emphasis). Tillich himself, of course, goes to pains to *deny* empirical connotations to his ontology.

The situation is, if anything, further confounded by Laing's comments in 'The Self and Others':

Although man is always poised between being and non-being, non-being is not necessarily encountered as *personal* disintegration. The insecurity attendant upon a precariously established personal unity is *one* form of ontological insecurity, if this term is used in its philosophical sense: that is, to denote the insecurity inescapably within the heart of man's finite being.

Tillich (1952) speaks of the possibilities of non-being in three directions... (of meaninglessness, guilt, and death).... The ontological insecurity described in 'The Divided Self' is a fourth possibility. Here, man, as a person, encounters non-being, in a preliminary form, as partial loss of the synthetic unity of self, concurrently with partial loss of relatedness with the other, and in an ultimate form, in the hypothetical end-state of chaotic non-entity, and total loss of relatedness with the other (pp. 35-6).

Let us try to see what is going on here. Laing is taking as the starting point the *philosophical* sense of the term ontological insecurity; which appears to be a generalized description of a universal human state. The ontological insecurity of 'The Divided Self', then, is merely an (empirical) phenomenal manifestation of this basic state. The insecurities described by Tillich are likewise alternative manifestations.

However, there is more involved here than a move from empirical particular to philosophical universal. For if it is the case that there is an 'insecurity *inescapably* within the heart of man's finite being', then it follows that the empirical *experience* of ontological insecurity *is a valid experience*. Equally, that the 'normal' experience, of ontological *security*, is an illusion. The similarity of this implication with the explicit position of 'The Politics of Experience' should be apparent without quoting chater and verse. But this implication remains *latent* in 'The Self and Others'; it is, I feel, both present but hidden in the concluding remark to the chapter from which the above quote comes: 'Not all who would, can be psychotic.'

But what of the implications of this vis-à-vis Tillich? Laing is much nearer to the basically 'pessimistic' existentialist than the optimistic Christian. For Tillich, anxiety and insecurity are *not* the ultimate depths - by virtue of man's capability for 'ecstatic reason', through which God-as-being-itself is revealed. Tillich shows that being-itself is not a particular finite being: the inclusion of the word 'finite' in 'within the heart of man's finite being' thus enables one to argue that Laing is adopting Tillich's position; insecurity is at the heart of man's *finite* being, one may argue, but

God, as being-itself, is the ground of all finite beings, and is thus beyond even this primal insecurity.

Such an argument is logically feasible. I do not believe, however, that it is one to which Laing adheres. For he gives no positive evidence of holding such a view. On the contrary, all the impressions given are that he regards insecurity, of being vis-à-vis non-being, as ultimate. And this view is surely supported, on the occasion of Laing's return to metaphysics, as when he says: 'We are afraid to approach the fathomless and bottomless groundlessness of everything' (1967a, p. 33).

I conclude, then, that Laing adopts a basically *negative* position towards Tillich: certain elements of Tillich's position carry over to Laing's; but the fundamental assertion is negated in the transformation.

We are now confronted with the elusive task of considering Laing's relation to Hegel.

Hegel has been the object of a considerable revival of interest in the last decade or so; the reasons for this revival itself would make a fascinating subject for study; but this cannot be undertaken here. It is remarkable, however, in view of Hegel's return to intellectual grace in the 1960s, that Laing should have been quoting him at length in 1957 (i.e. in 'The Divided Self'). Perhaps this merely boils down to Laing's awareness of continental philosophy, and the grossly retarded nature of British philosophy in relation to it.

At any rate, Hegel is quoted in 'The Divided Self': specifically, the discussion of the Act, from 'Phenomenology of Mind' (which is, in fact, the only book by Hegel that Laing does ever quote). His use of this passage is purely illustrative, however; there is no question of Laing employing the Hegelian system, either in its totality, or in its method (i.e. the use of dialectical triads). Indeed, we have already criticized 'The Divided Self' for its undialectical nature.

Hegel is again quoted in 'The Self and Others' - and again, merely illustratively. I have argued already, however, that there is a noticeable degree of general Hegelian influence here. This is undoubtedly so, if only by virtue of its intrinsically more dialectically nature. When viewed in a total context, however, it seems that the influence of Hegel is not so much direct, as via Martin Buber and Feuerbach.

Feuerbach is generally credited with establishing the distinction between the I-It relationship and the I-Thou relationship. (Why this is so, I am not quite sure. The distinction *can* be found in Hegel; but it was not relevant to his purposes to pursue it. It would be fairer to say that it was Feuerbach who appreciated the *relevance* of the distinction: which is to say he appreciated the relevance of materialism.)

This distinction is clearly of considerable importance to Laing; and indeed he pays tribute to Feuerbach in respect of it ('Interpersonal Perception', p. 4). In the same place, Buber is again mentioned as developing Feuerbach's insight. And in 'The Self and Others', it is Buber who is quoted at length on the crucial topic of confirmation (p. 88).

In stage 3, the Hegelian influence again is present but indirect:

this time via the Marxism of Sartre. Clearly, it is beyond the
scope of the present discussion to explore the fate of Hegel in the
inversions, coquettings, ruptures, not to mention ideological back-
trackings, of Marx and Sartre. We must note, however, that Sartre
makes absolutely central use of an insight of Hegel: that the
'world is a unity of the given and the constructed' (Hegel).
Sartre expresses this in his use of the terms 'field' and 'project',
and 'practico-inert'; it forms the basic insight of any phenomenological Marxism. (It is the same insight, incidentally, that is at
the heart of the crucial chapter Seven of 'Capital', vol. 1, on the
Labour Process.)

In stage 4, Laing himself begins to quote the above-emntioned
phrase of Hegel; as he still does in 'Politics of the Family'. In
fact, I would say it is still today an issue for Laing. For does he
not attempt to dissect this very unity, in his Reflections on Meditation (1973), when he says the problem is that of cultivating 'a
practice in which one simply looks at things as they are, without
presuppositions, or applications, or constructions.'

But to return to stage 4: it does not *embody* a Hegelian position;
as we have already established, philosophical positions are *used*,
not *embodied* in stage 4. But, granted that stage 4 is dialectical,
and also that it invokes idealism and metaphysics, it should come as
no surprise that a 'Hegelian reading' of 'The Politics of Experience' is a ready possibility. The most obvious example of such a
reading, I suppose, would be a consideration of the devious route
trailed by Being and Non-Being in 'The Politics of Experience', in
relation to Hegel's famous account of their relation in 'The Science
of Logic'.

A more interesting example, however, concerns the Family. Laing
never mentions Hegel in direct reference to the Family: yet consider
the account of the Family offered in 'The Politics of Experience' -
and indeed, the thread of discussion on the Family that runs from
Series and Nexus to 'The Politics of the Family' - in the light of
the following quote from Hegel.

> the *ethical* relation between the members of the family is not
> that of sentiment or the relationship of love. The ethical ele-
> ment in this case seems bound to be placed in the relation of the
> individual member of the family to the *entire* family as the real
> substance, so that the purpose of his action and the content of
> his actuality are... derived solely from the family life. *But*
> the conscious purpose which dominates the action of this whole...
> is itself the individual member (Hegel, 1949, pp. 468-9; emphasis
> in original).

Notice here: (a) the denial of the bourgeois myth of sentiment or
love as the 'ethical' element of family unification; (b) the notion
that Sartre generalized to apply to all groups, and which Laing re-
applies to the family, that (in Sartre's words) 'each and every person is produced and defined on the basis of this non-existent totality' (i.e. the 'Family'); (c) the denial of the reality of the
group action apart from the praxis ('conscious purpose') of the individual.

It is perhaps significant that Laing should have directly used
Hegel to sum up his own summing up of the Dialectics of Liberation
Conference (D.L. 13). In his own words:

There is, in the classical sense of Marx and Hegel, a 'Dialectic of Liberation'. It would take a long time to tell the whole story of dialectic, but Hegel had one famous example: the dialectic in relation to the Master and the Slave (Hegel, 1949, pp. 234-240). He pointed out that the more the master enslaves his slaves, in other words, the more he gets his slaves to do everything for him, the more he becomes himself helpless, until the slave wakes up one day and realises that *he* is the master, because the master has put himself in his power.

So today, Laing argues, this dialectic is active: the exploited people around the world are *beginning to realize* that they already have the power; they merely need the 'organizational means' whereby to use it. But the crucial moment is the realization.

This view, which seems to locate 'the problem' and its solution fairly and squarely in the realms of consciousness, is typically Hegelian: and typically Laingian. It certainly ties in with his view of activism propounded earlier; that, for us in the First World especially, the task is to see through the mystifying web, and that once we have done that, the battle is over, we simply 'dismantle' such institutions as the Police, the Army, and so on. Typically Hegelian, typically Laingian, typically idealist. Its convergence with his 'mysticism', reality as a maya-like web of illusion, is also apparent.

These convergences come out most strongly in the litte-known article The Terror of Security and the Security of Terror (Laing, 1967h). Its form is familiar to us now: it is that of 'Knots'. What appears somewhat strange is that it concerns not individuals but whole races: White and Yellow. (The context shows that these can be nationally identified as the USA and China.)

The knot concerns 'being afraid', starting from the point 'White is afraid of Yellow, and Yellow is afraid of White'. Laing moves on through a deductive dialectic (i.e. a *Hegelian* one) to the following point, which he says, 'requires sustained meditation upon':

White is terrified
not to be terrified of Yellow
and is terrified that
Yellow will *not* be terrified of White.
Yellow is terrified
not to be terrified of White
and is terrified that
White will *not* be terrified of Yellow

The first step seems paradoxically an increasing of terror. Each has to become terrified of terror, instead of being terrified of *not* being terrified, and of *not* terrorising. The problem therefore is: how can two parties... become... not terrified that each and other not be terrified.

The above was published the same month as the Dialectics Conference took place: it is scarcely surprising that Laing and Stokely Carmichael had such violent disagreements (which were apparently contributory to Laing's backing down from active radicalism).

Still on the subject of Hegelian radicalism, to coin a phrase to describe Laing's position; it is perhaps not too far-fetched to see in Laing's total orientation towards producing a conceptual synthesis, a mental picture-'of what the whole thing is like' (Laing,

1968b), the influence of Hegel's logical mountaineering in pursuit
of the Absolute. To identify the projects of Laing and Hegel would
be unfair; but in terms of influence, I think Hegel is undeniably
as strong in stage 5 as anywhere else in Laing's work, if not more
so. And of course, to the extent that stage 5 and stage 7 both
overlap and continue today, we must conclude that Laing is *still*
Hegelian. (He apparently still conducts the Philadelphia Association's study seminar on 'The Phenomenology of Mind'.) This remark
should, however, be qualified, with the comment that an exact measure of that extent is impossible for lack of information.

It is interesting that at this period Laing should show interest
in a notoriously 'Hegelian' Marxist: Marcuse. Laing's first reference to Marcuse occurs as early as 1964. In the Preface to the Penguin edition of 'The Divided Self', Laing invokes Marcuse's 'Eros
and Civilization', and refers the reader to his 'One-Dimensional
Man' (Marcuse, 1955; 1964). Thus he says:

Our civilization represses not only 'the instincts', not only
sexuality, but any form of transcendence. Among one-dimensional
men... it is not surprising that someone with an insistent experience of other dimensions... runs the risk of... being destroyed
(p. 11).

In the Introduction to 'The Politics of Experience', Laing makes
the following bizarre statement: 'It may be that dialectical theory
finds its present truth in its own hopelessness. See Herbert Marcuse, "One-Dimensional Man". This is not my view'(p. 11).

This would appear to be a reference to the extremely pessimistic
concluding chapter in 'One-Dimensional Man', where Marcuse says:

To be sure, the dialectical concept, in comprehending the given
facts, transcends the given facts. This is the very token of
its truth. It defines the historical possibilities, even neces-
sities; but their realization can only be in the practice which
responds to the theory, and at present, the practice give no
such response. On theoretical as well as empirical grounds, the
dialectical concept pronounces its own hopelessness.... No matter
how *obvious the irrational character of the whole* (cf. Laing's
'the Obvious'!) may manifest itself, and with it, the necessity
of change, insight into necessity has never sufficed for seizing
the possible alternatives (p. 198; my emphasis).

The relation between Laing and Marcuse is complex here. In 1964,
Marcuse saw 'no such response' in political practice to the theoretical awareness available through dialectic. As is well known, he
has since revised this pessimism. Laing, God knows, is pessimistic
in his descriptions of reality; yet, for apparently irrational reasons, he appears to believe there is some hope for the future. To
further complicate the issue, it is Marcuse who stresses that awareness is not a *substitute* for action; whereas, as we have seen, Laing
appears to move exactly in the direction of that substitution. Nor
should we forget that Marcuse was present at the Dialectics Conference, at which Laing propounded these views. There is possibly significant absence of any mention of Marcuse in Laing's writings
thereafter.

Laing's relationship to other figures of the New Left are even
more tenuous. Franz Fanon (1965) is referred to on various occasions (Laing, 1966a, 1967a, f), though in a way which strikes me

almost as voyeuristic. Speaking at the Dialectics Conference, he invoked Fanon, Mao, Ché Guevara, and Regis Debray as being those that epitomized the current theoretical 'orientation'. The necessity for 'hard core' political action implied by these writers (who significantly, are all active revolutionaries) was not, apparently, commented on by Laing. Yet Stokely Carmichael kept on chanting: 'What *have* you done? What have *you* done? What have you DONE?.... (D.L. 14).

We began this inquiry into Laing's philosophical roots by looking briefly at this relation to existentialism. We will end it by returning there (it was, after all, his 'main intellectual debt'); but to focus on a different aspect: the question of the meaning of human existence.

We shall approach this somewhat formidable topic by way of an opposition between two existential philosophers: Sartre and Merleau-Ponty. (Specifically, the pre-'Critique' Sartre.)

Spiegelberg, in his history of the phenomenological movement (1960) considers that the fundamental difference between Sartre and Merleau-Ponty resides in their views on the nature of 'meaningfulness', or 'sense' ('sens') vis-à-vis the human world. For Merleau-Ponty, sense and non-sense (which conveys absence of sense, rather than anti-sense) are a matter of degree:

> One cannot say that everything has sense or that nothing has sense, but only that there is sense.... *A truth against the background of absurdity,* an absurdity which the teleology of consciousness presumes to be able to convert into truth, *this is the primary phenomenon* (Merleau-Ponty, 1945, p. 324, quoted by Spiegelberg; my emphasis).

His desire for rationality recalls the writing of Foucault (1967); as when he talks of 'a new idea of reason, which does not forget the experience of unreason'.

Merleau-Ponty finds reason already in the world: because the world is, for him, (unlike Sartre) intersubjective; and because of the 'primacy of perception'. By the latter term is implied, among other things, that the 'matter' of perception - that is, the objects not yet unified, or synthesized by the act of their being perceived - are nevertheless already 'pregnant' with form and *thus with meaning.*

His use of the former term, intersubjectivity, derives largely from Husserl; at least, he says it does; several commentators (Spiegelberg, 1960; Wilson, 1965) have remarked on his disarming habit of using almost exclusively unpublished sources of Husserl; many of the most decisive and controversial 'quotes' have never been found in Husserl by anyone but Merleau-Ponty.

Already we can see strong divergences from Sartre: Merleau-Ponty could never agree to the doctrine of a meaningless being-in-itself, who can 'invent' meaning, by virtue of free choice. This divergence re-appears at a higher level when one considers history and dialectics. (Merleau-Ponty's criticisms of Sartre may have been influential in his production of the 'Critique', which renders most of the criticism redundant.)

For (early) Sartre, self and other are irreconcilable: 'Hell is Other People' ('Huis Clos'). The dialectic of history, then, is stuck at a presynthetic level, in the dualism of Cartesian subjectivity and meaningless objectivity (i.e. the pour-soi and the en-soi: their synthesis is stated to be impossible, logically, and to be identified with God, historically/mythically).

Merleau-Ponty, on the other hand, sees in history the very *affirmation* of the synthesis that Sartre denied. 'History is Other People' ('Primacy of Perception', 1964). The unity of pour-soi and en-soi, so far from being impossible, is for him ubiquitous: it is the very ontological structure of human existence: being-within-the-(intersubjective)-world.

What does all this mean for our appreciation of Laing?

I should like to argue that Sartre and Merleau-Ponty represent philosophically refined descriptions of two poles of feeling, or intuition, concerning being-human-in-the-world, that Laing appears to oscillate between, that can most simply be alluded to by the words 'pessimism' and 'optimism' respectively.

Consider, for example, some passages from 'The Politics of Experience'. In an abysmally pessimistic passage (chapter One, section VI) Laing writes:

> If there are no meanings, no values, no source of sustenance or help, then man, as creator, must invent, conjure up meanings and values... out of nothing.... The fate that awaits the creator, after being ignored, neglected, despised, is... to be discovered by the non-creative (p. 37).

This recalls Sartre (and Nietzsche, Beckett and many more) but would be quite foreign to Merleau-Ponty.

Yet just over the page, we find a passage that invokes, if anything does, the 'Mystery of Reason' (Merleau-Ponty); and, moreover, is potentially optimistic.

> From the point of view of a man alienated from his source, creation arises from despair and ends in failure. But such a man has not trodden the path to the end of time, the end of space, the end of darkness, and the end of light. He does not know that where it all ends, there it all begins (p. 38).

In Sartre's 'truncated dialectic', of 'Self and Other', we find a subjectivity, and an objectivity: and thus, a non-meeting. Sartre has described, brilliantly and accurately, the mass non-meeting which, in actual social life, constitutes human interaction - at least, as Laing portrays it in 'The Politics of Experience'. (See especially chapter Two.) But whilst this is in immediate historical terms the Truth, in potential transcendental terms it is a Lie, a denial of human Being. To oversimplify, then, I would say that Laing *uses* Sartre to point to what *is* the case (alienation, mutual estrangement, etc.); and uses Merleau-Ponty to point to what *could be* (and ought to be) the case.

For example, in chapter One, section IV Laing discusses Phantasy. Phantasy is part, we are told, of the 'sense' implicit in *every* action. (After the word 'sense' in this passage, Laing puts a note: '"le sens": Merleau Ponty'.) Thus, Laing is asserting, with Merleau-Ponty, that *all our actions are already and implicitly meaningful*. Where Laing makes an advance, however, is to point out that this meaning resides partly, *and sometimes entirely* in the experiential realm of phantasy: *and*, we are frequently 'unconscious' of this mode of experience (and therefore of the meaningful nature of our actions and existence). Finally, he insists that this need not be so; it is in no way necessary that we be split from our own phantasy, experientially.

Laing clearly has a high regard for Merleau-Ponty, despite the extreme rarity of explicit references. Indeed, he went so far as to hold him up as one of five people in whom 'truly contemporary experience and thought begin' (Laing, 1966a) - along with Artaud, Grass, Fanon and Marcuse. It is not exactly clear what he means by this; or on what criteria Merleau-Ponty is included. But it is my guess - informed, I hope - that it is because of the sorts of considerations discussed here. Merleau-Ponty finds meaning and reason in the world: but his is not a naive optimism; it is a reason, as we said, that 'does not forget the experience of unreason'. Is it too much to see in this 'Mystery of Reason', this journey from naive reason into unreason, and then back to a new reason, merely a description in different terms, of another sort of Journey?; one whose paradigmatic elucidation we associate with Laing?

If this is true, then I find Laing's description of Merleau-Ponty as 'truly contemporary experience and thought' one of the most *positive* aspects of 'The Politics of Experience'; for it is not a book overburdened by optimism.

We must finally return to Sartre. As we have said, the pre-'Critique' Sartre is used by Laing primarily to illustrate: he never uses Sartre's systematic position. (The nearest he comes to it, as may be expected, is in 'The Self and Others'. But even here, the fact that Sartre's dialectic was indeed so 'truncated', limits his applicability in a book which is pregnant with dialectic. This prenatal dialectic was seen to be manifest more through Hegelian/Feuerbachian influences.)

The influence of Sartre's 'Critique' has, of course, already been examined in detail. In summary, it was seen to be directly influential in stage 3; somewhat reflectedly so in stage 4; ideologically so in stage 5 (though by no means the only ideological influence) as well as theoretically so. In stage 7, there is virtually no trace whatever of Sartrean influence. We must say a few more words about stage 6, however; and this will lead us on to consider one particular theme, which derives from the 'critique', which cannot be identified with any single stage, but rather runs through several of them.

In *very* general terms, we can think of stage 6 as a 'marriage' between Sartrean existential-phenomenological Marxism, and a sort of psycho-analytic structuralism. As we noted earlier, this marriage is something of an intellectual achievement; a priori, one would have expected it to be somewhat unstable (or biased very strongly to one side or the other).

We noticed that the *internal* development *within* stage 6 appeared to indicate a marginal decrease of overt Sartrean Marxist influence, and a relative increase in structuralist tendencies. (This is reflected, incidentally, in stage 7: the form of 'Knots', and other similar sources (1967g and h, for example) indicate an increase of interest in formal conceptual topology, and a decrease of interest in the phenomenological analysis of concrete situations, clinical or otherwise.)

It is not possible, in the case of Laing, to assess the degree of success in holding the marriage together. This is simply because

Laing has not published enough clinical material recently to make the assessment particularly meaningful.

What we can say, however, is that (the ex-Kingsley Hall) Dr Schatzman's book 'Soul Murder', is most certainly successful in these terms - brilliantly so, in fact (Schatzman, 1973). Nor is it coincidence that Schatzman draws heavily on the work of Lacan; for if this 'marriage' is to work, it must surely be via Lacan, who is himself structuralist, Marxist, and psycho-analytic. (See Wilden, 1968, Althusser, 1971; Laing and Cooper, 1971.)

In conclusion, then, I see no reason to expect, still less to find already, a rejection of the basic concepts from Sartre's 'Critique'. What *will* have to happen, I am sure, is that Sartre's relation to psycho-analysis especially, and also to structuralism, will have to be reconsidered in detail. Sartre's own statements on the former, which date from 1953 (and are now to be found, curiously, in 'Being and Nothingness', 1958) are bizarre to say the least, and hardly satisfactory. But let it be re-affirmed that the 'Critique' is still considered to be the *theoretical* crux of the philosophical influences on Laing: which is to say that dialectical intelligibility is the central issue for Laing, and doubly so for us; that is, ontologically *and* epistemologically.

In leaving 'philosophical influences', we promised to consider one final theme from the 'Critique': it can perhaps best be referred to as the 'Them-versus-Us Game'.

The focal concept in this theme is what Sartre refers to as a 'bonded group': which is a nexus in Laing's terms. Laing has outlined, in *very* brief terms, the formation, or at least, the constitution, of a nexus, in the Series and Nexus article (Laing, 1962), and in greater depth in Individual and Family Structure (Laing, 1966b). The first instance of this Them-and-Us Game, then, occurs when Laing identifies 'Us' as 'The Family', and 'Them' as the outside world. Thus he says:

> The condition of permanence of such a nexus (i.e. the nexual family)... is the successful re-invention of whatever gives interiorisation its raison d'être. If there is no external danger, then danger and terror have to be invented and maintained.... Some families we have studied live in perpetual anxiety of what, to them, is an external persecuting world.... The 'protection' that the family offers its members seems to be based on several preconditions: (i) a phantasy of the external world as extraordinarily dangerous; (ii) the generation of terror inside the nexus at this external danger.... The stability of the nexus is the product of terror generated in its members by the violence done by the members of the group on each other (1962, p. 12).

Sartre used the example of a group storming the Bastille, Laing uses the family as his example. But the underlying dynamics are the same: group solidifcation as unification in the face of external danger, such that the unification - 'Us-ness' - is interiorized as well as objective. The subtlety of Laing's use lies in spotting its applicability; for families are not *formed* like this; *but they may be maintained like this*. Note, however, that Laing does not assert that *all* families are like this, only some. The phrase 'nexual family' would be redundant if all families were nexual.

Although Laing does not refer to schizophrenia in this paper, one strongly gets the impression that it is to families of schizophrenics that is he referring. (He had, incidentally, just completed the research for 'Sanity, Madness and the Family' at the time of writing the article.)

This view is supported by the evidence presented in 'Sanity, Madness and the Family'. Most, if not all, of the families discussed show signs of precisely those 'preconditions' specified by Laing; plus, of course, a *diminution* of internalized terror of the world, in one member: who by acting on that, comes to be seen as 'schizophrenic'.

Subsequently, Laing has implied that almost *all* families are terrorizing nexi (Laing, 1965c, d; 1967a; 1972b). Being challenged on this point (1972b) Laing referred to the research conducted at the Tavistock Institute on 'normal' families, the counterpart to the 'Sanity, Madness and the Family' research, claiming that this supported this assertion. In view of its obvious bearing on Laing's more radical assertions, one can only wonder at the fact that this research remains unpublished.

The next occasion for Laing's use of Sartre's theme was a chapter in 'The Politics of Experience', actually entitled 'Us and Them'; Laing himself recognizes that it is a 'revised version' (this is something of an understatement) of Series and Nexus. The prime difference, in this 'revision', is that the family is no longer the concrete point of reference.

The chapter does, as Laing says, owe a lot to the 'Critique'; not merely in its central theme, but also in its, so to speak, incidental comments. For example, the chapter starts with a discussion of the structures of shared experience, and the way that these come to be seen as objective. Laing refers to them, following Sartre, by saying 'these reified projections of our own freedom are then introjected' (p. 65). Our projects, (in the Sartrean idiom) are exteriorized through our praxis (that is, our freedom is objectified); and, via that form of relationship characterized as the practico-inert, they become interiorized again: but with the illusory appearance of totalities. Thus, as Laing suggests, Durkheim was *right*: phenomenologically speaking. But fundamentally, that is, ontologically, he was wrong. Social facts only *appear*, to consciousness, as things; in reality, they are merely internalized externalizations. (With a bit of sociological imagination, we can see Durkheim as the High Priest of maya, or Illusion. For it is this *illusory* confusion of phenomenological reality as ontological reality that Laing urges us to see through in his so-called mystical writings. The veil of maya is the non-existent *thinghood* of social relations, whether these be taken on the level of China's involvement with America's involvement with Vietnam's involvement with..., or my involvement, as a thesis writer, with you, as a thesis reader. This is not to say that Durkheim's accounts of this veil were themselves illusory in the sense of 'wrong' absolutely; merely that one cannot see Durkheim and his achievements until one can see beyond them.)

The chapter continues with a now familiar account of gossip and scandal, i.e. the serial group, the 'ubiquity of there's' as Sartre (and Laing) put it, in a word: Them; and the Sartrean group synthesis, the nexus, the interiorization of syntheses etc: Us.

Chapter 4

But then, for the first time in any significant depth, we are given an account of the phenomenon of groups *other* than the family (or its sub-units). The group, whether 'We, or You or Them' is not some sort of hyperorganism, we are told, but we know, from our experience ('we may shed our own blood... for this bloodless presence') that it is *some* sort of reality. What then is its nature?

From outside, a group of Them may come into view in another way. It is still a type of unification imposed on a multiplicity, but this time those who invent the unification expressly do not themselves compose it. Here, I am of course not referring to the outsiders perception of a We already constituted from within itself. *The Them comes into view as a sort of social mirage*. The Reds, the Whites, the Blacks, the Jews. In the human scene, however, *such mirages can be self-actualizing*. The invention of Them creates Us, and We may require to invent Them to re-invent Ourselves (p. 76; my emphasis).

This strikes me as a very important quote. We must go over it in detail, because, as I shall argue, Laing is employing a dialectical dynamic, expressed by Sartre in formal terms, to account for a crucial phenomenon that Sartre himself does *not* discuss, as far as I can make out.

The second sentence rules out the sort of nexual formation we are already familiar with, that of a family, in so far as the unification is not performed by one of those who is thus unified. The third sentence makes it clear that the group that is unified, or constituted, is not in the first place considered a unification by the members of the group at all. It is in this sense, then, a 'social mirage'.

What we are talking about is an *act* of unification that is totally external to the '*object*' that is unified. I think Laing detracts from the power of his case by using groups that have an undoubted objective existence, i.e. Jews, Blacks, etc. A better example, I should have thought, would be Witches. With certain qualifications, Reds, or Commies, or better, 'The Commie Conspiracy' is as good an example as Witches.

'Such mirages can be self-actualizing.' That is, by creating a *consciousness* a mythical group, such as Witches, one may *in fact* bring about the existence of something recognizable as that group. More important, however, 'the invention of Them creates Us'. That is, it may be in some obscure way necessary to invent a group against which one is opposed, in order to define and thus consolidate one's Own group. To take the obvious example, expressed banally but thus lucidly: a capitalist country such as the United States, beset by internal contradictions, falling apart from the *inside*, creates a Them, the Enemy, external to itself (geographically locatable as North Vietnam), defines it as a threat, and achieves some sort of consolidation of itself by doing so. That the astonishing *conviction* with which the Cultural Revolution was carried out is *partially* attributable to the same mechanism cannot be denied by anyone who has read Peking Review or China Reconstructs (sic!).

Laing goes on to consider some of the ways in which the invention, or 'reconstruction' of Ourselves may be brought about.

Perhaps the most intimate way We can be united is through each of us being in, and having in ourselves, the same presence.... We find this demonic group mysticism repeatedly evoked in the pre-war speeches at Nazi Nuremberg Rallies. Rudolf Hess proclaims: We are the Party, the Party is Germany, Hitler is the Party, Hitler is Germany, and so on.

We are Christians in so far as we are brothers in Christ. We are in Christ and Christ is in each one of us (p. 78).

But, remembering Durkheim's Illusion, we can see that the Party, the Christ, exists only in so far as it exists 'in' the members of the Party, or the Church. (Here again we see the almost unbelievable welter of social phantasy, the confusion of biological, interpersonal, and social modalities of experience: the Party is Germany; Germany is the *Father*land, Hitler is the Party/Germany, Hitler is the Father, We are the Sons of Germany; all in the context of father-dominated authoritarian family.) Or again; We are in Christ, Christ is in Us: This is my Body; The Church is the Body of Christ on Earth; and the Family of God; We are Brothers in Christ; God is the Father; I am the Son of Man. (For a brilliantly documented discussion of some of these links, see Schatzman, 1973, chapter eleven).)

But as Laing points out, this is not just a matter of the socio-political mysticism of the past. We are in danger of acting upon such 'mass serialized preontological phantasy', and of thus blowing our planet to smithereens.

I believe Laing's analysis of these matters is fundamentally sound as far as it goes. The problem is: what do we do about it? I cannot say I am impressed by his estimation of the possibilities:

It is just possible that a further transformation is possible if men come to experience themselves as 'One of Us'; if, even on the basis of the crassest self-interest, we can realize that We and Them must be transcended in the totality of the human race.... Shall we realize that We and Them are shadows of each other?... When will the veil be lifted? (p. 83).

It strikes me that this is expressing a thoroughly idealistic dialectic. That is, this expresses *only* the formal relationship of units of a very high degree of abstraction. Now, it may be true, on a global level, that We and Them are shadows of each other; there is, no doubt, a dialectic on this level; this is, indeed, Laing's discovery. But to pose the *solution* purely in those terms is to *deny* the existence of dialectics at lower, more concrete, levels of abstraction: relations of production, systems of education, of commodity distribution, of information control, of child-rearing, and so on.

It is, in fact, to negate what Laing himself is constantly negating: his own insight, expressed in 'The Obvious'; the total ubiquity of dialectic throughout all levels of the 'total social world system'. (We have already discussed some of the ways in which Laing's failure to be thoroughly dialectical lands him in an idealist stance: see Chapter 2, stage 5.)

'The Obvious', of course, is the next occasion for Laing to talk on Us and Them: he does not really say anything new in theoretical terms; though he adduces a considerable quantity of empirical material which gives the argument more body. And to be fair, he did on that occasion, go to the trouble of considering one of the mediating links, in its mediation: the phenomenon of obedience. Unfortunately, he does not consider how one might bring about sufficient civil disobedience to threaten the operation of the system on institutional levels, let alone a global level. Nor, to my knowledge, does he ever consider this mediating link anywhere else in his writings.

The final explicit reference to the Us and Them problem occurs in 'The Politics of the Family' (i.e. late 1968) - where it is referred to, incidentally, as a 'Knot' - but there is no discussion of it, and certainly no offered solution.

We have considered the evolution of this theme in considerable depth: for a specific reason. It can, I think, cast considerable light on one of the most problematical regions of Laing's development.

Summarizing this evolution (of the theme), we may say that it moves from the concrete application of portions of Sartre's 'Critique' to the understanding of certain sorts of families; to providing the barest framework, the pure abstract form, of an idealist intraplanetary dialectic. Its ultimate fate is to be found (via articles like The Terror of Security and the Security of Terror) in the almost totally abstract dialectics of 'Knots'.

This evolution has to be seen in the context of what we have termed Durkheim's Illusion. This term was originally coined, in all seriousness, to refer to a confusion of phenomenological and ontological accounts of social reality. But within the terms of Laing's career, this concept itself has undergone changes. In particular, one can perceive a tendency in Laing's more recent outputs to lose sight of the fact that *the Illusion is masking a Confusion*. That is to say, there is a tendency (and it is no more than that) to focus on the illusory nature of the social phenomenon *to the exclusion of* a consideration of the social ontology, i.e. the idealist notion that the world is *merely* illusion.

Adorno puts the point forcibly when he says: 'As the reflection of truth, appearances are dialectical; to reject all appearances is to fall completely under its sway, since truth is abandoned with the rubble without which it cannot appear'(Adorno, 1972, p. 84).

In terms of theoretical practice, this refers us back to the issue of an idealist formal dialectic versus a materialist concrete one. It was asserted that 'Knots' embodies an idealist dialectic. Is this to denigrate 'Knots'? Not necessarily: because an idealist dialectic can have a *heuristic* value in expressing, or pointing to, interpersonal or existential (and even 'spiritual/mystical') conditions. How else could Hegel's 'Phenomenology of Mind' say *anything* to us? How else, indeed, could Marx have found such wisdom in Hegel's discussion of the Master/Slave dialectic.

But this last point should alert us. Marx was not concerned to express existential etc. conditions; he was working on a different level of abstraction. Marx recognized what Laing now seems incapable of recognizing: that to talk about the 'human scene' even at an institutional level, let alone the global level Laing attempts on occasions, it is necessary to use a dialectic that is appropriate, epistemologically, to the ontological dialectic it is expressing: namely, a concrete, materialist, non-deductive, mediated-and-mediating dialectic. How to do this, as Laing himself once remarked, 'is by no means obvious' (DL 14). It must be admitted that he appears to have given up trying. Whether one blames him for that is another matter.

In conclusion, then, we are forced to say that what started out as one of Laing's greatest achievements - the application of Sartre's insights over a range of phenomena, from the family to international politics (demonstrating thereby the ubiquity of dialectics) - ended up as, at best, a limited if intriguing heuristic style of thought applicable in a limited though unexplored field; at worst, an idealistic metaphysical distortion of political reality, a stance that recalls to a frightenly accurate degree Ernst Fischer's brilliant description of Nihilism (Fischer, 1963, pp. 87-9). Laing's greatest success, perhaps, the globalization of dialectics, comes down to his greatest failure, the relapse into idealism.

THE NATURE OF PSYCHOSIS

> It would appear that once precipitated into psychosis the patient has a course to run. He is, as it were, embarked upon a voyage of discovery which is only completed by his return to the normal world, to which he comes back with insights different from those of the inhabitants who never embarked on such a voyage (Bateson, 1961).

We must now endeavour to give an account of Laing's views on the nature of psychosis; in particular, the nature of 'schizophrenia'.

Obviously, Laing's views have not been static; but they are not as mutually inconsistent as has sometimes been made out. The orientation of this section will be to focus on their consistency; we shall not review the gradual development in minute detail. Nevertheless, having established a historical perspective on Laing's work, we shall be employing this in broad terms before attempting a global summary. With these points in mind, then, we turn to stage 1 once more, to examine what view of schizophrenia is contained therein.

The most concise summary of Laing's view is given by himself: 'No one *has* schizophrenia, like having a cold. The patient has not 'got' schizophrenia. He is schizophrenic' ('The Divided Self', p. 34).

Schizophrenia is not, then, an illness (or a genetic defect, or a biochemical imbalance or whatever); it is a state of being, an existential condition. As Laing says (ibid., p. 17), 'Although retaining the terms "schizoid" and "schizophrenic"... I shall not, of course, be using these terms in their usual clinical psychiatric frame of reference, but phenomenologically and existentially.' As 'The Divided Self' concerns nothing but an elucidation of these existential conditions - in other words, as we have already (Chapter 2, stage 1) given an account of them - we have no need to spell them out again. For it is the view that schizophrenia is an existential condition *as such*, (not an illness), rather than the exact nature of this condition, that is characteristic of Laing's view.

Stage 2 sees the introduction of the crucial concept for the understanding of Laing's notion of psychosis: the social phantasy system.

Recalling that phantasy is a mode of experience, though not necessarily conscious, Laing went on to point out that this modality is not necessarily private and unsharable. That is, interpersonal relationships may be mediated by an interpersonal system of phantasy perceptions and attributions. I may experience you in phantasy terms. My behaviour towards you may be a function of my phantasy experiences of you. Further, your behaviour may be a function of your phantasies of my phantasies, etc.

Now the crucial point about a phantasy system is its appearance, phenomenologically, of reality. That is, a phantasy system is only recognizable (to the persons involved in it) retrospectively, i.e. to the extent that they have emerged from it. This involves a 'derealization' of the profound *illusion* of reality afforded by the system, and a 'rerealization' of a new sense of reality.

It is at this point that Laing proposes his new notion of psychosis:

> However, psychotically, a person placed in an alienated, false position within a social phantasy system, who is unable fully to apperceive his position, may give psychotic expression to his partial apperception of the actual phantasy state of affairs (though delusions).... *Such delusions are derealizations-rerealizations gone wrong* ('The Self and Others', p. 22; Laing's emphasis).

A psychotic breakdown, then, is viewed as a failed, or only partially successful, attempt to 'derealize' a false phantasy 'reality'.

Laing accounts for the more acute forms of psychosis by postulating the possibility of a person being placed, possibly from birth, in 'two or more mutually incompatible positions in dissonant phantasy systems within the same nexus' (p. 23). (This notion, of course, draws heavily on Bateson's Double Bind theory.)

Notice that it is not simply being in a state of conflict that is supposed to lead to a possible 'psychosis'. It is only so if this conflict is located in phantasy, and thus not resolvable except through a dissolution of phantasy; in other words, if the conflict is not readily apparent as such.

This distinction was spelt out in much greater detail in stage 3 in the paper Mystification, Confusion and Conflict (Laing, 1965a). It will be recalled that Laing used Marx's notion of mystification to describe the masking of real conflict and/or the invention of imaginary conflict. The possible resulting experience (of the mystified person) of 'confusion' was considered particularly likely to give rise to 'bizarre' behaviour, and thus the *attribution* of schizophrenia.

In stage 3, then, schizophrenia as an illness is rejected as an unwarranted assumption. In particular Laing (and Esterson) draw a distinction between the social fact of the label 'schizophrenia', and the experience and behaviour of individuals which receive that label. 'Sanity, Madness and the Family' was primarily concerned with the latter.

The concepts of praxis and process were introduced, and it was demonstrated that the supposed 'symptoms' of 'schizophrenia' were conventionally regarded as evidence of an unknown process, whereas they can be understood as praxis - albeit alienated, mystified, and confused praxis. The family was seen as the primary context for mystification; members of the family were seen as the active (though equally alienated and confused) agents of mystification.

The concept of praxis, then, emphasizes the *active* nature, both of mystification, and the confused attempts, on the part of the 'victim' at demystification. Laing and Esterson sum up this view by describing the so-called 'symptoms of schizophrenia' as 'a strategy adopted on the part of the "victim" to live in an unlivable situation.' This active view contrasts somewhat with the passive implications of prior formulations; it allows attention to be drawn to the fact that mystification (as well as demystification) is a strategy, it has a purpose, within the family context: namely, the maintenance of the family status quo.

To summarize so far, then: schizophrenia, or functional psychosis in general, is seen as a label that a group of people (psychiatrists) put on certain other people if they exhibit certain forms of behaviour. In their typicality, these behaviours are taken to be expressions of confused, half-mystified, half-demystified experiences. The latter occur, to some extent 'normally', but especially when an individual is seeking precisely to demystify himself: because certain families require their members to remain mystified in order to maintain the status quo, and thus, in effect, 'step up' the level of mystification should an attempt at demystification occur.

Research on 'normal' non-disturbed families, although never published, apparently indicated that mystification in families was far more prevalent than originally suspected. But if the vast majority of families practise mystification, why is it that only comparatively few families produce 'schizophrenics'? The question is frequently considered to be devastating to Laing's position; and indeed, if we look at it *out* of the context of his subsequent work, it is. For it is commonly assumed, on the basis of superficial differences, especially in the style of presentation, that Laing's subsequent views are incompatible with those expressed above. This is far from being the case. On the contrary, the apparent paradox just noted is only resolvable if we *do* incorporate Laing's subsequent views.

It will be recalled that one of the features of stage 4 was the notion of 'normality' as a state of chronic alienation. *Part of this 'alienation' is precisely the mystification and confusion that is typical of 'normal' families*. It must be emphasized that 'psychosis' was only postulated when an individual attempts to *demystify* himself. (This explains, incidentally, why there are two sorts of behaviour noticeable in 'Sanity, Madness and the Family' that are supposedly symptoms. The first is comparatively 'ordinary' behaviour which may nevertheless conflict with the particular views of the family of the person exhibiting it. Thus Ruth (Laing, 1965a) was considered obviously and seriously mentally ill by her parents because she wanted 'to wear coloured woollen stockings and go out with boys'. The stepped-up level of mystification that is often seen to accompany such attempts at individual autonomy then gives rise to greater confusion and thus the second sort of behaviour, which is more obviously 'bizarre'. The orthodox psychiatrist, failing to examine the family context, sees only the second kind, of course.)

So why do only some families produce schizophrenics? Part of the reason, of course, is that some families genuinely do employ greater degrees of mystification than others. But another part of the reason, Laing would surely wish to argue in stage 4, is that many individuals simply never attempt to demystify themselves. They just grow up to be mystified adults: 'normal' people.

We may say, then, that the concept of a social phantasy system has been extended: in range and context. For now this 'system' involves much more than conventional psycho-analytic phantasy. Phantasy was said to be unconscious: but as Laing points out in the Transcendental Experience paper (1965e) 'the Unconscious' is simply *all* that is within us that we are unconscious of; and that involves a lot more than just the phantasy mode. Furthermore, this state of being unconscious, of being literally 'out of our minds' is so widespread as to be constitutive of normality.

So what, in this context, is 'schizophrenia'? At this point, Laing found in a notion of Bateson's, the key to the understanding of much schizophrenic experience, as it had been described to him by his patients.

Bateson (1961) published the first truly modern commentary on a patient's own account of his psychosis. In it, Bateson suggested that psychosis be likened to a 'voyage of discovery' - see the quote at the beginning of this section -, and further, he compared it to death and rebirth initiation ceremonies. And then, with the extraordinary insight which is simply typical of Bateson, he continues:

> In terms of this picture, spontaneous remission is no problem. This is only the final and natural outcome of the total process. What needs to be explained is the failure of many who embark upon this voyage to return from it. Do these encounter circumstances either in family life or in institutional care so grossly maladaptive that even the richest and best organized hallucinatory experience cannot save them? (Bateson, 1961, p.xiv. Quoted Laing, 1967a, pp. 97-8).

Laing's comment: 'I am in substantial agreement with this view.'

So Laing takes over this view of psychosis; we have already examined Laing's exposition of it. As with the Double-Bind Theory, Laing's popularization of it often leads to the assumption of originality, on Laing's part; whereas, in both instances, he refers specifically to Bateson. In this case, however, Laing has subsequently made the following comments (in discussion with Maurice Carstairs, 1972):

Carstairs: 'If I ever suffer from an excruciating mental illness, as he (Laing) so vividly described, I hope I won't turn to a doctor who says you're experiencing a voyage into inner space and time.'
Laing: 'I never say that to people.'
Carstairs: 'But you write it in your books.'
Laing: 'I'm receptive to what people themselves tell me who are supposed to be, if you like, suffering from mental illness. *This is not something I've invented which I have attributed to them;* it's something that I've listened to many people, time and again, trying to convey to me what they've got into.... This is a

> metaphor used, coming, as it were, from the horses
> mouth, that I pass on' (Laing, 1972).

The fact that Laing chose to insert his own italics only in that section of Bateson's quote that concerns the idea of the family or the hospital inhibiting this process, suggests that it is this idea that Laing takes from Bateson, as truly novel; whereas the description of inner voyages are already familiar to him.

Incidentally, Bateson was not the first Westerner to remark on the similarity of madness to experiences described in anthropological literature; nor was Laing the first to explicitly suggest the role of guru for the psychiatrist. The following is Huxley's account of his mescalin experience:

> And once embarked upon the downward, the infernal road, one would never be able to stop...
>
> 'So you think you know where madness lies?' My answer was a convinced and heartfelt, 'Yes'... 'Would you be able', my wife asked, 'to fix your attention on what The Tibetan Book of the Dead calls the Clear Light?'...
>
> 'Perhaps', I answered at last, 'perhaps I could - but only if there were somebody there to tell me about the Clear Light. One couldn't do it by oneself. That's the point, I suppose, of the Tibetan Ritual - someone sitting there all the time and telling you what's what.'....
>
> What those Buddhist monks did for the dying and the dead, might not the modern psychiatrist do for the insane? Let there be a voice to assure, by day and even while they are asleep, that in spite of all the terror, all the bewilderment and confusion, the ultimate Reality remains unshakeably itself... (Huxley, 1959, p. 48).

And even Huxley was not the first: Aleister Crowley (who incidentally, studied psychiatry under Kraepelin, and took mescalin in 1906), although not normally venerated for making sensible statements on a reality level, was well aware that psychiatrists were often the blind leading the half-blind. And we cannot even begin to discuss the case of Jung.

We should note, returning specifically to Laing's views, that despite similarities, there *are* important points of divergence now from his earlier views of psychosis. Strangely, his view in stage 4 is *most* different from stage 3, rather than earlier steps: the issue is activity versus passivity.

We recall that in stage 3, 'schizophrenia' was viewed as an intelligible strategy, i.e. *praxis*, which, through an ignoring of its context, appeared superficially, as the meaningless outcome of a pathological process. It was an active, if confused, constitution of personal project.

However, in Is Schizophrenia a Disease? (1964b), the first occasion on which Laing propounds the Inner Voyage theory, he says the following: 'Without exception it seems to us that the experience and behaviour that gets labelled schizophrenic is a special sort of strategy...' (p. 187). So far, this sounds like stage 3. But then:

> When a person finds himself in a total impasse... Nature sometimes calls upon a healing process that has been available to mankind at all times and in all places.... I refer to the ceremonies of initiation practised all over the world until very

recently, when a person was conducted through an experience of
(i) death; of (ii) journeying in the Other World; of (iii) rebirth from that Place and that Time back into this world with
its here and now. Schizophrenia is a confused attempt to conduct such a sequence (p. 187).

Now this appears very strange. For, 'without exception', schizophrenia, or rather its supposed 'symptoms', are a *strategy*, an
action *by* the victim; and, at the same time schizophrenia is a 'confused attempt' to conduct the death-rebirth sequence. It seems
rather than Laing is confused; for we may ask:

(i) a confused attempt by whom or what? Clearly, either by
Nature or the Victim. But can Nature be 'confused'? If not, the
attempt is by the Victim. But in that case, why is it Nature that
'calls upon a healing process'. I think to avoid total logical
chaos we must assume that Laing for some reason chose to anthropomorphize 'Nature'; that it is in some sense Nature that *is* 'confused', i.e. that for some reason, Nature does not perform this
process 'properly'.

(ii) In that case, what exactly is meant by saying that schizophrenia is simultaneously a human strategic invention (praxis) and
a *process* of Nature? This dual assertion is obviously contradictory; unless one is prepared to assert that human intentionality
is logically reducible to a purely natural process, which presumably
Laing is not.

No further comment is forthcoming, and certainly no anomaly is
remarked on by Laing. Nor is there any attempt to qualify the staggeringly sweeping nature of his claims. There are a collosal
number of 'schizophrenics'; according to Laing, as he expressed himself here, all of them without exception are engaged in a confused
attempt to die and be reborn. I imagine that Laing received the
attacks for gross overgeneralization that he justly deserved, as
his next pronouncement on the matter was very much more reserved
(What is Schizophrenia? Laing, 1964g):

Some people labelled schizophrenic (not all, and not necessarily)
manifest behaviour ... that is unusual. Sometimes - not always
and not necessarily - this unusual behaviour... expresses,
wittingly or unwittingly, unusual experiences that the person is
undergoing. Sometimes - not always and not necessarily - these
unusual experiences... appear to be part of a potentially
orderly, natural sequence of experiences (p. 65).

This time there is no mention of 'strategies'; indeed, there is
no reference whatsoever to 'clinical' material. Rather, the above,
highly tentative connection between 'schizophrenia' and the 'natural
process' is followed by an account, in general terms, of such a process: under the heading 'Exploring inner space'. The confusion, or
rather ambiguity, of the previous paper is missing: 'The person who
has entered this inner realm will find himself going, or being conducted - *one cannot clearly distinguish active from passive here* -
on a journey' (p. 66).

In conclusion, we are told: 'this perfectly natural and *necessary*
process... is one, I believe, that all of us need, in one form or
another. This process would be at the very heart of a truly sane
society' (p. 68).

Notice here a very considerable change. Before, the inner voyage was a healing process that might spontaneously occur (thanks to Nature) if a person was in a total impasse, and that, in other cultures, had been deliberately sought. Now, it is a process that we all '*need*', it is in fact '*necessary*' - for positive 'mental health', presumably. Laing does *not*, however, as is commonly imagined, assert that all 'schizophrenics' who embark on this journey are, by that token, more 'healthy' than anyone else. On the contrary, they are likely to be all the more confused, frightened, etc., by our attempts to 'cure' them.

By 1965, yet another change has taken place, in that the nature of the necessity for such voyages is made more explicit. First, in the Transcendental Experience paper, we are given half political, half religious reasons:

> True sanity entails... the dissolution of the normal ego, that false self competently adjusted to our alienated social reality: the emergence of the 'inner' archetypal mediators of divine power, and through this death a rebirth... a new kind of ego-functioning, the ego now being the servant of the Divine, no longer its betrayer (Laing, 1965e, p. 15).

Later, in 1965, however, we are given a more overtly political justification; for instance, in the summary to the original version of A Ten-Day Voyage:

> Such an experience breaks down the entanglement in the thicket of false consciousness and pseudo-events that our society holds sacred. The need to *invalidate* such experience is because it is subversive. And it is subversive because it is *real*. Everything, as Peguy said, begins in mysticism and ends in politics... (Laing, 1965f, p. 35).

The retrospective irony of Laing's quote from Peguy notwithstanding, I think this quote (from Laing) really does epitomize the notion of 'The Politics of Experience'.

Laing gave the term 'metanoia' to this orderly sequence of experience, the Inner Voyage; the word appears particularly associated with Laing for those that knew him in 1967. It is uncertain when Laing first coined the phrase: it does not occur in 'The Politics of Experience', published in January 1967; the first public occasion for its use appears to have been in a paper to the First Rochester International Congress on the Origins of Schizophrenia (Laing, 1967c), delivered in March 1967. Laing spoke of metanoia as follows:

> The metanoiac sequence lends itself to the metaphor of a voyage, inwards and backwards, until it reaches a turning point, and the voyager returns through an accelerated neogenesis, forwards once more, and outwards into the world without loss of self.... It appears to be a sort of death-rebirth sequence, from which if successfully negotiated, the person returns to the world feeling new-born, refreshed, and re-integrated at a higher level of functioning than before (ibid., pp. 142-3).

He says that he has spoken in fuller depth of this voyage elsewhere, and gives two references: 'The Politics of Experience', and a book supposedly 'in press' entitled 'Schizophrenia: Sickness or Strategy'. This is also the title of a set of lectures given by Laing in New York during 1967. Unfortunately, the book was never published, and copies of the lectures are not available (Laing 1967k).

The last published reference to metanoia is Metanoia: Some Experiences at Kingsley Hall (Laing, 1968d). The paper starts with two hypotheses:
1 Whatever it is that clinically is diagnosed as acute schizophrenia or schizophreniform breakdown; may itself be a resource a human being calls upon when all else seems impossible. (See 'Sanity, Madness and the Family').
2 If the set and setting can be changed (from the mental hospital model), the experience may be so transformed, that it no longer need be regarded as 'psychotic' at all (1968d, pp.11-12).

Then follows the metanoia/LSD trip analogy, a repeat of what was said at the Rochester Conference, and a discussion of the case of Mary Barnes.

The Rochester paper was rewritten and included in the 1971 edition of 'The Politics of the Family' (in which version the term 'metanoia' is dropped - as is the reference to Laing, 1967k). If we examine the entire range of papers, which refer to the Inner Voyage, or metanoia, we notice that it starts out as a concept derived from clinical practice; it is first *presented* as an anthropological concept; it becomes more mystical, then political; and then, from 1967 onwards, there is a return to the clinical (the discussion of Peter (1967c); the examples of 1967i; the discussion of Mary Barnes (1968d); the 'clinical' statistics (!) offered in the 1971 edition, etc.). No longer do we find (after 'Politics of Experience') polemical exhortations to Take the Trip, nor psychedelic propaganda against the suppressive Society. Rather, we find a serious attempt to employ structuralist modifications of Freud's theory of defence, to understand *why* specific individuals are *prevented*, by the Knot, internal and external, of their family nexus, from undertaking this voyage that they so urgently need.

This is why we say there is no *fundamental* difference in the notions of schizophrenia presented in stages 4 and 6. The admittedly enormous difference in style merely reflects a different orientation towards the *same* notion. It should also be borne in mind that the earlier papers, by and large, were directed at a non-professional audience via radical journals; the later papers (March 1967 onwards) were largely lectures read to professional organizations, reprinted in academic journals.

So, to summarize this latest notion of schizophrenia that has been published, we may say that it often, though not necessarily, involves the individual becoming 'aware', or susceptible to, modalities of experience best described, for want of a better word, as 'inner', with which he may be extremely unfamiliar, and of which he may be terrified. It is thought particularly likely that those individuals who have internalized a paradoxical or contradictory *inter*personal social system as an *intra*personal phantasy structure, will be unable to allow these 'inner' modalities of experience to unfold in their natural ordered sequence. Such persons are said to be in a 'knot'; it is a state which we are all in, to a far greater extent that we realize - until we begin to try to untangle our minds. But as with many knots, the more one tries to loosen them, the tighter they get. The schizophrenic, then, on this basis, is one who is strangling himself in his own knot, by trying to undo it without knowing where the ends of the string are. It is the psychiatrist's job to show him where those ends are: to take him to the source of his tangled experience.

The 'dissolution' of the normal ego, the destructuration of the false self, which pervades, as we have seen, Laing's notions of positive sanity from, at least, 'The Self and Others' (the derealization of the social phantasy system) up to the present, does not only involve the 'inner' realms. In a fascinating though little-known paper, Ritualization in Abnormal Behaviour (Laing, 1967i) Laing offers one of his rare discussions of supposedly psychotic *behaviour*, as opposed to experience.

He notes that much 'abnormal' behaviour is simply behaviour that does not fit the structure of conventional social rituals. If we view such behaviour as a sort of strategy, we can see it, not as the outcome of pathology, but as an attempt at the subversion of normal ritual, a deritualization of convention, or a para-ritual.

Examples of this would include various forms of role reversal. Laing gives a suitable illustration:

> Thus one patient showed me that the psychiatric label for him was hypomanic or manic by entering my office for the first time in a breezy style, sitting on my chair, crossing his legs, clasping his hands and saying: 'Now, Dr. Laing, tell me what is troubling you today?' (p. 332).

The role reversals and abolitions of Kingsley Hall could, presumably, provide endless examples.

One convention that is particularly often subverted is that of language. Laing comments, with restraint untypical of 1967, that 'a mistake made by many psychiatrists in the first part of this century was to take behaviour woven out of the fabric of conventionally non-communicative action at its face value, that is, as having no communicative function' (p. 334). Some people, however, do form a 'tapestry' of communication out of kinetic and sonic 'left-overs'; it is these that Laing urges us to be sensitive towards.

It seems that Laing has out-Freuded Freud here. For part of Freud's genius was to see that there was a universe of discourse, a realm of meaning, beyond the conscious, rational aspects of the mind; for example, the meaningfulness of dreams.

Laing expands this universe, begins to chart new realms. For he is claiming that not only is there meaning in neurosis, manifest in dreams, phantasy etc: but there is meaning in *psychosis,* manifest in catatonic posture, word salads, and many forms of, as he says, kinetic and sonic left-overs. It is, perhaps, one of the most characteristic features of Laing's notion of psychosis, across the entire span of his career, that even psychotic experience and behaviour are always, in some way, meaningful. It is, indeed, the ever-present insight which guides the course of his work. (We have attributed this insight, in part, to Merleau-Ponty.)

It is a corollary, of course, of this view (that psychotic experience and behaviour is meaningful), that it can, in principle at any rate, be *understood*; more than that, it desperately *needs* to be understood. Its intelligibility *must* be restored.

So, here, at the very heart of one of the central issues in Laing's career, the nature of psychosis, we have come face-to-face, once more, with the concept that is, for this thesis, the central issue: Intelligibility.

Chapter 5

THE SOCIOLOGICAL USEFULNESS OF THE CONCEPT OF INTELLIGIBILITY

Science, so far, has been a bourgeois venture. There is nothing particularly dialectical about its form of reason.... But it is quite another thing when it is the human scene itself that is in question. Here, the dialectic is grasped by the practical consciousness.... It *has* to be the transcendence of a contemplative truth by a practical and efficacious one, the transcendence of atomizing and massifying truth by the synthetic unity of the combat group (Laing, 1964).

INTRODUCTION

In this last chapter, we shall be considering some of the implications of Laing's work for sociology, and the social scientific enterprise in general. We cannot pretend to be exhaustive, either with regard to the nature of sociology, or with the Laingain implications for it. In particular, we cannot even begin to examine the vast range of interconnections between Laing's work and anthropology; the former generates many hypotheses well worth investigation by the latter. Equally, it is clear that many of Laing's ideas stem from anthropology itself (see, for example, Kilton Stewart's book 'Pygmies and Dream Giants' (1955), which is remarkable for its anticipation of many of Laing's ideas).
   Our method in this chapter, then, will be to select merely one 'sociologist', and subject his work to criticisms, in the light of the insights derived from the review of Laing, especially as these are focused around the concept of intelligibility. (For, as we have seen, this is, methodologically, the central, unifying concept in Laing's work.) We shall then consider, more constructively, what the implications for use of this concept are, in the field of sociology. This will lead us to question the entire nature of the sociological enterprise.
   Who, then, is to be our sociological Aunt Sally? I have chosen Alfred Schutz, for a variety of reasons.
   First, he is a sociological theorist whose views are currently being taken as worthy of serious consideration. The interest in Schutz is, in fact, a part of the same contemporary revival of

interest in phenomenology as is the interest in Laing.

This leads us on to the second reason, namely that both Laing and Schutz have roots in the same tradition, that of phenomenology; although, due no doubt to other roots, they put phenomenology to radically divergent uses. Nevertheless, it provides us with at least something of a common base line for comparison.

It is probably from this common phenomenological origin that both Laing and Schutz are relatable to the sociological tradition, stemming from Weber, that considers 'subjective interpretation of meaning' as relevant. Purely on the latter basis, other choices of sociological theorists spring to mind, most notably Winch. I had, in fact, originally intended to use Winch, but rapidly came to the realization that to do so would involve an analysis of Wittegnstein's relation to the phenomenological movement. Fascinating as such an analysis would have been, I felt I had neither the space nor the ability to tackle such an undertaking in the context of this thesis. (Since making the choice, an excellent study has appeared with such an analysis. See Roche (1973) 'Phenomenology Language and the Social Sciences'.)

A final reason, which is primarily a negative one for choosing Schutz, is that he does not *appear* to have been a direct influence on Laing's own development; though it must be recognized that a negative assertion of this sort is unverifiable in the absence of a definitive statement by Laing himself.

All page references to Schutz refer to his 'Collected Papers', Volume 1. The main article used is Common Sense and Scientific Constructs; occasional reference is made to Concept and Theory Formation.

THE SOCIOLOGY OF SCHUTZ

We begin, then, by giving a *very* schematic outline of Schutz's position, as presented in the articles specified.

Schutz's starting point is a distinction between what he calls the 'constructs of common sense', and those of 'scientific thinking'. This distinction is derivative of one made by Husserl (see for example, Husserl, 1965) between what he calls 'the natural attitude', and that 'attitude' which can only result from a phenomenological reduction, and alone can provide the sound basis for a scientific philosophy (and hence, in Husserl's opinion, a basis for all other forms of scientific activity).

What is intended by this distinction? What, in fact, does Schutz mean by 'common sense constructs'?

Common sense constructs are those with which 'the wide-awake grown-up man looks at the intersubjective world of daily life within which and upon which he acts as a man amidst his fellow-men' (p. 7). They are those everyday notions which we take for granted; the constructs in terms of which the social and natural objects presented to us are 'pre-experienced' and 'pre-interpreted'. For example, if I see what is known as a bus approaching me, what I 'see' is not a red, cuboid, metallic structure containing a number of anthropoid mammals, etc. etc.: I 'see' a bus and its passengers. Furthermore, I know with at least a tolerable degree of certainty that if I fulfil certain conditions (stand at a bus stop, stick out my hand, etc.) the bus will stop for me to get on it. This is indeed 'common sense'.

On this view, a lot if not all of 'social reality' is based on common sense. A form of study of social reality, therefore, *which takes common sense for granted,* largely begs the question. This is the case, Schutz argues, for an 'ideally refined behaviourism'. The latter would duly record the regularly appearing red, cuboid structures, and probably with some accuracy predict the raising of hands, the stopping of the said structures, and the resultant locomotion of the anthropoid mammals. It would tell us nothing, however, of social reality as a *meaningful and relevant* structure for the people who comprise it.

A genuine social science, in Schutz's view, appreciates the importance of the question that behaviourism begs: how common sense constructs are constructed, and how they enable the pre-existing social reality to be experienced as meaningful.

Common sense constructs go together to yield common sense knowledge: this knowledge has for Schutz (following Husserl) one overridingly relevant feature: it is intersubjective.

Now to say that a given fact, *x*, is an intersubjective fact is to say that I know it, you know it, I know you know it; and you know I know it (presumably ad infinitum); in other words, it is 'common knowledge', it can be assumed (for everyday purposes). As Schutz puts it: 'this world is not my private world but an intersubjective one... therefore, my knowledge of it is not my private affair but from the outset intersubjective or socialized' (p. 11).

Now there are three particular properties attendant on this socialization of knowledge. These are:
(a) The reciprocity of perspectives or the structural socialization of knowledge;
(b) The social origin of knowledge;
(c) The social distribution of knowledge (p. 11).

These properties are the cornerstones of Schutz's position, in so far as they are the defining features of intersubjective common sense knowledge; and scientific thought, as we shall see, is so to speak meta-constructed upon common sense constructs. We must, therefore, examine them in some detail.

By the 'reciprocity of perspectives' Schutz appears to mean both of two very different things: first, that if two people change places, physically, one will see what the other saw, and vice versa; will be able to touch what the other was able to touch (given, presumably, a static environment); and second, that (in the absence of counter-evidence) one takes for granted that differences in perspectives 'originating in our unique biographical situations' are irrelevant for all practical purposes. Schutz makes it clear that by perspective he does not merely mean the optical properties of perception - if he did, the two propositions would be identical - as when he insists that the term 'object' (of a perspective) should be interpreted 'in the broadest possible sense as signifying objects of knowledge taken for granted' (p. 12).

Roughly, then, this proposition is to the effect that one takes it for granted that one's *biographical* position does not effect one's *physical* interchangeability with another person (of a different biographical position) vis-à-vis one's perspective on an object of 'common knowledge'. Another way of phrasing this is to say that one assumes that one's biography as a *unique* individual is not relevant in determining what one takes to be relevant when considering any given issue, social fact, object, etc., unless one has positive evidence to the contrary. I shall be arguing that this is a very dangerous assumption.

The phrase 'the social origin of knowledge' conveys the insight that only a very small part of our individual knowledge of the world originates within our own experience. The vast majority of it is second, third or nth hand. The term 'knowledge of the world' conveys not only bare facts, but also the typifying media - systems through which the facts are transmitted, notably of course, language. It embraces phenomena as different as political ideology, vocabulary, good manners, and the existence of public transport. Schutz makes no comments which might suggest that nth ($n > 1$) hand knowledge might be of a different epistemological status to first hand, direct experience knowledge. Again, this is a dangerous oversight.

Finally, Schutz claims, knowledge is socially, distributed; which at its most basic means I know some things that other people in the world do not know, and vice versa. The only refinement of this fairly obvious statement given by Schutz is that 'I am an "expert" in a small field and "layman" in many others, and so are you' (p. 14); and that knowledge of this distribution of expertise is itself an element of common sense experience.

Schutz next tackles the question of 'the structure of the human world and its typification by common sense constructs'.

There are, relative to any given individual, four broad categories of Others: predecessors, contemporaries, consociates, and successors. The first and last of these are those who precede and succeed our own existence chronologically, respectively. Concerning the other categories: 'Among my contemporaries are some with whom I share, as long as the relation lasts, not only a community of time but also of space. We shall... call such contemporaries "consociates" and the relationship prevailing among them a "face-to-face" relationship' (p. 16). Consociates, then, are mutually involved in each other's biographies; Schutz says they live in a 'pure We-relationship'.

In such a relationship, the Other is said to be grasped as a 'unique individuality', even though only a part of his personality is grasped thus. In all other forms of relationship, the Other's self can only be grasped in terms of a construct of typification: in so far as I grasp the existence of contemporaries whom I do not know personally, I grasp them, Schutz insists, in terms of typical patterns of behaviour, of motives, of attitudes, etc.

Clearly, there are varying degrees of anonymity, generality and accuracy involved in this process: my attributions concerning the motives of, say, the Assistant Registrar of Keele are *likely* to be more personal, more specific, and more accurate than, say, my attributions concerning the state of consciousness of an unspecified Chinese peasant; although I have met neither face-to-face.

We should note that Schutz parallels Sartre's concept of serialité (in fact, anticipates it) when in discussing this scale of anonymity of the other, he says 'In complete anonymization the individuals are supposed to be interchangeable' (p. 18).

Now this typification of the structure of the human world is based, in Schutz's view, on action and interaction. Action is defined as 'human conduct devised by the actor in advance, that is, conduct based upon a preconceived project' (p. 19). An act is defined as an accomplished action.

Interaction, on the other hand, depends on the 'idealization of the reciprocity of motives'. That is to say, if A is interacting with B, A must assume that his motives are in some degree understood by B, and further, that B actually has motives, which correspond to the motives A imagines or assumes B to have, and that together, these motives permit a 'meshing' as it were, of their individual actions into interactions. As Schutz points out, this reciprocity depends on the more general thesis of the reciprocity of perspectives.

However, this reciprocity of motives is not an all-or-nothing affair. Suppose A asks B if he would like a drink. B correctly understands the question, at its surface value, and concludes that A's motives in uttering those words were to find out whether he, B, would like a drink. Which indeed, A does want to know. Thus far there is a reciprocity. But then suppose that A is trying to get B drunk in order to seduce him/her. To the extent that A is trying that, and B is unaware, there is no reciprocity.

The implication of this is that the *meaning* of an action is different (a) for the actor, and (b) for the acted-upon-in-interaction. Even more so is it different for (c), an observer external to the relationship - say the barman in the above example.

This leads us on to what is perhaps Schutz's most important contribution to sociological theory: a three-fold distinction in what is involved in the problem of the 'subjective interpretation of meaning' for the actor; that is, adopting, as Schutz does, Weber's terminology, the problem of Verstehen. In Schutz's words:

> The whole discussion suffers from the failure to distinguish clearly between Verstehen (1) as the experiential form of common-sense knowledge of human affairs, (2) as an epistemological problem, and (3) as a method peculiar to the social sciences (p. 57).

(1) has just been outlined: we all employ Verstehen all the time, in so far as we live together in an intersubjective world which, for most of us, most of the time, makes some semblance of sense. That you, the reader, can, I presume, derive some meaning from the sentence you are now reading, is Verstehen (1) in action.

The second aspect, the epistemological problem, can be most succinctly summarized by asking: how is it that Verstehen (1) is possible? I can only agree with Schutz that it is a 'scandal of philosophy' that so little attempt has been made to even think about this problem - Husserl and Whitehead notwithstanding. This is not the place, however, to examine in detail the epistemological advances already established.

We must rather turn to examine Verstehen (3); or, what is the same thing, the methodology of social science as seen by Schutz.

Schutz begins to tackle this by noting an apparent paradox: (granted that we, as social scientists are concerned with subjective meaning for the actor)

First, we have seen... that the subjective meaning an action has for an actor is unique and individual because it originates in the unique and individual biographical situation of the actor. How then is it possible to grasp subjective meaning scientifically? Secondly, the meaning context of any system of scientific knowledge is objective knowledge but accessible equally to all his fellow scientists and open to their control, which means being capable of being verified, invalidated, or falsified by them. How is it, then, possible to grasp by a system of objective knowledge subjective meaning structures? Is this not a paradox? (p. 35).

Schutz answers himself as follows. Considering the first point, he takes what I can only see as the 'easy way out' and denies it is relevant at all - a stance reminiscent of Flew's 'No True Scotsman Move'. The thought objects of social science do not refer, we are told, to unique acts of unique individuals; it is not, apparently, the concrete analysis of concrete situations. The second problem is a real one, Schutz concedes - though not insurmountable. For he insists that the

attitude of the social scientist is that of a mere disinterested observer of the social world. He is not involved in the observed situation... it is not the theatre of his activities, but merely the object of his contemplation. The social scientist has no 'Here' within the social world (pp. 36-9).

So what, in the midst of this welter of negation, *does* the social scientist do? Again, to be as fair as possible to Schutz, I shall quote his words:

He begins to construct typical course-of-action patterns corresponding to the oberved events. Thereupon he co-ordinates to these typical course-of-action patterns a personal type, a model of an actor whom he imagines as being gifted with consciousness. Yet it is a consciousness restricted to containing nothing but all the elements relevant to the performance of the course-of-action patterns under observation.... He ascribes, thus, to this fictitious consciousness a set of typical in-order-to motives corresponding to the goals of the observed course-of-action patterns and typical because-motives upon which the in-order-to motives are founded. Both types of motives are assumed to be invariant in the mind of the imaginary actor-model (p. 40).

Via this invariant psyche (or rather psyches - the social scientists create whole systems of interacting 'puppets' or 'homunculi' as Schutz himself calls them) predictions can be made, tested and verified or rejected. Verification is then taken as proof that the imputed consciousness, motives etc. - in short, the meaning structure - of these puppets is in fact the meaning structure as experienced by the real actors initially observed.

Schutz puts forward three extremely important 'postulates' which act as governing principles in the construction of these social scientific 'models'. They are (a) the postulate of logical consistency, (b) the postulate of subjective meaning, and (c) the postulate of adequacy. These must now be examined.

The postulate of logical consistency requires that the system of typical constructs, created by the scientist, must be 'established with the highest degree of clarity and distinctness of the conceptual

framework implied and... fully comparable with the principles of
formal logic' (p. 43). Schutz appears to think that this secures
the construct system's 'objectivity'; and that its adherence to the
principles of formal logic establishes its status as scientific,
as opposed to common sense, thought.

The second postulate requires that the system devised must be
capable of explaining all observed behaviour 'as a result of the
activity of such a mind in understandable relation'. It is not entirely clear *precisely* what this means; but it appears to mean simply
that the imputed contents of the fictitious consciousness must be
sufficiently broad to account for *all* observed behaviour *purely* as
a result of the activity of that consciousness.

Finally, the postulate of adequacy insists that every term in
the scientists model must be of such a nature that a human act performed in the way the model predicts would be understandable to the
actor himself, and his fellow actors, in terms of common sense
interpretation. In other words, the scientists' constructs must be
consistent with the constructs of common sense experience of social
reality.

In this way, then, Schutz thinks, he has satisfied both the need
for subjective interpretation, and the canons of objective scientific procedure, which he does not question; in fact, he reaffirms
them. He also believes he clarifies Verstehen (1), and Verstehen
(3).

I shall now attempt to illustrate that Laingian insights can be
applied to Schutz; that in the course of so-doing, we shall find
that Schutz ignored the problem of Verstehen (2) at his peril; that
much of Laing's theoretical work has bearing on Verstehen (2), and
that when it is brought to bear, Schutz's Verstehen (3) collapses.
We shall also be using Laing, more empirically, to question, and
indeed reject, many of the assumptions of Verstehen (1). Our use
of Laing to do all this should not be taken to imply that any or all
of the criticisms of Schutz that will follow would be *impossible*
without Laing; but it is to suggest (a) that the criticisms will
have a greater mutual coherence if we do; and (b) that this procedure might indicate that Laing has implications for sociology at a
profounder level than that usually recognized (i.e. as a critical
figure in a sub-branch of medical sociology).

LAING AND SCHUTZ

It would seem logical to return to Schutz's starting point, and to
adhere, initially at least, to Schutz's order of presentation,
bringing in Laingian points as we progress. With this in mind, we
turn to Schutz's original distinction between common sense and scientific constructs.

Laing, of course, does not make a distinction in precisely those
terms. Nevertheless, there is apparent in Laing the notion that
everyday thinking does not provide us with adequate means of conceptualizing everyday life: because the 'natural attitude' is predominantly an attitude from an alienated standpoint. The degree of alienation considered prevalent varies, as we have seen, throughout
Laing's career. The issue clearly revolves around what sort of

deviation from a 'true' perception of social reality is involved in the everyday perception of it. We are obliged, therefore, to bracket the implications of Schutz's original distinction (as indeed Schutz does) to consider in greater depth this question of the everyday perception of social reality.

Laing and Schutz agree that the social world, and knowledge of it, is intersubjective. But as soon as we look more closely at what this term implies, we begin to see differences. Consider the three properties of intersubjective knowledge that Schutz isolates.

The first, it will be recalled, was the reciprocity of perspectives. Schutz assumes the congruency of the 'systems of relevances' between two perspectives - 'until counter-evidence'. We said earlier that this was a dangerous assumption; Laing can help us see why.

Consider a family (an everyday phenomenon if ever there was one) comprising a father (F), a mother (M), and a daughter (D). Schutz's assumption means that, *unless we have reason to believe otherwise*, F's perspective on M is 'empirically identical' to D's; that the differential biographical situations of F and D are irrelevant. This is quite obviously false - and we hardly need 'Sanity, Madness and the Family' to realize this.

It may be objected that this is too extreme an example; that where the 'common social object' is, for both parties, an intimately known human being, we must *always* expect to have counter'evidence'. But then, I ask, does this human being have to be intimately known? Or even known at all? What grounds does Schutz have for *assuming* that any two people, each with their unique biographical histories, will have the same perspective on a total stranger that they pass in the street?

But then perhaps it will be argued that in *every* case where a person is the common object, we must make this proviso, of expecting counter-evidence. Unfortunately, this leads one to the somewhat whimsical position that the fundamental assumption of Schutz's theory of perception of social reality excludes people as an element of that reality! It would seem to be a bankrupt assumption.

If we turn now to Laing, we find a very different assumption. For Laing says:

Each person not only is an object in the world of others but is a position in space and time from which he experiences, constitutes, and acts in *his* world. He is his own centre with his own point of view, and it is precisely each person's *perspective* on the situation that he shares with others that we wish to discover.... People have identities. But they may also change quite remarkably as they become different others-to-others. It is arbitrary to regard any one of these transformations or *alter*ations as basic, and the others as variations (Laing and Esterson, 1964, pp. 19-20).

The assumption that Laing makes, then, concerning the nature of the intersubjective world (which, as with Schutz, is inevitable logically prior to the methodology of Intelligibility/Verstehen) is almost diametrically opposed to Schutz's; Laing's asserts the logical necessity of the uniqueness of each person's perspective, Schutz's denies it.

It would seem that underlying even these, apparently basic, assumptions, are another pair of opposed assumptions. For Schutz seems to assume, given a sufficiently deep level of abstraction, a fundamental homogeneity of consciousness in society; Laing, on the other hand, assumes an equally fundamental heterogeneity.

We have seen the background to Laing's assumptions; Schutz's seem to have come more or less directly from Husserl. Consider, for example, the following quote from 'Cartesian Meditations', probably the most important Husserl text for social scientists, being more or less the birth place of 'intersubjectivity':

> The existence-sense of the world and of Nature in particular, as Objective Nature, includes after all *thereness-for-everyone*. This is always cointended when we speak of Objective actuality.... Thus it is in the case of *all cultural Objects* (books, tools, works of any kind, and so forth,) which carry with them... the experiential sense of thereness-for-everyone (Husserl, 1973, p. 92).

The plain fact is that cultural objects are not 'there-for-everyone'; there is acute and antagonistic disparity in the distribution of cultural goods within one 'culture'. So, too, the analogy, whereby Husserl constitutes intersubjectivity as a special case in which human beings are the shared cultural 'objects' (that are also subjects), is ultimately misguided. The shift worker is 'there-for' the company boss in a *radically* different way to that in which the company boss is 'there-for' the worker. Sameness is the special case of difference, rather than difference being an exception to sameness.

It is beyond our scope to delve deep enough to explore the preconditions of these assumptions; at the risk of being dogmatic, I would merely say that these reflect, possibly, Schutz's and Laing's adherences to essentialist and existentialist traditions respectively.

Moving on now to consider the second of the three properties outlined by Schutz, of intersubjective knowledge, we recall that Schutz, like Laing, recognizes that the vast majority of any individual's knowledge is socially mediated. Unlike Laing, however, Schutz does not appear to see this particularly relevant - certainly not as epistemologically problematic. Laing, on the other hand, does recognize a severe epistemological problem, that is limiting in his own field, and almost annihilating at a broader, sociological level.

In The Obvious (Laing, 1967e), he notes that 'almost all social scientists' now realize that the intelligibility of a given social event requires its being placed in its spatial and temporal context. The paradox, he says, is that this is often as impossible as it is necessary. For the *visibility* of social events is remarkably low. We cannot see in social space any further than our senses - we are limited to our perceptual mode of experiences. And in time, we are limited to the memory modality, which is not normally considered to pre-date our birth. Beyond these, our 'knowledge' is indirect. But, as Laing points out elsewhere (1968b), the more removed the source of our knowledge, the more unreliable it becomes. The media really do mediate our knowledge of 'what is going on'. And this, of course, is a corollary of Laing's assumption above, that one cannot, and must not, assume a homogeneity of perspectives, amongst individuals, or amongst groups and even nations. Our knowledge of the Vietnam War will vary according to whether we live in Russia, America, or North Vietnam. Similarly, our reconstructions of history will be partially determined by *whose* records we have access to - regardless of whether this is the history of the Roman Empire or of a schizophrenic breakdown. This would appear to give a somewhat pessimistic outlook for sociology: but realistic pessimism is preferable, is it not, to naive optimism?

The third property Schutz considers is the social distribution of knowledge. Schutz is, of course, right to insist on this property. But it is one that is far more pervasive than Schutz implies. In particular, Schutz notes that 'not only *what* an individual knows differs from what his neighbour knows, but also *how* both know the "same" fact. Knowledge has manifold degrees of clarity, distinctness, precision, and familiarity' (p. 14). All this is true; but it goes much deeper than this. 'Knowledge' of the 'same fact' - say, a social situation - can, for two parties, be so disjunctive (as again, 'Sanity, Madness and the Family' illustrates) that to describe it as a 'distribution' is scarcely adequate. Again, we are confronted by Schutz's apparent inability to recognize the existence of outright contradictions in the Lebenswelt. A better term than distribution would be the social control of knowledge. Trevor Pateman (1972) extracts an interesting point from 'Sanity, Madness and the Family', showing that in one of the cases at least (that of Maya Abbott), her parents effectively acted as 'epistemological authorities' for her - of a very oppressive nature. Pateman says:

'Maya, like most children, regarded her parents as epistemological authorities.... Her parents consistently deny the truth of her statements and thereby undermine any developing mastery of epistemological criteria and/or her perceptions themselves.... When Laing and Esterson say that 'She could not know...', this 'could not' is a *logical* could not: it is not that the girl failed to exercise her cognitive skills; she simply had no cognitive skills to exercise (pp. 22-3).

Once again, the relevence of this fascinating point is frustrated by the fact that Laing and Esterson's work on non-schizogenic families remains unpublished. Nevertheless, it would seem apparent that this is not an all-or-nothing situation; this epistemological violence is undoubtedly prevalent in varying degrees. But regardless of exactly how prevalent it is, can it really be called a 'distribution'? Does this term not mask something a little more antagonistic?

We must turn now to consider Schutz's contribution to sociological methodology; for it is here that Laingian insights are most pertinent.

In section IV, Constructs of Thought Objects by the Social Sciences, Schutz asks: how is it possible to grasp subjective meaning scientifically? He then asks what is in effect a meta-question to the effect that *granted* scientific knowledge is 'objective' *and* openly accessible to fellow scientists (for purposes of verification) how, again, can subjective meaning structures be grasped in this fashion?

The answers appear to be two-fold: first, social science does not deal in unique events, but in typicalities; second, the social scientist is a 'disinterested observer'. We will return to the first point shortly; immediately, we must discuss this question of the place of the observer.

Recalling the quotes we gave earlier from this section, we find that Schutz has a somewhat extraordinary attitude to this problem. The simple answer to his assertions that, for instance, the observer does not act within the observed situation, is that this is just not possible. Of course he acts in the observed situation; his mere act of observation is indeed an act, as any anthropologist will testify. It is significant that Schutz never descends to such basic problems as data-collection; his sole concern seems to be data-processing. But the process that he is advocating is one that ignores the fact that data can only be collected by *people*.

It would seem that there are two sorts of approach to this 'observer interaction' problem: one is to endeavour to minimize this effect as much as possible. This may involve supposedly 'objective' techniques of data-collection - hidden video equipment, statistically rigorous questionnaires etc.; or it may involve Cartesian exhortations to the observer to be unbiased, and generally to try to be socially invisible. Pretending there is no problem is a highly unsatisfactory sub-class of this first general approach.

The other, second sort of approach is to recognize that this observer interaction phenomenon is inevitable, and to take essentially *theoretical*, as opposed to practical, steps to control it, or otherwise take it into account. The rationale for this second approach is that it is easier to know the extent of one's control over theoretical issues than it is over practical ones.

The Laingian position is, of course, a strong form of the latter approach. Strong, because it not only asserts the inevitability of this phenomenon, but also its desirability:

> I said that we are all implicated in this state of affairs of alienation.... Under these circumstances, our relationships... are our research. A re-search, a search, constantly reasserted and reconstituted for what we have *all* lost.... Our re-search is validated by the shared experience of experience regained... in the here and now (Laing, 1965b, p. 65).

It seems to me that Schutz negates his own basic insight: or else his insight is not, in fact, basic enough. To anticipate what is really the entirety of my criticisms: he wants intersubjectivity without dialectics. For what Schutz is *implying* is that the observer does not exist in a dialectical relation to what he observes. His negation of himself resides in the fact that although he recognizes the intersubjective (and thus, as our review of Laing has shown us, synonymously dialectical) nature of social reality, he thinks a social scientist can simply step outside this reality, and view it objectively. Schematically, then, my argument goes: social reality is constitutively dialectical; the *study* of social reality is itself an aspect of that social reality; it consequently exists in a dialectical relationship with all aspects of social reality other than itself.

But surely, one may say, this is obvious enough; it cannot have escaped Schutz's notice. To an extent, this is true; and we must not leave the matter with the impression that Schutz is simply blind to this. It is more a question of what Schutz does with this vision. Consider the following statement from Schutz:

Surely, scientific activity itself occurs within the tradition of socially derived knowledge.... But insofar as scientific activity is socially founded, it is one among all the other activities occurring within the social world. Dealing with science and scientific matters within the social world is one thing, *the specific scientific attitude which the scientist has to adopt towards his object is another* (p. 37; my emphasis).

As we have said, Schutz does not see the scientist as an actor in the social world; this precludes him from commenting on the absurdity of this position as he would have to do if he ever considered the theoretical problems attendant on the actual practice of data-collection. But even if we overlook this oversight and consider only what Schutz says about data-processing, there are problems. Let us turn now to our main concern: Schutz's attempt to use Verstehen as a social scientific tool.

We have already seen how Schutz wants to create 'models' of typical situations, populated by 'homunculi' endowed with 'fictitious consciousnesses' in accordance with three 'postulates'. Further, let us remember that his espousal of a refined ideal typical methodology precludes him, as he correctly points out, from talking about unique situations. We thus have two major lines of attack on Schutz's enterprise: first, we can examine these postulates, to see exactly what sort of model they would produce; second, when we are propounding some first steps to a solution of the problems inherent in Schutz, we will criticize his more basic assumptions underlying his whole approach, of not considering unique events in their uniqueness.

Turning first, then, to the postulates. The first postulate is that of logical consistency. The system of typical constructs must be fully compatible with the principles of formal logic, we are told. This warrants their objectivity. Well, true enough, it warrants that; but that is precisely what is wrong with it!

We have spelt out earlier, at some length, how the dialectic is both the ontological and the epistemological principle of social reality. In both spheres, the dialectic is manifest as contradiction. Dealing, as we are here, with the epistemological sphere, we can see that *any* verbalized account of social reality that is 'fully compatible with the principles of *formal* logic' is doomed to be a lie, and a denial of the ontological nature of that of which it is a verbalization. There is no question of a change in the type of logic as one moves from the concrete everyday to the abstract (social) scientific. It cannot be that one is intersubjective, the other formal and objective: both are dialectical (constitutively and regulatively). As Laing says:

> The dialectic is a method of knowing, and a movement in the object known.... To the necessity and the intelligibility of dialectical reason is joined the obligation to discover it empirically in each case, and this can only be achieved dialectically. Nothing can become dialectic seen from the point of view of analytic reason, that is, exterior to the object considered e.g. the passivity of the scientist to a system, and the passivity of the system to him. The dialectic is revealed only to an observer situated inside the system (Laing and Cooper, 1964, pp. 94 and 101).

So, the real meaning of this postulate is that if the model (for which the postulate is a regulative principle) is to grasp social reality in its actual ontological status (i.e. as an intelligible totalization of a multiplicity of intelligible praxes), it negates itself in its inevitable transcendence of the principles of formal logic. Put more bluntly, the postulate defeats its own object (to regulate the understanding of reality); it is itself contradictory, but in an inert, non-dialectical way.

It will be recalled that we had reservations as to the clarity of the second postulate: it appeared to mean that the system devised by the scientist must be such that *all* observed behaviour was to be accountable for by reference to the imputed subjective states of the actor. It would be naive to suggest that by this Schutz wishes to deny the relevance for action of the 'outside world'. For it is implicit in his account of common sense thought that the relevance of physical externality is interiorized by the individual; this is, indeed, a large part of what Schutz means by 'common sense thought'. The ambiguity lies in his use of the phrase 'takes for granted', rather than 'interiorizes'. We saw that the intelligibility of social reality resides in the dialectic between personal project, and the field of possibilities (which is the dialectic of Freedom and Necessity). Biographically, the leading insight here, for Laing, (through Sartre) is Engels': 'Men make history, on the basis of anterior conditions.'

I see no reason why this second postulate of Schutz's is incompatible with this; though once again, his lack of explicit dialectics does not enhance the clarity of his insight.

The third postulate was that of adequacy, which basically insisted upon the consistency of scientific constructs with common sense ones. In effect, it means that the system must not cause the homunculi to do anything which a real person, in that situation, would not be able to understand. Further, the homunculi must not be caused to do anything that his fellow homunculi would not understand, on the same basis.

This has a number of very serious implications. For a start, it has been *my* experience (and I take it I am a real individual actor) that the vast majority of my 'fellow men' appear not to understand a great deal of my actions. Similarly, I find it impossible to understand, in terms of subjective meaning, how anyone can drop napalm on innocent Vietnamese children, or bundle millions of Jews into gas ovens. As Laing says, 'normal men have killed perhaps 100,000,000 of their fellow normal men in the last fifty years'(1967b, p. 24). I find that utterly and irredeemably incomprehensible. That, as Laing reminds us, *is* 'normality' in the present age. Perhaps I am abnormal - God help me if I'm not - but am I for that reason any the less open to social scientific study? It would seem to be the implication of Schutz's last postulate that I am. If mass genocide is normality, 'common sense', then common sense will never understand me.

Another point which this postulate raises is whether individuals understand themselves, and their own actions. For instance, it has been the burden of much of Laing's writing, from 'The Self and Others' onwards, that phantasy is a highly relevant mode of experience that is yet in some way 'unconscious'. Further that this is by no means a purely intra-individual matter. We have social phantasy systems; we even have:

> A 'being' phantasied by 'The Russians' as what they are in, which they have to defend, and phantasied by the non-Russians as an alien super-subject-object, from which one has to defend one's 'freedom', is such that if we all act in terms of such *mass serialized preontological phantasy* we may all be destroyed (1967a, pp. 79-80; my emphasis).

When we are on that level, postulates which insist that explanatory systems of action must be hypothetically understandable to all parties involved sounds a bit hollow. Not all of social reality is as unproblematic as putting a letter in a letter-box - Schutz's favourite example.

Another way of saying some of this is to point out that, taken together, at least, the first and third postulates preclude people from being inconsistent, especially between what they say and what they do. Ernest Gellner's brilliant article, Concepts and Society, shows lucidly how such inconsistency, if 'frozen' in a concept, can be socially functional, and thus, pragmatically, apologetic for an exploitative status quo. I would merely add to that that any proposed social scientific methodology which effectively precludes the exposure of such a phenomenon is itself apologetic in a similar (though less direct) way.

It should be apparent, I think, that we are once again confronted here with Schutz's blindness to heterogeneity in consciousness, and to the whole question of contradiction. The gist of these specific criticisms of Schutz, that we have just offered, has been to the effect that by attempting to put Verstehen on an analytic, objective epistemological basis, Verstehen as a social scientific methodology (i.e. Verstehen (3)) obscures more problems than it solves. The remedy consistently proposed was that a more appropriate methodology was to be found focused round the dialectical concept of Intelligibility, as propounded in 'Reason and Violence'. As the review showed us, Laing himself never in fact made a full formal application of this, his interests leading him towards other areas. His ex-colleague Esterson, however, has pursued this line, and 'The Leaves of Spring' - a grossly ignored book - will eventually go down in intellectual history as the first thorough-going example of dialectical intelligibility applied to a specifically social scientific problem. (By thorough-going, I mean one that descends, via a phenomenologically-guided psycho-analysis, to explore the phantasy components of experience, which alienate praxis from project, in the actual individuals studied.)

THE GHOST OF SCHUTZ: OR, THESES ON GARFINKEL

We have dealt at length with Schutz: we must now tackle his ghost, for it haunts sociology today.

Whilst there have been numerous attempts since Schutz to present phenomenological sociologies, success has been extremely limited. As Heap and Roth (1973) - to whom the reader is referred - point out, this has been largely due to a thorough-going ignorance of what Husserlian phenomenology actually is. This, in turn, I would think, has been due to the remarkable dearth of translations of basic phenomenological texts, at least until the later 1960s. And it was with the eventual availability of phenomenological texts that sociologies began to appear for which the label 'phenomenological' was other than spurious.

We cannot attempt here to deal with all the recent uses that Husserl and/or Schutz have been put to in the service of social science. Heap and Roth's article is very well referenced, for those who wish to follow the divergent strands.

Our purpose here will be to look in some depth at what is undoubtedly the most influential legacy of Schutz's approach: ethnomethodology.

One is invariably told that the starting point, as far as ethnomethodology goes, is Garfinkel's 'Studies in Ethnomethodology' (Garfinkel, 1967). If one survives the traumatic effect of an unprepared dip in the murky waters of Garfinkel's book, one may be lucky enough to reach Paul Attewell's brilliant article (1974) Ethnomethodology since Garfinkel (which in fact documents both Garfinkel's position and its immediate forerunner, symbolic interaction, in addition to post-Garfinkelian ethnomethodology, to wit Zimmerman, Pollner, Wieder, Sacks, Blum, McHugh and Cicourel).

Ethnomethodology started out as a critique of orthodox sociology; in Attewell's words:

> Other sociologies accept social facts as things. That is, they accept the ontological nature of the social world, of social institutions etc., in exactly the way that members do. As such, standard sociology totally reifies social existence and sociological concepts. It blinds itself to the fact that social facts are produced and managed by the ongoing process of members' activities (p. 197).

By neglecting, then, to look at *how* individual members constitute themselves as a 'society', standard sociology takes for granted precisely the most problematic thing, namely the 'accomplishment' of society *at all*.

A crucial term in ethnomethodology, that was pertinent in the critique of standard sociology, but has now become something of an embarrassment, is Indexicality.

Indexicality refers to a property of words; specifically, any given word has a generally understood, agreed-upon meaning (roughly speaking, its dictionary definition), and a set of specific meanings present by virtue of the context in which the word is used, on each particular occasion. The indexicality of a word, phrase or sentence (or any communicational unit) is that portion of its total meaning which is specific to its particular contextual occurrence, and which is unknowable without knowledge of that particular context.

Garfinkel (1967) uses the concept of indexicality to point to the poverty of standard sociology. He notes that any set of social practices that one observes, including accounts of those practices given by members, occurs in a particular context of biography, time, place, etc. Accounts, interactions, etc., are thus highly indexical, yet this indexicality is negated by the generalizing tendency of the (social) scientific attitude. But further, the social scientist, Garfinkel claims, is in the same position vis-à-vis his own categories. The only way he can subsume a particular event under a general category is by appeal to the context of the event. In other words, a social scientist uses his own concepts and taken-for-granted knowledge, which derive from his society, when he studies that society, and further assumes his readers share that same 'background' knowledge.

Ethnomethodology attempts to undercut both this problem and standard sociology by (in Attewell's words) 'recognizing that situations were understood through members' practises of dealing with situations of indexicality. Furthermore, it purported to set as its object of study exactly those practises (p. 199).

Clearly, ethnomethodology moves headlong into its own criticism. Ethnos say on the one hand that all social activity is indexical, and seek to discover how this is possible; yet how are they to produce an account which is not itself equally indexical, but rather is 'objective' in the scientific sense of universally unambiguous?

The variety of reactions to this paradox is bewildering. Blum and McHugh, with their self-consciously idealist orientation, say it doesn't really matter, as knowledge is radically other than what it describes. They abandon all hope of science, but consider ethnomethodological analysis as worth while as a thing in itself. 'It's all in the mind' seems to be their motto, and they see ethnomethodology as potentially revealing, or 'displaying' the nature of mind. But then, Blum and McHugh are clearly not too bothered about theoretical paradoxes; for Blum writes: 'Note in passing that the different sorts of questions that are asked of theorizing in this game (Is it correct? Does it work?) are senseless, for how do you speak of reacting to a display of mind' (Blum, 1970, p. 304).

Sacks' 'solution' is even more drastic, and nothing like as amusing. He simply ignores indexicality by disregarding *what* people say, and concentrates on *how* they are saying it (e.g. sequencing in dialogues, etc.). This indeed removes most of the indexicality (though by no means all of it) along with most of the data too.

However, even if Sacks left himself with any interactional data worthy of the name, his programme would still be doomed, were it not for his own inconsistency. For he proclaims as a *rule* to be constantly attended to that: 'Nothing we take as subject can appear as part of our descriptive apparatus unless it itself has been described' (Sacks, 1963).

Clearly then, we have to just wait around for descriptive apparatus to fall out of the sky, as we are logically prohibited from starting at all on this basis. What happens of course, is a compromise. The ethnomethodologist promises to do his very best to make explicit any common sense assumptions he makes in finding words to describe other people's common sense assumptions. But how realistic is this? For every step that is taken towards making such descriptions feasible is a step *away* from the radical goal which distinguishes ethnomethodology from other sociologies. And just suppose it was faithfully carried out, this promise. The sheer long-windedness, not to mention the banality, of such a meta-account would be overwhelming.

A more realistic approach taken by some workers, is to admit the existence of indexicality, but to deny its relevance: i.e. to define the object of one's study as *totally* other than this embarrassing indexicality. This involves then a study of, or rather a search for, universals, invariants.

This appears to be Zimmerman and Pollner's stance. They 'descend' from the observation of unique situations, via intervening concepts (corpuses etc.) to 'members' practices'. They say:

> The practices through which a feature is displayed and detected however are assumed to display invariant properties across settings whose substantive features they make observable. It is to the discovery of these practises and their invariant properties that inquiry is to be addressed (Zimmerman and Pollner, 1970, p. 95).

But as Attewell lucidly points out, this leads to problems when one considers the temporal cumulative nature of understanding. How, on this model, can anyone learn from experience? For in their eagerness to avoid the reification problem, they insist that each new situation is handled from scratch as it were, but from a set of invariant processual practices. They have no way of expressing the influence of one process upon another over time. If then, they deny understanding as pre-constituted knowledge, they cannot ever account for understanding as a temporally accruing phenomenon. Accounting for (or even describing) socialization becomes very tricky on this basis.

Cicourel (who now apparently disowns the label of ethnomethodology in favour of cognitive sociology) likewise has recourse to invariants, which he calls interpretive procedures, and considers innate pre-conditions attributes, present in children (and presumably, in a foetus, and a fertilized ovum?), and underlying all social learning.

Despite the noble heritage of Man's search for universal properties of himself (a task which structuralism is pursuing with infinitely greater sophistication and success), it is hard to see exactly how success in this search would help the ethnomethodological programme. For clearly, any invariants that might be found, are going to be at several levels of abstraction away from immediate experience; they will not be a part of the 'natural attitude', as phenomenologists would say. Even supposing then, that invariants are found of such potency that they are truly situationally transcendent, *and* even, that a way is found to express these non-indexically, will this really help? For surely their very abstractness, their otherness-than-normal- experience, requires a vast system of intervening liguistic activity before they can be comprehended. The doing of sociology *is* an indexical activity. From a rigorously *self-consistent* ethnomethodological attitude, either indexicality prevents the discovery of invariants, or, if one removes indexicality first, and discovers invariants, then indexicality creeps back in when trying to express, communicate or understand them. It either stops you getting to them, or stops them getting to you.

It would be a long and arduous task to document all the difficulties, practical and epistemological, that confront the ethnomethodologist in his 'every-day life'; and a task that is tangential to our purposes here. For we promised to confront 'the ghost of Schutz'. Let us look now, therefore, at the programmatic pronouncements of ethnomethodology, to examine their dependence on Schutz; in particular, to note how the contradictions we have already discovered in Schutz's own work, undermine the ethnomethodological programme.

Silverman (in Filmer et al., 1972) has this to say:

> Our commitment to sociology involves a rejection of sociologism

and psychologism... our focus is primarily on the shared world of social meanings through which *social* action (understood in Weber's sense...) is generated and interpreted. As sociologists we are not concerned with analysing inner mental processes...; we seek to understand instead the rules used to locate meanings in the other's actions, expressions, gestures and thoughts (p. 4).

Their indebtedness to Schutz thus lies primarily in his demonstration of the pre-constituted nature of the Lebenswelt, its 'availability' as a pre-given, and his demonstration of the need to analyze precisely this pre-giveness as a prerequisite to accounting for the empirical nature of the Lebenswelt. This debt is clearly visible in Garfinkel: 'study is directed to the tasks of learning how members' actual, ordinary activities consist of methods to make practical actions, practical circumstances, common sense knowledge of social structures, and practical sociological reasoning analysable' (Garfinkel, 1967, pp. vii-viii).

Or again: 'I use the term ethnomethodology to refer to the investigation of the rational properties of indexical expressions and other practical actions as contingent ongoing accomplishments of organised artful practises of everyday life' (Garfinkel, 1967, p. ii).

Schutz, it will be recalled, found language to have the crucial and primary role in rendering possible common knowledge, and intersubjectivity generally. Although he was ambivalent - or at least, non-committal - about it, it is fairly clear, when reading Schutz *against* a reading of Husserl's later work, that Schutz was not impressed by Husserl's attempts to constitute intersubjectivity in the transcendental plane.

Garfinkel radicalizes - if that is the right word - this constituent shift, till it is no longer a question of constitution but of identity. In a blaze of what might be called linguisticism, Garfinkel states that: 'the activities whereby members produce and manage settings of organized everyday affairs *are identical with* members procedures for making those settings "account-able" ' (Garfinkel, 1967, p. 1). Elsewhere he uses the phrase 'visibly-rational-and-reportable-for-all-practical-purposes' to describe those everyday activities which are the proper field of sociology, and asserts that language is the principal mechanism with which members make their life so rational-and-reportable. As Paul Filmer sums it up:

> For ethnomethodology, then, the basis of the systematic character
> of social life would appear to be found in Schutz's explanation
> of the origins of knowledge held in common by collectivity mem-
> bers; that is, in the linguistic typification of its constituent
> phenomena (Filmer, op cit., p. 222).

I think it should be clear that we are really right back with Schutz here; specifically, his notorious postulates. Garfinkel's identity (summarized neatly by Attewell as 'to do interaction is to tell interaction') is quite clearly based on Schutz's postulates, as when he (Schutz) claims that interaction depends on 'the idealization of the reciprocity of motives'.

But we have already spelt out how the very assumptions that Schutz uses (fundamentally, what I have alluded to as 'the heterogeneity of consciousness in the Lebenswelt') are virtually bankrupt. *To precisely the extent that ethnomethodology bases itself on Schutzian assumptions, to that extent it is doomed.*

To take a concrete example: Garfinkel states that the 'doing' of interaction is identical with the actors' methods of making the interaction 'analysable' or 'accountable'.

But can one not imagine an everyday scene where quite the opposite is happening? Consider a board meeting of an advertising company. They are struggling to find some new way of 'describing' their product, searching for a new set of statements, at best half truths, with which to sell their products.

Now, regardless of what their actual interaction consists of, are not their accounts, even the methods they use to provide accounts, going to be very different according to whether they are talking to (a) the studio producer about to make their promotional film, (b) their wives, (c) a competing firm (d) the Consumer Council and (e) an ethnomethodologist studying advertising (if there be such a beast...).

The point I am trying to make is that *within* any one system of interaction, some people may be endeavouring to give one 'account' or impression to one sub-system, and a totally opposite account to a different sub-system, and perhaps a different account again to systems outside their own, but all of the same interaction. Which account is the interaction supposedly identical with?

I can imagine an ethnomethodologist would say, Ah, but the interaction going on between the actors and one sub-system is a *different* interaction to that between the actors and the other sub-system (thus allowing each sub-interaction to be identical with each account).

To which I would reply: Yes that is so: but it only holds if you refuse to recognize *as a system* any multiplicity of sub-systems which, when taken 'together', exhibit contradictions (either verbal, at the accounts level, or on a direct antagonistic level). And this is to go right back to our criticism of Schutz (and thus ethnomethodology): the refusal to recognize contradiction and dialectic in the everyday social world.

Let's get blatant about this: as I write these words, thousands of people are butchering each other in South-East Asia, in Chile, in Belfast, in Glasgow, in Brixton. Mass violence and genocide *is* a part of everyday life, and we had better believe it. So, consider the interaction of the GI and the Viet Cong fighter. Whose account of the war is identical to the bullet? But back to ethnomethodology....

It is, of course, particularly the third postulate which renders Schutz's position invalid; yet it is also the third which ethnomethodologists seem to take as their hall-mark. It is not necessary to repeat the argument at this juncture; rather we shall take the ethnomethodologist's use of it as a starting point; for their problems are only just beginning.

The postulate of adequacy becomes, in ethnomethodological hands, a dictum that the sociologist may not use terms and concepts to account for the action he observes that would be incomprehensible to the actors themselves. Methodologically, the second order scientific constructs must be consistent with and grounded upon the (first order) common sense concepts of the 'natural attitude'.

Now it seems to me that if adhered to *absolutely*, this dictum alone would abolish sociology. For can we not ask: comprehensible to the actors *after how long*? If, say, one submitted all one's actors to a three year sociology course, then one could (theoretically!) use all the technical terms one wished. But this is obviously not permissible. Are we to say then that the account, given by the sociologist, must be such that, at least in theory, it would be *immediately* comprehensible? *Absolutely* immediately? Then surely, the 'sociological' account becomes *at best* literally identical with the conceptual aspect (which is a small enought part, to be sure) of the actors' total being, at the time of interaction. Sociology, far from being a social science, becomes merely an attempt at partial transcription.

No, that can't be it, either. So, one is forced to recognize *as a problem* the issue of the actors' comprehension (potential or actual) of the sociologists' account. Crucially, two aspects must be dealt with. First: what time lag is permissible between the observed action, and the hypothetical comprehension of the account of the action (for I know that I now comprehend, say, my experience at primary school, in terms that I could not possibly have grasped at the time; it is even likely that if I could somehow be presented now with how it *felt* to be me then, I would deny it, or refuse to comprehend it - there is such a thing as repression). Second, what, if anything, is the sociologist permitted to *do*, other than (a) attempt to passively observe and (b) present written (and perhaps, taped or videoed) accounts, using demonstrably 'everyday' concepts. We will return to this point shortly.

Indeed, it is not at all clear exactly what this talk of being 'comprehensible to actors', 'grounded in concrete experience', etc. is actually talking about. Is it, on the one hand supposedly referring to an ongoing modality of cognition which for some reason (far more mysterious than any found in Merleau-Ponty) 'occurs' at the time of the action? This would seem to follow from Garfinkel's position - it is consistent with his accountability of interaction equation, and with his notion of understanding as always being a *process* not a *state*. But it is somewhat heretical, from a phenomenological point of view: one would imagine that Husserl would want to know exactly what was noema and what was noesis. Garfinkel identifies his notion of understanding with Weber's begreifen: what, the phenomenologist would want to know, is the ontological status of begreifen, as used by Garfinkel, how does it relate to intentionality; and how does Garfinkel see the phenomenology of internal time consciousness? (Cf. Husserl, 1966.)

To these questions - absolutely central to an enterprise claiming to be phenomenological - there is a sad lack of answers.

On the other hand, however, perhaps the understanding is, as orthodox phenomenology would want to say, a *reflective* noetic act, logically and actually (temporally) subsequent to the interaction being reflected upon. This seems to be the position taken by some ethnomethodologists, and it certainly seems more fruitful than Garfinkel's. But even here, there are problems.

In the first instance, we may ask: to what extent do people, in their everyday life, 'reflect' on what they are doing? I am not advocating a statistical analysis; on the contrary, I merely ask the reader to consider his own life. When I consider mine, I find that I do many things which *if* I stop to think about, I can find no rational accountability for at all. Furthermore, I find that I simply *do* the vast majority of things with only the thinnest film of awareness. I get 'into' things; I have to get 'out' of them to even be aware of, let alone understand, how I got into them. Finally, my experience of other people tells that they experience things (including themselves) in much the same way.

This all seems obvious enough; but the point is that I, at least (and I assume it is so for others) *feel*, often, very differently about things if I do reflect on them. They appear to me to *mean* very different things. The very life I am living is a different life if I reflect on it and thus if I attempt to 'understand' it, in this sense (the 'other hand' sense, above). *This has absolutely crucial import for the criterion of the sociologist's account being 'understandable'.*

Here we begin to see the very real danger in the ethnomethodologist's espousal of the search for that sociological Grail, invariants. We have noted, following Attewell, the difficulty inherent in conceptualizing the *temporal* augmentation of understanding. But now we can see that this is not merely problematic when the ethnomethodologist orients himself to obviously historico-biographical substantive issues, such as socialization: it strikes a blow at the very heart of the enterprise. For if temporality is, as we have just seen, inextricably linked with understanding, *then temporality must be an irreducible element in the criteria of validity*. And in the essentially static (and, one can say, the statically essentialist) conceptions of the ethnomethodologists, this is not the case. And so it is to criteria of validity that we turn now, to finally lay to rest the ghost of Schutz.

In the Schutzian scheme of things validity is ensured essentially by adherence to the third postulate. Michael Phillipson, in one of the better papers from within ethnomethodology, asserts that validity in conventional sociology is usually determined by criteria internal to the enterprise of sociology generally, such as internal logic, and consistency with similar studies. The narrowness of this perspective, he argues makes it,

> difficult, if not impossible, to show the relationship and connections between the reconstructed logic of the explanation and the logic-in-use of the members who created the realities. Phenomenological sociology specifically concerns itself with these connections and offers a new criterion of validity; from this perspective the ultimate validity of a sociological interpretation rests on how far the sociologist's idealized and formalized second-order constructs truthfully reconstruct the essential processes of meaning-construction from which the project to be understood actually emerged. In other words, to establish validity the following question must somehow be answered: What is the relationship between the retrospective reflections of the sociologist and the past realities he is trying to understand? (Phillipson, p. 149; in Filmer et al., 1972).

So far I would agree entirely with Phillipson. But so far, the crucial question of *how* validity is established is not considered; and I cannot say I am happy with the answer when it comes. For, Phillipson goes on to talk about Schutz's postulate of adequacy, and decides that: 'Validity is established by developing methods which show that, for all practical purposes, the sociologist's reconstructions are consistent with members' constructions' (ibid., p. 151).

But what methods could these possibly be? For sociology has already been defined as concerned solely with meaning construction; presumably, then, in the initial process of interpretation the sociologist will have judged that his interpretation is consistent with the members'. To simply re-make the judgment again clearly does not help: and even in the event of the sociologist showing his written up piece to the members and saying 'Is that what you meant?' (and how often in practice does that happen?) there are still the questions of (a) the members' interpretation of the sociologist's account, and (b) the sociologist's interpretation of the members' reaction to the account. To insist that sociologists use the same terms as their subjects in no way ensures that both mean the same thing by them. When it comes down to this - which we may term the infinite-regress-of-indexicality-crunch - we see the ethnomethodologists slipping back into their Schutzian (and ultimately Husserlian) assumptions that we reject from the start: that of the reciprocity of perspectives; that, unless there is evidence to the contrary, it is safe to assume a homogeneity of perspective and subjective meaning between two individuals. As we are about to see, it is one that leads to some very odd paradoxes.

Discussing the limitations of sociology, Phillipson concludes that, because of the temporal, reflective nature of social science, the latter must be restricted to an interpretive role: 'Thus, while practical action in the world is forward-looing or prospective in character, social science is a process of retrospective reflection and this limits social science to an interpretive role' (ibid., p. 155).

We shall return to this point in its own right in a minute; for the moment, let us note that when this *ideal* of social science is compared to the practice, we find what Phillipson describes as a 'problem'.

> One problem of developing a dynamic sociology which tries to establish validity by taking its explanations back into the world and to members themselves is that the very process of validation may itself produce changes in the phenomenon being studied; these changes would by definition invalidate the original explanation and require a new interpretation (ibid., p. 160).

It is interesting that this is seen as a 'problem'. For it will be argued that within social phenomenology, this fact is recognized, and, as it were, celebrated. For in *dialectical* terms, *the only test of validity is praxis, practical action.*

It is really quite ironic: Phillipson is recognizing (and all credit to him for it) dialectic after dialectic - but it seems he cannot call them that, and cannot thus recognize them for what they are. Thus he says: '... a central paradox for sociology: the very process of validating an explanation at the level of intentionality may *create new understandings* among members which in themselves require fresh interpretation and appropriate validation by the sociologist.'

But for dialectical sociology, this is no paradox: this is 'what it's all about!' It seems that Phillipson labours, ultimately, under the Schutzian notion of the sociologist as desituated with respect to 'his' subjects. For this issue raises the (ultimately political) question: sociology *for whom*? It seems that the ideal, for Phillipson, would be if he could say, 'Well, *that's* how it is with these people'; but, he would say it to somebody other than his subjects.

From the dialectical viewpoint, however, things are a little different. For dialectical sociology *asserts* the situatedness of its adherents; it rejoices if those people apprehended as 'subjects' (i.e. as objects, in fact) assert *their* subjectivity through the 'created new understandings' referred to above.

As we shall see in the last section of this chapter, the formal test of validity, within dialectical social phenomenology, is that the totalizations produced 'in theory' should enable the sociologist *to act effectively within the siuation,* in the direction of the resolution of inherent contradictions. Such action is indeed only possible in so far as subjects do come to new understandings. Truly, this is the locus of validity - and in a double dialectical sense. First, it is, in formal terms, the criterion of validity in the logical sense, as used above. But also, beyond that, is a second sense of validity. For such concrete changes in real living people: it is these, ultimately, that can alone 'validate' the entire enterprise of sociology. Mere academic sociology, that turns its subjects into objects, steals their consciousness merely to file it away per HM ad infinitum - that is invalid sociology. Sociology in the service of an elite, that is actually turned against its subjects, to control them rather than to free them - that is anti-valid.

And here we can return, as promised, to the quote from Phillipson, p. 155. It is invalid, in this second sense, to distinguish between action in the world, on the one hand, and social science as a literally re-actionary enterprise on the other. In practice, it simply isn't like that, as Phillipson himself points out, and in theory, it shouldn't be like that, as I have just pointed out. Ethnomethodology, it seems, perpetuates this false dichotomy, at least in theory; social phenomenology pledges to transcend it.

Again we have an irony: for all the fuss the ethnomethodologists make about positivist sociology 'escaping' into predictionism, they commit the same mistake by their insistence that social science is 'limited to an interpretive role'. For the error in fact lies neither in the prediction nor the interpretation - both are indeed necessary in certain circumstances - *but in the escape itself*. The question is: escape from what? The answer, surely is: effective social action on the part of the sociologist.

Certainly Phillipson (and Winter, whose ideas Phillipson is perpetuating) are not alone in this. Silverman, for example, uses a quote from Goodenough, in his passage entitled A Basis for Validity. Thus:

To 'know' a culture is, then, to have learned: 'whatever it is one has to know or believe in order to operate in a manner acceptable to its members and to do so in any role that they accept for any one of themselves' (Goodenough, 1966, p. 36) (Silverman, in Filmer et al., 1972, p. 11).

But how can this be? What sort of validity does this 'knowing' possess? For it implies that every person who is able to 'operate in a manner acceptable etc.', in a word, anyone who is able to *conform*, understands their society, at least to the extent that a sociologist wants to understand it. This is truly bizarre. For it would seem to follow that everyone (except 'deviants') *already* knows everything that a sociologist could wish to know. What, one wonders, could possibly be the point of doing sociology at all, on such a basis; because presumably the sociologist also already knows it. But perhaps such sociologists are simply more stupid than everyone else....

The intelligence or otherwise of sociologists apart, however, we would surely be wise to question a theoretical orientation that concludes that obedience is equivalent to understanding. And it is the orientation that is at fault: for we can see in Goodenough's prescription something like a weak case of the dialectical criterion of validity, but based on radically different assumptions. For he is right to assert that being able to act in the situation is the crux of validity: the dialectic of knowing and doing asserts itself, even if it is not known for what it is. But here we see more clearly than anywhere, the ideological dangers of those assumptions that go back from ethnomethodology, through Schutz, to Husserl, of the homogeneity of consciousness in the Lebenswelt. For it is precisely on the basis of those assumptions that we end up in ethnomethodology, with the *practical* criterion that the ability to *conform* indicates accuracy and establishes validity.

In dialectical social phenomenology, however, with its polar opposite assumptions of heterogeneity and contradiction, we find ourselves ending with the practical criterion of the ability to act towards change and the transcendence of contradiction as the indication of an accurate, valid, totalization.

And so, in conclusion, I would present as my final thesis on Garfinkel et al.: 'The ethnomethodologists have only *interpreted* the world, in various ways; the point, however, is to *change* it.'

NON-DIALECTICAL DIALECTICS: THE CASE OF LÉVI-STRAUSS

Before we leave pre-existing sociology, we still have one trend of extreme importance to consider: modern structuralism.

This is certainly not the place to recount once again the history (or is it now a myth?) of the development of the modern structuralist programme, or its functionalist lineage. Indeed, a structuralist would probably find our considerations below disconcertingly negative: for we shall content ourselves with a prolonged discussion of what would seem to be the problematic crux of structuralism - at least of the Lévi-Strauss variety - rather than attempt the futile task of precising the precises already available of the structuralist mode of operation in general.

The issue is synchrony and diachrony. In practice, structuralism is overwhelmingly synchronic; the question is: if structuralism is to be a valid approach in social science, can it and should it be diachronic as well as synchronic? Phrased in disciplinary terms: what is the role of history in anthropology?

We can also state the problem more concretely: given that, in many cases, the object of anthropology is a society apparently without 'history', what is the anthropologist to make of an epistemology which claims universality, yet which found its own preconditions in the transparency of history? What in fact, is the relation between history and dialectical reason?

Happily, Lévi-Strauss's position on this is made very clear to us; for he devotes the last chapter of 'The Savage Mind' (Lévi-Strauss, 1962) - entitled History and Dialectics - to defining his position relative to Sartre's, as given in the 'Critique'. Our familiarity with the latter, and a detailed consideration of the former will thus enable us to shed considerable light on this gloomy area of structuralism.

The Sartrean position rests on the relative mutual autonomy of analytic and dialectical reason. Lévi-Strauss denies it from the start. For him, dialectical reason is merely an aspect of analytical reason, albeit perhaps the most important one. In his own words, dialectical reason is

> the bridge, forever extended and improved, which analytical reason throws out over an abyss; it is unable to see the further shore but it knows that it is there, even should it be constantly receding. The term dialectical reason thus covers the perpetual efforts analytical reason must make to reform itself if it aspires to account for language, society and thought; and the distinction between the two forms of reason in my view rests only on the temporary gap separating analytical reason from the understanding of life.... I believe the ultimate goal of the human sciences is not to constitute, but to dissolve man...: the reintegration of culture in nature and finally of life within the whole of its physico-chemical conditions (pp. 246-7).

He might as well have come right out and called it soul; but as he reminds us a few lines later, he is an agnostic....

It is not clear exactly on what grounds Lévi-Strauss denies the discontinuity between dialectical and analytic reason proposed by Sartre; for he does not discuss any of the formal aspects that are definitive of this distinction (see above, the section on Sartrean Marxism). Indeed, upon a couple of pages' reflection he concludes: 'So it would follow that all reason is dialectical, which for my part I am prepared to concede, since dialectical reason seems to me like analytical reason in action' (p. 251).

And Lévi-Strauss even goes so far as to admit that Sartre puts his dialectical reason into action, 'with incompatable artistry', but insists that the lessons to be learned from him are practical, not theoretical.

He is never specific about it, but he seems to recognize totalization as a 'requirement' (at least for science); yet there is here no mention of analytic reason which patently does not totalize. His constant emphasis on the 'active' nature of dialectical reason almost leads one to suppose he makes a naive conjunction of analytic with thought and dialectical with (physical) activity. But what then of dialectical reason's aspiration to 'account' for language, society, etc? Dialectical reason seems verging on synonymity with mere consciousness as such. (Whereas the latter is its *precondition*.)

Lévi-Strauss jibes at Sartre that whereas the need for 'totalization' may be a novelty for historians, sociologists and psychologists, it is nothing new for anthropologists, who've been 'taking it for granted' ever since Malinowski. Exactly. It is 'nothing new', in the ontological sense for *anyone*, in that social reality is constituted dialectically; in this (ontological) sense, 'dialectical' refers simply (and indeed complexly!) to the social mode of being - intersubjectivity, if you like - wherein one is conscious of others as being conscious of oneself. But this has indeed been 'taken for granted', and long before Malinowski. For, at least for western civilization, it was necessary to wait for Marx to reveal the second, epistemological sense of dialectical reason, its *transparency to itself*. This distinction, which Lévi-Strauss does not mention, would appear to be the key to this issue. Without this second sense, dialectical reason is incomplete, other than itself, alienated into blind social ontology, in a word: lost. Perhaps this 'loss' coincided with the western world's 'fall' in history; perhaps non-historical societies have not (yet) lost it. But the point is not critical here; the existence of societies such as ours must surely render the distinction vital for Lévi-Strauss.

Certainly, in the field of anthropology, credit must be given to Malinowski for his totalizing vision. But a vision is not a rigorous technique, still less a theory; it was the pre-conditions for the second and the presence of the third that Sartre had been laying in the 'Critique'. And that is why Lévi-Strauss is right when he says that we have in Sartre the beginning (or at least, the possibility of it), not the end. But was this not Sartre's fervent hope, the very reason for his attack on 'dogmatic Marxism'? (See also Sartre, 1974b).

And in the end, Lévi-Strauss destroys his own position. For he says: 'it does not follow from the fact that all knowledge of others is dialectical, that others are wholly dialectical in every respect' (p. 250). Certainly, 'others' have non-dialectical attributes. But if all knowledge of others is dialectical, then their knowledge of themselves as others to each other is dialectical; it is, in fact, the dialectic that they all are! Yet such knowledge by no means exhausts the capacity of consciousness - it may even be largely unconscious, as Laing has shown us repeatedly. We are thus back with the distinction as firmly as ever.

Lévi-Strauss introduces history into the debate as follows: 'And indeed what can one make of peoples "without history" when one has defined man in terms of dialectic and dialectic in terms of history?' (p. 248).

Not much, to be sure. But has Sartre really done this? I do not think so. Admittedly, there are passages that could be interpreted that way, especially if taken out of the broad context. But surely, the important passages render that interpretation - which depends on an ambiguity in the word 'history' - highly implausible. The absurdity of such a position would be double for Sartre, as it runs counter to the very aim of his enterprise: Lévi-Strauss's interpretation contradicts the very context that it is taken out of.

Specifically, Lévi-Strauss's criticism would be pertinent, indeed, devastating, if Sartre had defined dialectics in terms of history, *and* had defined history as an unfolding process, the units of which were *transcendental with respect to individual men*, as, for example, in the Althusserian notion of history as a process without a subject. For in such a schema, there is no place for men who do not act out their relationship via the mediation of changes in the ownership of the means of production.

But this is *precisely* Sartre's advance: that he insists on constituting the relevant units of history by totalizing the praxis of individual men. The bulk of the 'Critique' is devoted to showing the conditions for group formation which in its turn is the condition for history.

There is no a priori reason (as Lévi-Strauss implies Sartre holds) for groups to form in such a fashion as to occasion history. As Laing puts it, summarizing Sartre:

Scarcity is the basis of the possibility of our history, not its concrete reality. Other factors are necessary to produce history, and there could even be other possible histories without scarcity. There could even be societies without history, based on repetition. History is born from an abrupt disequilibrium which fissures society at all levels. History is not necessary or essential' (Laing and Cooper, 1964, p. 113).

Elsewhere (Lévi-Strauss, 1968) Lévi-Strauss calls Marx and Engels to his own defence, under attack from Rodinson. Certain Asiatic societies maintain a stability, Marx thought, derived from their economic self-sufficiency and simple division of labour, and the fact 'that the individual does not become independent of the community'. Such a tribe is already a unified group; there is no other grouping. Kinship rather than economics is the governing principle.

Levi-Strauss draws from this that 'If these societies were not destroyed from without, they might endure indefinitely. The temporal category applicable to them has nothing to do with the one we employ to understand the developments of our own society' (1968, p. 337 in 1972 edition).

Two points confront this: first, it is not necessary as Marx pointed out, that the society be *destroyed* from without. An apparently innocuous external change can precipitate an internal contradiction which leads to change of the society itself, and to history.

The second point is that in practice a history-less society is impossible *as an object for us*. For every society we know about, there are these 'external influences', namely ourselves, in the process of observing them (and usually, exploiting them). But no matter if the arrival of the ethnographer is the first event in their history: it is already too late.

Sartre's theory of history is certainly compatible with Marx's - indeed it is a rigorous development of crucial aspects of it. In particular, it allows one to be quite rigorous *at different levels of abstraction*. We have seen how Sartre's schema enables us to obtain simultaneously a synchronic and diachronic perspective on an individual's life. This should be of immense interest to Lévi-Strauss as it is the locus of the reality of the praxis that only appears as the praxis of say, the tribe, by virtue of the ethnographer's totalizing praxis; but it seems it is not.

Let us consider the words of C. Wright Mills: that sociology is situated at the interface of biography and history. So, for a society with no history, it would appear to be just biography, or better, at the interface of biography, and biography. Better still, the 'history' *is* the biography. For a person living in a 'timeless' world (as Lévi-Strauss calls it), his lifetime is eternity. But this eternity is structured diachronically as well as synchronically: the archetypal repetitions play out their cosmic sequence *in the spacetime of each individual's life span*. This fact is irreducible. The danger in Lévi-Strauss's position is that he identifies diachronicity with history, whereas it is identical with temporality. And it is the phenomenology of temporality that is culturally specific, but omnipresent in some form.

The value of the Sartrean 'Critique' of Lévi-Strauss, or indeed, the structuralist programme in general, then, is that, as Laing shows us, it provides a rigorous schema for the simultaneous grasping of the synchronic *and* diachronic structures that are somehow present for all members of all societies.

But what of the 'value' of the structuralist programme itself? I think we must be careful to avoid a particular confusion here. The problem lies more in what structuralism *isn't* than in what it is.

If the structuralist programme yields positive empirical fruits, then of course these are not to be denied on the grounds that the theory behind the research was wrong. But we should have to be extremely careful about what we claim the results mean. It seems to me highly likely that structuralism will indeed prove highly fruitful in certain limited areas; particularly, those in which human *universals* are prominent. (It is easy, in these Althusserian days, to forget that there *are* human universals: the need for food, to take a certain case; or certain aspects of transcendental or archetypal symbolism, to take a more contentious case.)

But we must not allow ourselves to be seduced by the contingent success of the structural exploration of these areas. For, as Sartre's 'Critique' - not to mention the bulk of Marx's work - indicates and theoretically establishes, we can know and demonstrate a priori the irreducibility of the temporal/historical order, and its manifestation in dialectics. And just as Lévi-Strauss finds it necessary to consider Sartre's 'Critique' as a cultural product, an aspect of twentieth century French mythology, so, too, will it be necessary when examining the structuralist findings, to keep in mind the dialectics-in-action that are, amongst other things manifestations of the structural relations established.

In conclusion then, we wish the structuralists every luck; there is, no doubt, a level of reality/conceptualization where structuralist concepts and methods are those most suited to producing comprehensible conclusions. But we insist that this is by no means the case for all levels of interest to social scientists, and further, that structuralism is demonstrably inadequate in cases where a diachronic perspective is essential, these in fact being the majority.

LAING AND THE POSSIBILITY OF SOCIOLOGY

In this, the last section of the thesis, we will be looking at the a priori pre-conditions of a viable sociology - a sociology, that is, that is neither a conceptual nor a political betrayal of society.

As such, our main textual sources will be the more theoretical ones of those already considered - notably 'Reason and Violence', and Part 2 of Esterson's 'Leaves of Spring'. Once again, we must reiterate our reservations as to the degree that this enterprise can be called Laingian. It is Laingian only in the sense that these ideas follow logically from some of the things Laing has said; in particular, it is fairly apparent that Laing himself would most likely not agree today with what I shall be saying.

Laing, following Sartre, conceives of sociology as an 'auxiliary discipline' capable of, and required to, provide 'vital mediations'. How could it do this? Sartre calls on Henri Lefebvre: his contribution, in Laing and Cooper's words, is as follows:

> Lefebvre notes that in studying, for example, the reality of a peasantry there is first of all a *horizontal complexity* which concerns a human group with its agricultural productive techniques, its relation to these techniques and the social structure they determine which in turn conditions the group. The group depends on collectivities on the national and international scale, and so on. Then there is a *vertical complexity* which is historical, the co-existence in the rural world of formations of different age and duration. These two complexities act and react on each other (Laing and Cooper, 1964, p. 43).

Then follows a brief account of the so-called 'regressive-progressive method', the nature of which we discussed, in its bare outline, earlier in the thesis. It is now time to return to it in much greater detail.

The regressive-progressive method, or RPM, involves a three-stage totalization. The best account of this that I know of is Esterson's; I shall be paraphrasing it.

The first moment consists of 'registering phenomenologically' the social situation and the contradictions it contains. In micro-social situations, e.g. a family, this would involve collecting verbal data as well as behavioural data, on the interexperience and interaction of all parties concerned, including the observer. For example, the observer would record disjunctions between the way, say, a mother talks *about* her child, and the way she talks *to* her child (as well as other aspects of her behaviour towards her). Generally, then, a picture is drawn up of how each relevant party 'sees' the situation in the present.

The second moment is a regressive-analytic one: the observer analyses all the issues in historical terms, both in terms of the history of the system itself, and the history of his participation/observation within it.

At this stage, the observer formulates a hypothesis, which synthesizes the initial, contradictory phenomenological account with the historical analysis. This is the progressive-synthetic moment, which moves from past to present, exposing the intelligibility of the present as a partially historically determined totalization of partially free, partially alienated, praxes.

Esterson appears to be employing some of Mao Tse Tung's theoretical insights - especially in relation to this question of forming and verifying the hypothesis. For the hypothesis, as Esterson presents it, is always, (relative to the given situation, defined by the first moment) the *likely principal contradiction*. Concerning verification, Esterson says:

With the totalization (i.e. the synthesizing hypothesis), the observer enters the practical stage. By synthesizing the contradictions of action and experience in the system into a more comprehensive view, the problematic praxis is rendered intelligible. But a gestalt that makes contradictory behaviour intelligible is not, by that token, necessarily correct.... How may one verify intelligibility?

Since the totalization is for action, it constitutes a type of working hypothesis. And its validity, which is also the truth of (its) intelligibility... may be tested by the criterion of practical realization. A valid totalization should always enable the observer to act effectively in relation to the field (Esterson, 1972, p. 232).

As Mao put it: 'Start from perceptual knowledge and actively develop it into rational knowledge; then start from rational knowledge and actively guide revolutionary practise to change both the subjective and the objective world ('Selected Works', Vol. 1, p. 308).

Social reality is dialectical. If science is a form of knowledge adequate to the object of knowledge, social science is dialectical knowledge. But, as Marx, Lenin, Mao, Sartre, Laing, Esterson and I have pointed out, dialectical knowledge ceases to be dialectical if it suppresses or ignores the dialectic between knowing and doing. Is it not *the* fundamental tenet of dialectical materialism that there is a unity, not a dualism, of the ontological and the epistemological, which is the dialectic itself. As Laing, with typical eloquence, puts it: 'dialectic is the living logic of action'.

The implication of this, as Esterson and Mao have just shown for us, is that dialectical knowledge can only be verified in praxis. We are, presumably, familiar with this implication in the sphere of Marxist politics; hopefully, we are also now familiar with it in the sphere of micro-social 'therapeutic' situations. If the educators must be educated, so too must the analyst be analysed (not once, as Freud thought, but continually) and so too, must the therapist allow himself to be changed.

But what of the dialectical sociologist? It is hardly a question of him becoming more 'socialized' - at least not in the normal sense of the word. However, praxis is the last term in the RPM ('without revolutionary theory there can be no revolutionary practice'); let us return, once more, to the beginning, and review the situation for sociology.

We start, as Mao put it, with perceptual knowledge - 'registering phenomenologically the situation and its contradictions', as Esterson says. However, as Laing pointed out, this creates a difficulty at a sociological level, because of the 'low visibility' of social events. But one thing is clear: it is to *concrete real situations* that we must look, if we are to open our eyes at all. (Remember Lenin: 'the most essential thing... the concrete analysis of concrete conditions'.) As Althusser points out, dialectical science takes complexity, not abstracted essences, as its principle. We reject, therefore, Schutz's assertion that the social scientist does not deal in unique situations: *all social situations are unique*. This is the burden of Sartre's critique of what he calls 'dogmatic Marxism'; it has substituted dogmatic principles for concrete analysis. It mistakes regulative principles for concrete facts.

Not that Schutz is a dogmatic Marxist - yet there is a parallel: his denial of a *dialectical* intersubjectivity does parallel, to an extent, the hypostatized dialectic that Sartre correctly perceives in the dogmatic Marxists. Both stem from this withdrawal from reality which is involved in their respective refusals to deal with concrete situations in their concreteness.

But if sociology is not to deny the dialectic of complexity, how is it to proceed? Clearly, one cannot hope to grasp the entirety of the social world in its full, structured interdependence, 'all in one go'. The *beginning* of the problem (that is, dialectically, the beginning of its solution) is really arbitrary: if sociology is a mediating discipline, at what level of structuredness does it begin to look?

Now it seems to me that sociology of a sort is possible at a fairly high level of abstraction. I am thinking of the level at which it is the mediating link between history and economics. It is undeniable that existing sociology has made significant advances in accounting for 'what goes on' at this level. Nevertheless, social reality is meaningful to social actors; if we are not to implicitly deny the epistemological gulf between the natural world and the social world, we must take this into account. In other words, if sociology is to be more than a highly abstract form of socio-economic behaviourism; if, in fact, it is to be, as C. Wright Mills would want, a mediation between history and *biography*, it must be prepared to 'come down' a bit in level, and study the *intelligibility of group praxis*.

To expand: it is an urgent requirement that sociology looks to the institutional structures of society, not only as they function one with the other to make up 'Society'; but as forms of intelligible totalizations of mutliplicities of individual praxes. As Laing and Cooper put it, presumably in critical reference to certain sorts of so-called 'Marxist' sociology: 'Thus, a whole theory of society will be elaborated starting from the conflict between classes, without any adequate grasp of the classes themselves being constituted by a prior dialectic beginning with praxis' (1964, p. 16).

It is possible, even likely, that a concept like 'class' is still too broad to serve as a starting point for this particular exercise - which is not to deny the importance of class analyses. On the contrary, it is a step towards not only recognizing, but providing the pre-conditions for the realization of, their crucial importance.

Historically, the development in this field has so far been more or less limited to one institution: the Family. And this is hardly surprising. Marx and Engels recognized clearly the importance of this institution - as did the early Russian revolutionaries. More recently, Althusser, in his brilliant paper Ideology and the Ideological State Apparatus (in Althusser, 1971), puts great emphasis on the Family, along with the educational system.

Without implying that all has been said that needs to be said about the Family, I think it is time that dialectical sociology, or to give its slightly more well-known name, social phenomenology, began to look at other institutional structures. Cohen and Taylor's

'Psychological Survival' is a step in the right direction here, presenting what is basically a social phenomenological analysis of a long stay prison.

In view of the established importance of the Family, and its highly ideological role, it would seem to me to be a matter of some urgency to undertake a social phenomenological analysis of the commune. As with families and prisons, this will involve prolonged contact with a commune; and it will involve the researcher in an unknown range of 'metanoic' experiences.

So what, in general, then, is to become of the dialectical sociologist? We have established that to grasp the dialectical nature of social reality, the sociologist himself must exist the dialectic of knowledge and action (to employ Sartrean syntax). What he does will therefore be dependent on what he chooses to study; but he should always remember that the truth of the intelligibility he establishes can only be put to the test through praxis.

In conclusion, then, what is the 'sociological usefulness of the concept of intelligibility'?

This question can be answered on a number of levels.

It is 'useful' in a theoretical sense in that it exposes the fallacies of many approaches to social reality that pass for sociology. It reminds us, should we need it, of the 'Universality of Contradiction'.

It is useful again in a negative sense, in that it warns us against being over-optimistic about our achievements to date. As Laing pointed out in 'The Obvious', social reality is a hierarchy of contexts, sub-contexts, meta-contexts etc. The intelligibility of any phenomenon requires it be placed in *its* (meta)-context. Complete intelligibility, like perfect enlightenment, is impossible till every aspect of the total system is simultaneously rendered intelligible (or enlightened). Buddha realized that Hegel's Absolute Idea was a contingently unrealizable abstract ideal.

More positively, the concept of intelligibility, by virtue of that moment of it which Sartre calls comprehension, can, heuristically, subsume C. Wright Mills' notion of sociological imagination. This is not the place to write about dialectics as a Way of Life, or intelligibility as an individual's epistemological mode of being-in-the-world; simply to assert that one could so write. If Wright Mills' term is not a misnomer, this feature is indeed an aspect of the 'sociological usefulness' of the term intelligibility.

Finally, our reflections on the regressive-progressive method, which is nothing but the methodological reality of intelligibility, has shown us that sociology is no mere academic abstraction. For sociology is, literally, the Logos of the Socia, and we, - you and I -, are parts of that Socia. If we are sociologists we must be, by definition, committed to its Logos; that is, its unfolding manifestation. A sociologist can only be one who is committed to living this manifestation; to living, in its full, contradictory, thus political, entirety, the dialectic of human social existence. The sociological usefulness of Intelligibility is thus that is tells us what Sociology could be.

BIBLIOGRAPHIES

CHRONOLOGICAL ORDER OT LAING'S TEXTS

(N.B. In cases where there are many texts in the same year, notably 1964-5, and 1967, the chronological order given is only approximate, as exact dates of publication are not always known.)

* co-written with Cameron and McGhie
† co-written with A. Esterson
≠ co-written with D. Cooper
co-written with Phillipson and Lee
╱ co-written with D. Cooper and A. Esterson

1955*   Patient and Nurse Effects of Environmental Changes in the Care of Chronic Schizophrenics.

1958†   The Collusive Function of Pairing in Analytic Groups.

1960   'The Divided Self'.

1961   'The Self and Others'.

1962   Series and Nexus in the Family.

1964
    a   Schizophrenia and the Family.
    b   Is Schizophrenia a Disease?
    c   Introduction to M. Coate's 'Beyond All Reason'.
    d   Statement on Marijuana (unpublished letter to British Medical Association).
    e   Preface to Penguin edition of 'The Divided Self'.
    f   Psychotherapy: The Search for a New Theory.
    g   What is Schizophrenia?
1964†   'Sanity, Madness, and the Family'.
1964≠   'Reason and Violence'.

1965
    a   Mystification, Confusion, and Conflict.

- b Practice and Theory: The Present Situation.
- c Violence and Love.
- d The Massacre of the Innocents.
- e Transcendental Experience in Relation to Religion and Psychosis.
- f A Ten-Day Voyage.
- g Foreword to F. MacNab's 'Estrangement and Relationship'.
- h† Results of Family-oriented Therapy with Hospitalized Schizophrenics.

1966
- a Book review: E.H. Erikson's 'Insight and Responsibility'.
- b Individual and Family Structure.

1966#
- a 'Interpersonal Perception'.
- b Institute for Personal Management Questionnaire.

1967
- a 'The Politics of Experience'.
- b The Bird of Paradise.
- c The Study of Family and Social Contexts in Relation to the Origin of Schizophrenia.
- d Book review: S. Freud's and W. Bullitt's 'Thomas Woodrow Wilson'.
- e The Obvious.
- f Dialectics of Liberation Records.
- g Appearances and Disappearances.
- h The Terror of Security and the Security of Terror.
- i Ritualization in Abnormal Behaviour.
- j Family and Individual Structure.
- k Schizophrenia: Sickness or Strategy?
- l The Kodak Mantra Interviews.

1968
- a Interview with 'International Times'.
- b Interview: Our Present Madness.
- c Book review: Liberation by Orgasm (Reich's 'Function of the Orgasm').
- d Metanoia: Some Experiences at Kingsley Hall.

1969
- a Intervention in Social Situations.
- b Book review: Watzlawick et al.'s 'Pragmatics of Human Communication'.
- c Introduction to Mary Barnes Art Exhibition Catalogue.
- d 'Self and Others' (2nd edition).
- e 'The Politics of the Family' (USA and Canada only).
- f The Ghost in the Weed Garden (revised edition).

1969† Preface to 2nd edition of 'Sanity, Madness, and the Family'.

1970
- a Religious Sensibility.
- b 'Knots'.

1971   'The Politics of the Family and Other Essays'.
1971≠   Introduction to 2nd edition of 'Reason and Violence'.

1972
   a   Interview: After Freud and Jung, now comes R.D. Laing.
   b   Interview: Something to Say.

1973
   a   Interview with 'Radio Times'.
   b   Interview: Qui est fou?

BREAKDOWN OF LAING'S TEXTS, BY TYPE, WITH SOURCE REFERENCES

(i)   Books

1960   'The Divided Self'. Tavistock.
1961   'The Self and Others'. Tavistock.
1964†   'Sanity, Madness, and the Family'. Tavistock.
1964≠   'Reason and Violence'. Tavistock.
1966#   'Interpersonal Perception'. Tavistock.
1967   'The Politics of Experience'. Penguin.
1967   Schizophrenia: Sickness or Strategy. Unpublished.
1969   'The Politics of the Family'. CBC.
1970   'Knots'. Tavistock.
1971   'The Politics of the Family and Other Essays'. Tavistock.

(ii) Papers not subsequently appearing in Laing's Books

1955*   Patient and Nurse Effects of Environmental Changes in the Care of Chronic Schizophrenics (in 'Lancet', ii, 31 December 1955).
1958†   The Collusive Function of Pairing in Analytic Groups (in 'Brit. J. Med. Psychol.', 31).
c.1960   Infancy and Ontological Insecurity (unpublished manuscript).
1964   Statement on Marijuana (unpublished letter to British Medical Association).
1965   Mystification, Confusion, and Conflict (in L. Boszormenyi-Nagy and J. Framo (eds), 'Intensive Family Therapy').
1965≠   Results of Family Orientated Therapy with Hospitalized Schizophrenics (in 'Brit. Med. J.', 18 December 1965, pp. 1462-5. Reprinted in Cooper 1967a).
1966   Individual and Family Structure (in P. Lomas, 'Psychoanalytic Studies of the Family').
1967   Family and Individual Structure (in P. Lomas, 'The Predicament of the Family').
1967   Ritualization in Abnormal Behaviour (in 'Ritualization of Behaviour in Animals and Men', Proceedings of the Royal Society, Second Series).
1967   The Obvious (in D. Cooper, 'The Dialectics of Liberation').
1968   Metanoia: Some Experiences at Kingsley Hall (in H. Ruitenbeek, 'Going Crazy').
1970   Religious Sensibility (in 'Listener', 23 April 1970).

(iii)   Papers subsequently revised as parts of Laing's books

1962   Series and Nexus in the Family (in 'New Left Review', 15).
1964   Is Schizophrenia a Disease? (in 'Int. J. Soc. Psychiat.', Spring 1964).
1964   Schizophrenia and the Family (in New Society, 16 April 1964).
1964   What is Schizophrenia? (in 'New Left Review', 28).
1964   Psychotherapy - The Search for a New Theory ('New Society', 1 October 1964).
1965   Practise and Theory: The Present Situation ('Psychother. Psychosom.', 13).
1965   Violence and Love (in 'J. of Exist.' 5, 20).
1965   The Massacre of the Innocents ('Peace News', 1491).
1965   Transcendental Experience in Relation to Religion and Psychosis ('Psychedelic Review', 6).
1965   A Ten-Day Voyage ('Views', 8).
1967   The Study of Family and Social Contexts in Relation to the Origin of Schizophrenia (in J. Romano, 'The Origins of Schizophrenia').
1967   Appearances and Disappearances; The Terror of Security and the Security of Terror ('Fire', 1).
1969   Intervention in Social Situations (Pamphlet published by the Association of Family Caseworkers, and the Philadelphia Association).

(iv)   Prefaces, introductions, and forewords

1964   Introduction to M. Coate's 'Beyond All Reason' (Coate, 1964, Lippincott).
1964   Preface to the Penguin edition of 'The Divided Self' (Laing, 1965, Penguin).
1965   Foreword to F. MacNab's 'Estrangement and Relationship' (MacNab, 1965, Tavistock).
1969   Preface to 2nd edition of 'Self and Others' (Laing, 1969, Tavistock).
1969† Preface to 2nd edition of 'Sanity, Madness, and the Family' (Laing and Esterson, 1969, Tavistock).
1969   Introduction to Mary Barnes Exhibition Catalogue (quoted in Barnes and Berke, 1971, MacGibbon & Kee).
1971≠ Introduction to 2nd edition of 'Reason and Violence' (Laing and Cooper, 1971, Tavistock).

(v)   Book reviews

1966   E.H. Erikson's 'Insight and Responsibility' ('New Society', 28 April 1966).
1967   S. Freud and W. Bullitt's 'Thomas Woodrow Wilson' ('New Society', 18 May 1967).
1968   Liberation by Orgasm: Reich's 'Function of the Orgasm' ('New Society', October 1968).
1969   Watzlawick, Beavin and Jackson's 'Pragmatics of Human Communication ('New Society', 3 April 1969).

(vi) Interviews

1967   The Kodak Mantra Interviews ('The Kodak Mantra Diaries', Sinclair, 1971).
1968   Interview in 'International Times' (Spring 1968).
1968   Our Present Madness. Interview with Rod Stokes (in 'Unit', 11).
1972   After Freud & Jung, now comes R.D. Laing.... (P. Mezan in 'Esquire', January 1972).
1972   Something to Say. Interview with John Morgan and Maurice Carstairs. (Edited transcript in the 'Guardian', 27 December 1972; complete transcript, personal communication Udi Eichler, Thames Television.)
1973   Discussion of 'Knots' ('Radio Times', 21 April 1973).
1973   Qui est fou? (In 'L'Express', 23 July 1973. Trans. John Tillich).

(vii) Radio and television broadcasts

1964   Tonight - Interview on Causes and Cures of Schizophrenia. (BBC TV 28 April 1964.)
1964   Short Circuit - Logic Game. (BBC TV 6 May 1964.)
1964   Way of Life: Priest or Psychiatrist. (BBC Radio 22 May 1964.)
1965   Synanon. (BBC Radio 12 March 1965.)
1966   Science Review. (BBC Radio 3 March 1966.)
1966   New Release - Conversation with Dr Mercer. (BBC TV 8 November 1966.)
1966   Horizon - Filmed Interview. (BBC TV 30 December 1966.)
1967   Line-Up - Discussion of 'In Two Minds'. (BBC TV 1 March 1967.)
1967   Frontiers of Knowledge. (BBC Radio 2 March 1967.)
1967   William Blake - Tiger, Tiger. (BBC TV 21 June 1967.)
1967   Panorama - Discussion of Dialectics of Liberation. (BBC TV 7 July 1967.)
1967   Your Witness - Marijuana. (BBC TV 24 August 1967.)
1968   Towards Tomorrow. (BBC TV 5 February 1968.)
1968   The Politics of the Family. (Canadian Broadcasting Corporation. 5 Radio Talks, November-December 1968.)
1970   Religious Sensibility - Is There a Future for Religious Belief? (BBC Radio 27 March 1970.)
1972   Something to Say. (Thames Television 21 December 1972.)
1973   Knots - Stereo Workshop, dramatized muscial version. (BBC Radio 27 April 1973.)

(viii) Unpublished lectures, etc.

1960   The Development of Existential Analysis (Royal Medico-Psychological Association).
1967   Dialectics of Liberation Discussion Seminars (mostly available on DL records see below).
1968   Psychology and Religion: Descriptions of Inner Space in

Greek, Christian and Egyptian Mythology (Anti-University of London, 10 May and 7 June).
1972   Lecture Tour of USA.
1972   Reflections on Psychiatry (public lecture on behalf of the Philadelphia Association).
1973   Reflections on Meditation (public lecture on behalf of the Philadelphia Association).

(ix) Films

'Asylum'.
'Breathing and Running'.

(x) LPs

Dialectics of Liberation Conference Records (1967).
DL 4 The Obvious.
DL 13 and 14 Open Discussion (with S. Carmichael and A. Ginsberg).
DL 20 Anti-Institution Seminar.

ARTICLES, BOOKS, ETC., DIRECTLY OR INDIRECTLY RELATING TO R.D. LAING

(N.B. This is not intended to be an exhaustive survey. Much of what has been written on Laing is of such a low standard as to be not worth quoting. What follows is a list of articles, etc., which, if not to be agreed with, are at least *worth* disagreeing with.)

AGEL, J. (ed.) (1971) 'The Radical Therapist'. Ballantine Books, New York.
BARNES, M. (1970) Flection and Reflection. 'Fire', 10. Also in Boyers and Orrill (1972), Agel (1971), and Ruitenbeek (1972).
BOYERS, R. and ORRILL, R. (eds) (1972) 'Laing and Anti-Psychiatry'. Penguin.
CLARE, A. (1973) Laing Returns to the Fold, 'Spectator', 3 February.
COLES, R., FARBER, L., FRIEDENBERG, E. and LUX, K. (1970) R.D. Laing and Anti-Psychiatry: A Symposium (reprinted in Boyers and Orrill, 1972).
EYSENCK, H.J. (1970) The Ethics of Psychotherapy. 'Question', 3, January.
FRIEDENBERG, E. (1973) 'Laing'. Fontana.
GILLIE, O. (1969) Freedom Hall. 'New Society', 27 March.
GORDON, J. (1971a). Who is Mad? Who is Sane? R.D. Laing: In Search of a New Psychiatry. 'Atlantic Monthly', January. Also in Ruitenbeek (1972).
GORDON, J. (1971b) The Meta-Journey of R.D. Laing. In Boyers amd Orrill (1972).
HERNTON, C. (1968) In G'ahdhi's Room. (N.B. This is a poem about Hernton's meeting with Laing, not an article.) 'Fiba', 1, Spring. (Reprinted in 'Fire', 10, 1970.)
HOLBROOK, D. (1968) R.D. Laing and the Death Circuit. 'Encounter', August.

INGLIS, B. (1969) The Remarkable Ronald Laing. 'Vogue', 15 September.
JACOBY, R. (1973) Laing and Cooper, and the Tension between Theory and Therapy. 'Telos', 17, Fall.
JACOBY, R. (1975) 'Social Amnesia: A Critique of Conformist Psychology from Adler to Laing'. Beacon Press.
LIDZ, T. (1971) Schizophrenia, R.D. Laing and the Contemporary Treatment of Psychosis. In Boyers and Orrill (1972).
LYNCH, W. (1970) Review of 'Divided Self' and 'Self and Others'. 'Commonwealth' 25 September.
MARTIN, D. (1970) R.D. Laing: Psychiatry and Apocalypse. In Maurice Cranston (ed.), 'The New Left', World Publishing Co.
NELSON, B. (1971) Afterword: a Medium with a Message: R.D. Laing. In Boyers and Orrill (1972).
RACHMAN, S. (1973) Schizophrenia: a Look at Laing's Views. 'New Society', 26 April.
RAPAILLE, G.C. (1972) 'Laing'. Editions Universitaires, Paris.
RATNER, C. (1970) Laing's Psychology. 'Telos', 5, Spring.
ROSSABI, A. and BERKE, J. (1970) Anti-Psychiatry: An Interview with Dr. Joseph Berke. In Boyers and Orrill (1972), Agel (1971) and Ruitenbeek (1972).
RUITENBEEK, H. (1971) R.D. Laing and the Young. Reprinted in Ruitenbeek (1972).
RUITENBEEK, H. (ed.) (1972) 'Going Crazy: The Radical Therapy of R.D. Laing and Others'. Bantam Books, New York.
SAYERS, S. (1972) Sanity, Madness and the Problem of Knowledge. 'Radical Philosophy', 1, January.
SAYERS, S. (1973) Mental Illness as a Moral Concept. 'Radical Philosophy' 5, Summer.
SCHATZMAN, M. (1970) Madness and Morals, in J. Berke (ed.), 'Counter-Culture: The Creation of an Alternative Society'. Peter Owen and Fire Books. Also in Boyers and Orrill (1972), and Agel (1971).
SCHATZMAN, M. (1973) Reply to Rachman (1973). 'New Society', 3 May.
SEDGWICK, P. (1971) R.D. Laing: Self, Symptom, and Society. In Boyers and Orrill (1972).
SIEGLER, M., OSMOND, H. and MANN, H. (1969) Laing's Model of Madness. 'British Journal of Psychiatry' 115, 525. Also in Boyers and Orrill (1972).
SINCLAIR, L. (1971) 'The Kodak Mantra Diaries'. Albion Village Press.
SPECK, R. (1972) 'The New Families'. Tavistock.
TYSON, A. (1971) Homage to Catatonia. 'New York Review of Books'. 11 February.
WARRINGTON, J. (1973) A Critique of Laing's Social Philosophy Part 1. 'Radical Philosophy', 5, Summer.
ZEE, H. (1972) Laing's Changed Views on Schizophrenia - a Latterday Discussion. 'Journal of the National Association of Private Psychiatric Hospitals', 4, 1, Spring.

GENERAL BIBLIOGRAPHY

(All items published in Britain unless otherwise stated.)

ADORNO, T. (1972) 'Prisms' New Left Books.
AGEL, J. (ed.) (1971) 'The Radical Therapist'. Ballantine Books, New York.
ALDISS, B. (1969) 'Barefoot in the Head'. Faber & Faber.
ALTHUSSER, L. (1969) 'For Marx'. Allen Lane.
ALTHUSSER, L. (1971) 'Lenin and Philosophy'. New Left Books.
ATTEWELL, P. (1974) Ethnomethodology since Garfinkel, 'Theory and Society', 1.
BARNES, M. and BERKE, J. (1971) 'Mary Barnes: Two Accounts of a Journey through Madness'. MacGibbon & Kee (Penguin, 1972).
BATESON, G. et al. (1956) Towards a theory of Schizophrenia, 'Behavioural Science', 1, 4. Reprinted in Bateson (1972).
BATESON, G. (1961) 'Perceval's Narrative'. Stanford University Press.
BATESON, G. (1972) 'Steps to an Ecology of Mind'. Ballantine Books, New York.
BERKE, J. (ed.) (1971) 'Counter-Culture: the Creation of an Alternative Society'. Peter Owen and Fire Books.
BLIGH BOND, F. (1924) 'The Company of Avalon'. Blackwell.
BLUM, A. (1970) Theorysing. In Douglas (1971).
BOYERS, R. and ORRILL, R. (eds) (1972) 'Laing and Anti-Psychiatry'. Penguin.
BOSZORMENYI-NAGY, L. and FRAMO, J. (eds) (1965) 'Intensive Family Therapy'. Harper & Row, New York.
CARROL, L. (1958) 'Symbolic Logic and the Game of Logic'. Dover, New York.
COOPER, D. (1967a) 'Psychiatry and Anti-Psychiatry'. Tavistock (Paladin, 1970).
COOPER, D. (1967b) The Dialectics of Revolution, 'Fire', 1.
COOPER, D. (1968) 'The Dialectics of Liberation'. Penguin.
COOPER, D. (1971) 'Death of the Family'. Allen Lane (Penguin, 1972).
COOPER, D. (1974) 'A Grammar of Living'. Pantheon.
CUMMING, R. (1965) 'The Philosophy of Jean-Paul Sartre. Random House. Methuen, 1968.
DESAN, W. (1966) 'The Marxism of J.-P. Sartre' Doubleday Anchor, New York.
DOUGLAS, J. (ed.) (1971) 'Understanding Everyday Life'. Routledge & Kegan Paul.
DYLAN, B. (1973) 'The Writings and Drawings of Bob Dylan'. Cape.
ELZEY, R. (1971) Founding an Anti-University. In Berke (1971).
ESTERSON, A. (1970) 'The Leaves of Spring'. Tavistock (Penguin, 1972).
FANON, F. (1965) 'The Wretched of the Earth'. MacGibbon & Kee.
FEUERBACH, (1957) 'The Essence of Christianity'. Harper & Row, New York.
FILMER, P. et al. (1972) 'New Directions in Sociological Theory'. Collier-Macmillan.
FISCHER, E. (1963) 'The Necessity of Art'. Penguin.
FOUCAULT, M. (1967) 'Madness and Civilization'. Tavistock.

GARFINKEL, H. (1967) 'Studies in Ethnomethodology'. Prentice-Hall, Englewood Cliffs, New Jersey.
GELLNER, E. (1962) Concepts and Society. In Wilson (1970).
GOFFMAN, E. (1968) 'Asylums'. Penguin.
GOODENOUGH, E.R. (1966) Cultural Anthropology and Linguistics. In Hymes (1966).
HALEY, J. (1963) 'Strategies of Psychotherapy'. Grune & Stratton, New York.
HEAP and ROTH (1973) On Phenomenological Sociology, 'American Sociological Review', 38.
HEATON, J. (1972) Insight in Phenomenology and Psychoanalysis, 'J. Brit.Soc.Phenomenol.', 3, 2.
HEGEL, G. (1929) 'Science of Logic'. Muirhead Library of Philosophy.
HEGEL, G. (1949) 'Phenomenology of Mind'. Muirhead Library of Philosophy.
HEIDEGGER, M. (1949) 'Was ist Metaphysik'. Trans. W. Kaufmann in his 'Existentialism from Dostoevsky to Sartre'. New American Library, New York.
HEIDEGGER, M. (1949) 'Existence and Being'. Vision Press.
HEIDEGGER, M. (1962) 'Being and Time'. SCM Press.
HENRY, J. (1963) 'Culture Against Man'. Random House, New York. Penguin, 1972.
HESSE, H. (1970) 'Glass Bead Game'. Cape.
HESSE, H. (1960) 'Journey to the East'.
HUSSERL, E. (1964) 'The Idea of Phenomenology'. Martinus Nijhoff, The Hague.
HUSSERL, E. (1965) 'Phenomenology and the Crisis of European Philosophy'. Harper Torchlight, New York.
HUSSERL, E. (1966) 'The Phenomenology of Internal Time Consciousness'. Martinus Nijhoff, The Hague.
HUSSERL, E. (1973) 'Cartesian Meditations'. Martinus Nijhoff, The Hague.
HUSSERL, E. 'Gesammelte Werke'. 'Husserliana'. Adler.
HUXLEY, A. (1946) 'The Perennial Philosophy. Constable.
HUXLEY, A. (1959) 'The Doors of Perception and Heaven and Hell'. Penguin.
HYMES, A. (1966) 'Language in Culture and Society'. Harper & Row, New York.
JACQUES, (1955) Social Systems as Defense against Persecutory and Depressive Anxiety. In M. Klein, P. Heimann and R. Money-Kyrle (eds), 'New Directions in Psycho-Analysis'. Tavistock.
KAPLAN, B. (ed.) (1964) 'The Inner World of Mental Illness'. Harper & Row, New York.
KIERKEGAARD, S. (1941) 'Concluding Unscientific Postscript'. Princeton University Press.
KIERKEGAARD, S. (1946) 'The Sickness unto Death'. Princeton University Press.
LAFARGE, R. (1970) 'Jean-Paul Sartre: his Philosophy'. Gill & Macmillan, Dublin.
LEARY, T. (1970) 'The Politics of Ecstasy'. Paladin.
LÉVI-STRAUSS, C. (1962) 'The Savage Mind'. Weidenfeld & Nicolson.
LÉVI-STRAUSS, C. (1968) 'Structural Anthropology'. Penguin.
LOMAS, P. (1966) 'Psychoanalytic Studies of the Family'. Hogarth Press.

LOMAS, P. (1967) 'The Predicament of the Family'. Hogarth Press.
MACNAB, F. (1965) 'Estrangement and Relationship'. Tavistock.
MAO TSE-TUNG (1967) On Contradiction, and On Practise. In 'Selected Works', vol. 1, Foreign Languages Press, Peking.
MARCUSE, H. (1955) 'Eros and Civilization'. Beacon Press (Sphere Books, 1969).
MARCUSE, H. (1964) 'One-Dimensional Man'. Routledge & Kegan Paul (Sphere Books, 1968).
MARX, K. (1951) '18th Brumaire'. New York Labour Co., New York.
MARX, K. (1971) 'Early Texts' (ed. D. McClelland). Blackwell.
MARX, K. and ENGELS, F. (1968) 'Selected Works'. Lawrence & Wishart.
MASLOW, A. (1962) 'Towards a Psychology of Being'. Van Nostrand.
MERLEAU-PONTY, M. (1962) 'The Phenomenology of Perception'. Routledge & Kegan Paul.
MERLEAU-PONTY, M. (1964) 'Primacy of Perception'. Northwest University Press, Evanston, Ill.
MOUNIER, E. (1952) 'Personalism'. Routledge & Kegan Paul.
NICHOLLS, W. (1969) 'Systematic and Philosophical Theology'. Penguin.
NUTTALL, J. (1970) 'Bomb Culture'. Paladin.
PHILADELPHIA ASSOCIATION (1969) 'Philadelphia Association Report, 1965-1969'. Stott Brothers.
REICH, W. (1968) 'The Function of the Orgasm'. Panther Books.
ROCHE, MAURICE (1973) 'Phenomenology, Language and the Social Sciences'. Routledge & Kegan Paul.
ROMANO, J. (ed.) (1967) 'The Origins of Schizophrenia'.
RUITENBEEK, H. (ed.) (1970) 'The New Group Therapies'. Avon Books, New York.
RUITENBEEK, H. (ed.) (1972) 'Going Crazy'. Bantam Books, New York.
SACKS (1963) Quoted in Attewell (1974).
SARTRE, J.-P. (1947) 'Huis Clos'. Gallimard, Paris.
SARTRE, J.-P. (1958) 'Being and Nothingness'. Methuen.
SARTRE, J.-P. (1960) 'Critique de la raison dialectique'. Gallimard, Paris.
SARTRE, J.-P. (1963) 'Saint Genet'. W.H. Allen.
SARTRE, J.-P. (1964) 'The Problem of Method'. Methuen. ('The Search for a Method'. Knopf, 1963.)
SARTRE, J.-P. (1973) On Maoism, 'Telos', 16, Summer.
SARTRE, J.-P. (1974a) 'On a Raison de se Revolter'. Gallimard, Paris. Trans. Doug Kellner.
SARTRE, J.-P. (1974b) 'Between Existentialism and Marxism'. New Left Books.
SCHATZMAN, M. (1973) 'Soul Murder'. Allen Lane.
SCHUTZ, A. (1962) 'Collected Papers', vol. 1, Martinus Nijhoff, The Hague.
SEARLES, H. (1959) The Effort to Drive the Other Person Crazy. 'Brit. J. Med. Psychol.', 32, I.
SILVERMAN, D. (1972) In Filmer et al. (1972).
SINCLAIR, I. (1971) 'The Kodak Mantra Diaries'. Albion Village Press.
SNYDER, G. (1968) Buddhism and the Coming Revolution, 'Fire'. 1.
SPECK, R. (1972) 'The New Families'. Tavistock.
SPIEGELBERG, H. (1960) 'The Phenomenological Movement', vols I and

II. Martinus Nijhoff, The Hague.
STEWART, K. (1955) 'Pygmies and Dream Giants'. Gollancz.
SZASZ, T. (1972) 'The Myth of Mental Illness'. Paladin.
TILLICH, P. (1952) 'The Courage to Be'. Nisbet.
TROCCHI, A. (1965) Why Drugs?, 'New Society'. May.
TURNER, R. (1973) Dialectical Reason. 'Radical Philosophy', 4, Spring.
WATTS, A. (1962) 'The Way of Zen'. Penguin.
WILDEN, A. (1968) 'The Language of the Self'. Johns Hopkins University Press, Baltimore.
WILSON, B. (ed.) (1970) 'Rationality'. Blackwell.
WILSON, C. (1965) 'Beyond the Outsider'. Pan.
WINCH, P. (1958) 'The Idea of a Social Science'. Routledge & Kegan Paul.
WITTGENSTEIN, L. (1947) 'Tractatus Logico-Philosophicus'. Kegan, Paul, Trench, Trubner.
WITTGENSTEIN, L. (1953) 'Philosophical Investigations'. Blackwell.
WRIGHT MILLS, C. (1970) 'The Sociological Imagination'. Penguin.
ZIMMERMAN and POLLNER (1970) The Everyday World. In Douglas (1971).

INDEX

Aletheia, 21, 144
Alienation, 19, 28, 55, 61-2, 67-8, 128
Althusser, L., 39, 119, 204
Analytic versus dialectic logic, 198
Anti-psychiatry, 80
Anti-university, 69-71
Arbours Association, 5, 71
Attewell, P., 188-90

Barnes, Mary, 52, 59
Bateson, G., 21-4, 31, 43, 98, 164, 167-8
'Bird of Paradise', 65-6
Berke, J., 69, 130
Buber, M., 23, 30-1
Buddhism, 60-1, 90-1, 97

Carmichael, S., 71-3, 156
Carstairs, M., 98, 167-8
Collusion, 20-1
Common-sense constructs, 176
Communes, 52; see also Arbours Association; Kingsley Hall; Philadelphia Association
Communication, 31, 110
Comprehension, 105, 122
Cooper, D., 32, 45, 52, 65, 69, 70, 80, 85, 123, 127, 138
'Critique de la raison dialectique', 31ff, 45, 113ff, 158, 160

Dasein, 143ff, 148
Death and Rebirth, 50ff, 59; see also Inner voyage
Desan, W., 123
Dialectic, 116, 203
Dialectics of Liberation conference, 69-72, 124, 130, 153
'Divided Self', the, 7-17, 112, 141ff
Double Bind, 21-2, 31, 167
Dreadful, the, 146-8
Durkheim's Illusion, 38, 160, 163
Dylan, Bob, 49, 132

Elusion, 19
Engels, F., 186
Engulfment, 11
Esterson, A., 5, 7, 27, 32, 43, 45, 115, 118, 127, 202
Ethnomethodology, 3, 188, 190-7
Existentialism, 14-17, 22-3, 67, 142

Feuerbach, L., 31, 152
Freud, S., 56, 78, 87-8, 172, 203

Garfinkel, H., 187-92, 197
Genet, 19
God, 54, 94, 96, 157
Goffman, E., 43

217

Heaton, J., 112
Hegel, G., 13-14, 23-4, 30, 60ff, 152ff, 205
Heidegger, M., 21, 30, 142ff
Henry, J., 56
Hippies, 71, 73
Homogeneity of Consciousness, 197
Husserl, E., 13, 16, 112, 176, 182
Huxley, A., 96, 168
Hysteria, 19

Implosion, 11
Indexicality, 188, 190, 195
Induction, 85
Inner space, 58, 169
Inner voyage, 55, 58
Intelligibility, 1, 2, 41-2, 45, 63, 69, 89, 172-4, 205
Internalization, 79, 83
Interpersonal method (IPM), 20-30, 112
'Interpersonal perception', 26, 29-30, 90, 111
Intersubjectivity, 10, 106, 108, 181

Jung, C.J., 56

Kierkegaard, S., 142
Kingsley Hall, 5, 52-3, 67, 70, 76, 115, 128
'Knots', 5, 90-2, 132, 140
Kraepelin, 10, 50, 168

Lacan, J., 125, 159
Leary, T., 1, 5, 75, 128
Lefebvre, 202
Lévi-Strauss, C., 3, 89, 126, 197-201
Love, see 'Violence and Love'
LDS, 5, 74-6, 93-4, 128

MacNab, F., 53, 143
Madness, 55, 168
Mao Tse Tung, 202-3
Mapping, 82, 85-6, 88
Marcuse, H., 128, 155
Marijuana, 5, 74-5

Marx, K., 37, 46, 57, 68, 163, 200
Marxism, Sartrean, 31-2, 40, 72, 158
Maya, 90, 92-3
Meditation, 97-9, 101
Merleau-Ponty, M., 121, 156-8
Metanoia, 76, 80, 85, 98, 170-1
Mysticism, 132ff
Mystification, 32, 46-8, 165-6

'New Left Review', 17, 31, 60
Nexus, 5, 17, 18, 23, 31, 35-43, 110, 159
Nirvana, 91
Normality as alienation, 55-6, 123
Nuttall, J., 70, 75

'Obvious, the', 124, 135, 162, 182, 205
Ontological insecurity, 11, 150-2

Patient-and-Nurse Effects, 7, 8
Perspectives, reciprocity of, 176
Petrification, 11
Phantasy, 13, 18, 20, 25, 31, 75, 85-7, 157, 164-5
Phenomenology, 13-17, 22-3, 67, 88, 99
Philadelphia Association, 5, 27, 52, 71, 75, 80, 87, 112
Phillipson, M., 194-6
Piaget, J., 39-40
Poetry, 63-4
Police, the, 71-3, 130
Political radicalism, 68
'Politics of Experience', 50, 59-66, 123, 170
'Politics of the Family', 82, 125
Postulates, Schultzian, 175
Practice, inert, 40
Praxis, 32-47
Process, 32-47
Progressive-regressive method, 1, 202
Psychoanalysis, 2, 78, 91, 105, 109

Psychosis, 19, 31, 70, 85, 141, 164ff
Psychotherapy, 131

Radicalism, 68
'Reason and Violence', 45-6, 116, 123, 202
Redler, L., 69
Reich, W., 77, 87
Religion, 54-5, 89, 94-6, 102-3, 139
Revolution, 70
Rules, 84, 87

'Sanity, Madness and the Family', 114-15
Sartre, J.-P., 1, 2, 30-1, 34-43, 67, 113ff, 134-5, 156, 164, 198ff
Schatzman, M., 89, 105, 159, 162
Schizoid state, 9-13, 164ff
Schizophrenia, 8, 10-13, 50-9, 77, 80-2, 138, 164, 169
Schizophrenia as inner voyage, 52-67, 124, 127, 169
Schizophrenia as strategy, 50, 127, 172
Schutz, A., 23, 174-88
Searles, M., 21
Sedgwick, P., 92, 100, 103
Self and others, 17-31, 85
'Self and Others, The', 7, 17-31, 108ff
Series, 5, 17, 31, 40, 42, 114
Social phantasy system, 187
Social phenomenology, 2, 59-62, 67, 70, 118-19

Sociology, 201
SOMA, 75
Speck, R., 43
Structuralism, 88, 104, 126
Synchrony versus diachrony, 197, 201
Szasz, T., 50

Taoism, 90-1
Tavistock Institute, 4, 17, 26-7, 43, 46, 112, 160
Tillich, P., 15, 150-2
Totality, 38, 121, 136
Totalization, 37-8, 42-5, 121, 124-5, 136, 203
Transcendental experience, 54-5, 75, 170
Transcendental meditation, 99

Underground movement, British, 5, 70, 73
Understanding, 107, 109ff

Verstehen, 178, 180-1, 187
'Villa 21', 52, 80
'Violence and Love', 56, 138

Watts, A., 92
Winch, P., 176
Wittgenstein, L., 93
Wright Mills, C., 200, 204-5

Zen, 64, 91-2